Operation Heartbreak

The Man Who Never Was

OPERATION HEARTBREAK

A STORY BY DUFF COOPER

THE MAN WHO NEVER WAS

BY EWEN MONTAGU

With an Introduction by

JOHN JULIUS NORWICH

SPELLMOUNT

A catalogue record for this book is available
from the British Library

ISBN 978-0-7524-5775-8

This combined edition first published in the UK by Spellmount in 2003.
Paperback edition first published in the UK in 2007; this edition published in
2010 by
Spellmount Publishers,the military history imprint of The History Press
The Mill, Brimscombe Port
Stroud, Gloucestershire. GL5 2QG

Tel: 01453 883300
Fax: 01453 883233

www.thehistorypress.co.uk

1 3 5 7 9 8 6 4 2

About the Authors

Duff Cooper (1890–1954) joined the Foreign Office in 1913 and was released only in late 1917 to take part in the First World War. During his six months in France he won the DSO. On his return he entered Parliament, holding several posts in successive Conservative governments including those of Secretary of State for War and First Lord of the Admiralty. He was Ambassador in Paris 1944–47. He wrote several books, among them a famous biography of Talleyrand and an autobiography, *Old Men Forget. Operation Heartbreak* is his only novel. He was created 1st Viscount Norwich in 1951.

Ewen Montagu (1901–1985) was educated at Westminster School, Harvard and Trinity College, Cambridge. Called to the Bar in 1924, he became a KC in 1939, the youngest of his year. He was Recorder of Devizes and Southampton, Chairman of Hampshire Quarter Sessions, Chairman and later Presiding Judge of Middlesex Sessions. From 1945 to 1973 he was Judge Advocate of the Fleet. He served in the Royal Navy during the War, from 1940 in the Navy Intelligence Division at the Admiralty. He was appointed OBE (Military) for his work there and subsequently promoted to CBE.

John Julius Norwich was born in 1929, the son of Duff Cooper. He too spent time in the Foreign Service, but resigned in 1964 to be a full-time writer. He has written the histories of Norman Sicily, Venice and Byzantium, together with other books on Shakespeare, architecture, music and travel. He has also made thirty historical documentaries for BBC television. For some thirty years Chairman of the Venice in Peril Fund, he has chaired the World Monuments Fund in Britain. His most recent books are *The Middle Sea: A History of the Mediterranean* (Chatto and Windus, 2006) and *Great Cities in History* (Thames & Hudson, 2009, ed.).

Operation Mincemeat in the News

Lt-Cdr Montagu inspired the secret plan, which resulted in fake documents ending up in German hands and persuaded them to move troops away from the South of Sicily where the Allied forces successfully invaded in July 1943.

After the war Lt-Cdr Montagu immortalised the episode in his book *The Man Who Never Was*, which was also made into an acclaimed film.

Daily Telegraph, 2003

The tale of the deception, codenamed Operation Mincemeat, became a best-selling book and a classic film – *The Man Who Never Was*.

Daily Mail, 2002

Perhaps the most decisive bluff of all time, Operation Mincemeat had but one purpose, to cover up the Allies' true objective, to attack Southern Europe through Sicily … This operation was of course, top secret, however before long it became legendary.

Skirmish, 2004

Reviews of the Spellmount edition:

The factual and fictional stories of how the Germans were deceived into believing that the Allied invasion of Sicily would, in reality, take place in Greece, are gathered here in one volume for the first time … This volume is essential reading for all WWII buffs.

The Officer, 2003

The government had tried to suppress Cooper's novel, but its publication prompted the intelligence services to pressurise Montagu to publish an official version. Running both volumes together the publishers have supplied a splendid read about this most curious scheme of World War II.

Nautical Magazine, 2004

Leo Cooper and Jamie Wilson at Spellmount have had the brilliant idea of publishing together two books that cover one of the most extraordinary stories of World War Two ... In 1950, Duff Cooper published a fictionalised account of the early part of the mission called *Operation Heartbreak*. With its appreareance came pressure on Ewen Montagu to tell the real story. With these two titles published together, it is a wonderful opportunity to see how the two stories tie together.

Military Illustrated, 2004

Montagu's tale is fascinating ... Throughout, he is remarkably good at portraying the thought processes and judgments that he and his team put into the plan's preparation and execution, along with the many unforeseen challenges they had to overcome, and he frequently displays a professional's pride in the artistry it demanded.

The Spectator, 2004

Goebbels thought the documents were fake but he was eventually won round by the torrents of corroborating disinformation that the British were sending out.

The Daily Express, 2010

The creativity of so many would-be authors added nuance and credibility to the workings of official deception.

The Telegraph, 2010

Acclaim for *Operation Heartbreak*:

This is a rare book, written with wonderful economy and perfect timing.

Manchester Guardian

A work of jewel-like brevity and intensity more expected in French than in English.

New York Herald Tribune

Operation Heartbreak ... should take its place beside other, similar classics such as *Reunion* by Fred Uhlman, *Strange Meeting* by Susan Hill and *A Month in the Country* by J L Carr – short novels about war which are quiet, domestic, poignant and understated.

The Persephone Quarterly

Introduction

by John Julius Norwich

On 30 April 1943, at half-past four in the morning, the dead body of a man in his early thirties was slipped overboard from His Majesty's Submarine *Seraph*, 1,600 yards off the south-west coast of Spain. Picked up a few hours later by a fisherman, it was easily identified by the local authorities as that of Major William Martin, Royal Marines. At noon on the following day it was interred, with full military honours and in the presence of the British Vice-Consul, in the cemetery at Huelva. There the grave can still be seen, having been tended by a local Anglo-Spanish lady for the past sixty years.

What the Vice-Consul was not told was that there had also been found, chained to the body through the belt of its trench-coat, a locked leather briefcase. Now Spain, as a technically neutral country, had a clear duty to return this case unopened to the British Embassy in Madrid; and when after urgent representations by the Naval Attaché it was duly delivered to him nearly a fortnight later, it showed no sign of having been tampered with. Subsequent events, however, proved that in fact it had, and that within a week of its first discovery translations of the two principal letters it contained were being studied with some care by the German Intelligence Service in Berlin.

The first of these letters, addressed to General Sir Harold Alexander, in Tunisia, was signed by the Vice-Chief of the Imperial General Staff, Sir Archibald Nye. The second was from Vice-Admiral Lord Louis Mountbatten, Chief of Combined Operations in London, to Admiral Sir Andrew Cunningham, Commander-in-Chief Mediterranean. Both letters were genuine; it was only the information they contained that was not – for, read together, they made it clear that the Allies were planning two simultaneous attacks on Europe, one through Sardinia and the other through southern Greece, to cover which they intended to try to deceive the enemy into thinking that the real target for their attack was Sicily.

Since Sicily was indeed the target, this was a perfect double-bluff; and, thanks to the ingenuity with which it was planned and the meticulous care with which it was carried out, it worked superbly. Those responsible for it in London had counted on the strong pro-Axis sympathies of Franco's Spain to ensure that the planted documents found their way into German hands, and on German efficiency to do the rest. As a result, the Allied invasion of Sicily on 10 July – just ten weeks after the finding of 'Major Martin's' body – caught the Germans utterly unprepared, with the defence forces that had been intended for the island diverted at the last moment to Corsica, Sardinia and the Balkans. Even after the invasion was in full swing, the German High Command insisted on looking upon it as a feint; and as late as 23 July we find the Führer himself – always notoriously slow to change his mind once an idea had become fixed in it – appointing his most trusted general, Erwin Rommel, to the defence of Greece.

Such, briefly and baldly, is the story of 'Operation Mincemeat' – as the scheme was named, with a nice sense of the macabre, by its principal begetters, planners and executors, a team led by Lieutenant-Commander Ewen Montagu RNVR. A decade later Mr Montagu – no longer a lieutenant-commander but Judge Advocate of the Fleet – was to write the true story of the operation in a book which he called *The Man Who Never Was*; and it is that book which occupies the second half of the present volume.

It was an apt and admirable title, which was very wisely retained for the most successful film that followed; but it was also in one sense something of a misnomer. 'Major Martin', to be sure, never existed. His name, like the whole *persona* with which he was brilliantly and imaginatively endowed – by means of keys, photographs, an invitation to a nightclub, theatre-ticket stubs, a tailor's bill (paid, somewhat improbably), letters from father and fiancée, a bank and a solicitor – was an invention of Lt-Cdr Montagu's. But the body which was slipped from the *Seraph* that spring night – that, surely, was real enough. And if it was not William Martin's, whose was it? Who was this man, obscure and nondescript as he must have been, whose single moment of glory occurred after his death, and whose dead body achieved more than most men achieve in their lives?

Speculation continues to this day. In 1996 previously secret papers became available in which it was suggested that the body was actually that of a Welsh tramp named Glyndwr Michael, who had died in January 1943 after drinking rat poison. Some doubts, however, still persisted: what if the Spaniards had carried out a post mortem and found traces of the poison? Such a discovery would have rendered the entire operation useless; would those who planned it really have taken such a risk? The book, *The Secrets of HMS Dasher* by John and Noreen Steele, claims that when that ship – an aircraft carrier – blew up in mysterious circumstances in the Clyde in 1943 with the loss of 379 lives, the number of recovered bodies officially listed was greater than that of those buried by the Commonwealth War Graves Commission; they believe that 'Major Martin' was one of the former, possibly that of Sub-Lieutenant John McFarlane, whose father's request for his son's body for private burial was refused. In support of this theory they point out that according to Admiral Norman Jewell, who as a young lieutenant had commanded the *Seraph*, he had received last-minute orders to sail to Holy Loch, only eight miles from where *Dasher* went down.

At the time of writing, the most recent evidence to have come to light takes the form of a letter to the *Daily Telegraph* published on 13 August 2002. In it Mr Ivor Leverton, proprietor of a well-known firm of undertakers, tells of how some sixty years ago he had been instructed by the St Pancras coroner – secretly, and at 1 a.m. – to transfer a corpse from the local mortuary to that of Hackney. He adds that the body measured six foot four inches. But was it 'Major Martin'? Would a body so unusually tall have been selected for such a mission?

All these questions remain unanswered; but let me quote Mr Montagu:

> At last, when we had begun to feel that it would have either to be a 'Burke and Hare' after all or we would have to extend our enquiries so widely as to risk suspicion of our motives turning into gossip, we heard of someone who had just died from pneumonia after exposure: pathologically speaking, it looked as if he might answer our requirements. We made feverish enquiries into his past and about his relatives; we were soon satisfied that these would not talk or pass on such information as we could give them. But there was still the crucial question: could we get permission to use the body without saying what we proposed to do with it and why? All we could possibly tell anyone was that we could guarantee that the purpose would be a really worthwhile one, as anything that was done would be with approval on the highest level, and that the remains would eventually receive proper burial, though under a false name.
>
> Permission, for which our indebtedness is great, was obtained on condition that I should never let it be known whose corpse it was.

Nor did he; and, as we have seen, historians have been speculating ever since. Even if we discount the rat poison and accept the facts as he gives them – as surely we must – we are still no nearer to the truth. Welsh tramps can easily die of 'pneumonia after exposure'; so can young naval officers after disasters such as that suffered by the *Dasher*; so – given the right circumstances – can almost anybody. When Mr Montagu died in July 1985 he took the secret with him; and I for one am very glad that he did.

Reading his words, I cannot help thinking that if I were the next of kin from whom such permission were requested – or if authority to use my own body for such a purpose had been sought from me on my deathbed – I should not only have agreed with pleasure and pride; I should have wanted the whole world to know about it as soon as security considerations allowed. But that is by the way. There is another question, more challenging and infinitely more rewarding than the simple issue of whose the corpse was. Whose, ideally, should it have been?

This was the question to which my father, Duff Cooper, tried to provide an answer; and *Operation Heartbreak* – which takes up the first part of the book which you now hold in your hands – was the result. He began it on 21 October 1949, and five months later wrote to his nephew and publisher, Rupert Hart-Davis: 'I have just finished the story – a moment of exultation – and had a drink on it.' He must have felt that drink to be well-deserved; in later years he was always to claim that *Heartbreak* – his first and last venture into fiction – had lived up to its name and had proved, of all his books, the hardest to write. But his real troubles over it were only just beginning.

Word now reached Whitehall, probably through my father himself, of the subject of the story that he was intending to publish; and strong pressure was put on him not to do so. Just what form that pressure took I have not been able to establish, but I am virtually certain that the Prime Minister – Mr Attlee – was personally involved. On the other hand I remember perfectly well my father telling me two of the reasons – there may have been others – that had been advanced in an effort to make him reconsider. One was the harm that the publication of the story might do to Anglo-Spanish relations; he had replied pointing out that Generalissimo Franco was still in power and that there was no reason for us to be over-solicitous about Spanish feelings. The other argument was that in the event of any further outbreak of hostilities we might wish to repeat the operation. To this his answer had been that such an idea would be madness. The war had already been over for five years; the Germans had long ago woken up to the deception; and full details of the operation must by now be presumed to be equally well-known to the Russians. In short, this was the kind of trick that could never, by its very essence, be played twice. He had further pointed out that his was a work of fiction, containing nothing to suggest that the events described in the penultimate chapter had the slightest foundation in fact, and that meanwhile Winston Churchill himself was known to be holding dinner parties spellbound with his own distinctly baroque version of what had taken place. For all these reasons he considered the objections to be ridiculous. He would publish and be damned. *Operation Heartbreak, a Story by Duff Cooper* was accordingly published on 10 November 1950. It received one bad review – by John Raymond in the *New Statesman*, who wrote that a veil of rich fatuousness hung over it like a Scotch mist – but Compton Mackenzie hailed it as 'a little masterpiece', and within a few months it had gone into four editions and sold 40,000 copies. I am not aware that the national interest suffered, either then or later, in consequence.

My father described it as, quite simply, a story. He might have been more precise and called it a love story, for that is essentially what it is: the story of a man in love with his regiment and with a passion to serve his country who, partly through ill luck and partly through his own shortcomings, is disappointed and frustrated at every turn – until at last, after his death, he achieves his heart's desire. The long, basically unsatisfactory affair with the girl he loves follows the same pattern in an interwoven strand, ending with the short but almost unbearably moving scene of her last letter to him – three pages which I can never read without tears.

That scene, with the short final chapter – a single paragraph – that follows it, rounds the story off with all the inevitability of a play by Sophocles. Suddenly, everything falls into place. One understands that although the great enterprise that gives the book its name is introduced only in the last twenty pages, nothing could be less of a *deus ex machina*; every incident that has gone before, every sentence almost, from those quiet opening words 'Nobody ever had fewer relations than Willie Maryngton' – points inexorably towards the plot's culmination and is essential to it. This compression extends even to the style of writing. The whole thing is deliberately understated. There are no loose adjectives, never the suggestion of a purple patch. Not a word is wasted. As in the real-life Operation Mincemeat, every detail has its own reason for being there, its own contribution to make to the finished work.

And yet, for all the discipline in its style and construction, the book is written from the heart. It would be impossible for anyone who knew my father to see the faintest resemblance between him and Willie, but he had a rather touching affection for – and an absolute loyalty to – several of his friends who had turned out not unlike his hero, whose character he could therefore draw with understanding and at times even with love. And though he loathed war as much as Willie worshipped it, he too knew the frustration of feeling it passing him by. On 17 May 1917 he had written in his diary:

The Government want more men for the Army and we in the Foreign Office are all to be medically examined. I think they will have to let some of us go. If anyone is allowed to go I shall be, as I am the youngest of the permanent staff, unmarried and I should think perfectly fit. The thought fills me with exhilaration. I don't own to it, as people would think it was bluff, and I dare say that I shall very soon heartily wish myself back. But I am eager for a change. I always wished to go to the war, though less now than I did at first. I envy the experience and adventure that everyone else has had. I am not afraid of death, though I love life and should hate to lose it. I don't think I should make a good officer. The only drawback is the terrible blow it would be to Mother. I don't know how I should dare to tell her. I think Diana too would mind.

She did. A few days later he continued:

I explained to her that it was no nonsense about dying for my country or beating the Germans that made me glad to join, but simply the feeling that I have had for so long that I am missing something, the vague regret that one feels when not invited to a ball even though it be a ball that one hardly would have hoped to enjoy.

Twenty-two years later, in September 1939, the frustration was far worse. He had resigned the post of First Lord of the Admiralty after the Munich *débâcle* and, though still a backbench MP, was otherwise out of a job. 'I took Terence O'Connor out to luncheon at Buck's. We both envied the people we saw there in uniform. He at least has something to do – and plenty to do. I have nothing.'

At this time, too, he tried to relieve his feelings in a poem:

As autumn fades and winter comes
    With menace deep and dire,
We sit and twiddle useless thumbs
    And chatter round the fire.

When young we fought with might and main,
    Our comrades by our side.
They were the noblest of our strain –
    Those friends of ours who died.

We mourned them, but we still believed
    They had not died in vain.
And there was glory while we grieved –
    The noblest of our strain.

But doubts begin to rise today
    Like ghosts beside the grave.
Have we in weakness thrown away
    All that they died to save?

We ask. We hear the answer bold
    And know again the tone
Of voices that have not grown old
    With years, as ours have grown.

'Though much be lost which we had won,
    Not yours, old friends, the blame.
The battle is but re-begun,
    The quarrel is the same.

'We fought that men might still be free,
　As men have fought before,
Nor hoped for final victory
　In any single war.

'Man's life, at best, is sad and brief,
　What matters loss or gain?
Whoever dies for his belief
　Will never die in vain.'

We hear their words; we know their truth,
　And feel through ageing blood
The impulse of eternal youth
　Surge like a rising flood.

Oh England, use us once again,
　Mean tasks will match the old;
Our twiddling thumbs can hold the skein
　From which the wool is rolled.

More gladly though would we give all
　That yet we have to give.
Oh let the old men man the wall,
　And let the young men live.

It may not be. Not ours to fight,
　Not unto us, O Lord,
Shall twice in life be given the right
　To serve thee with the sword.

Yet our deep love and fierce desire
　Must aid our country still –
The steadfast faith, the quenchless fire,
　The unconquerable will.

Willie Maryngton would have known what he meant.

So much for *Operation Heartbreak*. Its publication put, as was expected, the cat among the pigeons; and no one suffered more – and less deservedly than the one man who was, more than anyone else, responsible for that other operation which inspired it. Ewen Montagu would, I imagine, have been only too happy to tell the story of so superbly successful an enterprise, had he not known full well that he would never be given permission to publish it. But then, with my father's decision to ignore the Government's grotesque attempts to suppress him, everything changed overnight. Among its indirect consequences was that the journalist Ian Colvin sniffed a good story and set himself to find out exactly what had really happened. The Government in panic decided that if they couldn't shut him up they must immediately mount a spoiling operation. Mr Montagu partially explains the situation in the second paragraph of his preparatory Author's Note; he is too polite – and too modest – to reveal that the security authorities, having for years withheld permission to write the story at all, now ordered him to produce it at once. He accordingly wrote *The Man Who Never Was* in a single weekend – a *tour de force* second only to Operation Mincemeat itself. It was first published as a series of articles in the *Sunday Express* in 1953; Colvin's *The Unknown Courier* appeared later the same year.

Now, for the first time, Heartbreak and Mincemeat are published in a single volume. I am endlessly grateful to my old friend Leo Cooper – whose idea it was – not just because they complement each other so beautifully but because I feel that their joint publication somehow sets the seal on the friendship between Ewen Montagu and myself. I first met him only in 1973, when – thanks again to Leo – *Operation Heartbreak* was given a second edition, to which I contributed an introduction on which the present one is closely based. He kindly invited me to lunch, and I was able at last to offer him family apologies for all the hot water in which, through no fault of his own, he had found himself immersed. He has been dead, alas, for nearly twenty years; but my gratitude to him – as well as my admiration for the patience and good humour with which he endured the ridiculous and quite unnecessary tribulations that he was called upon to suffer – remains as warm as ever, and it is to his memory that this first joint edition of two great books is dedicated.

John Julius Norwich
London, 2003

OPERATION
HEARTBREAK

A STORY BY DUFF COOPER

To The Lady Caroline Duff

Contents

Prologue

It was a long way from the capital to the coast, and they had been obliged to leave very early in the morning. It had been cool then, but now, although it was not yet midday, the three occupants of the car were suffering from the heat.

The Military Attaché was also suffering from the wound which had incapacitated him for further active service. It still caused him, at times, acute pain. He would have thought it unmanly to say so, although it would have secured him sympathy and forbearance. He preferred to vent his misery by bullying his subordinates, being rude to his equals and insolent to his superiors. He had recently arrived at his new post, and was anxious to lose no time in becoming acquainted with his work. He therefore resented bitterly having to spend a whole hot day attending the funeral of a brother officer whom he had never liked.

The Chaplain was equally unhappy. During a residence of several years he had acquired the habits of the country, which did not include long drives over bad roads in the heat of the day. He had put on weight recently, which he regretted, but he had no wish to lose it in the way he seemed likely to do in the next few hours. He was beginning to wonder in what state his collar would be when it came to conducting the service. Not that it would matter much what he looked like or said, he reflected bitterly, as nobody except his two companions would ever see him again or understand a word he was saying.

The third occupant of the car had been looking forward to the day's outing, and was determined to enjoy it. The Assistant Military Attaché was a very young officer, whose health had caused him to be sent abroad, in the hope that he might benefit from a dry climate. He was well aware of the growing discomfort of his elders, which afforded him a good deal of amusement.

'It's getting nice and warm,' he said cheerfully, as the Chaplain for the third time mopped his brow. 'I suggest we stop somewhere and have a drink.'

The Chaplain and the Military Attaché hesitated. Each was determined to take the opposite line to the other and therefore waited for the other to speak first.

At last the Military Attaché said, 'There's nothing fit to drink in this damned country, and there aren't any decent pubs.'

The Chaplain pursed his lips. 'I think that a glass of cold water would be very refreshing.'

'As good a way of getting typhoid as any other, I suppose,' grunted the Military Attaché.

'The ordinary water in this district is singularly pure,' said the Chaplain. 'If you won't take my word for it, you can doubtless obtain mineral water.'

'Well, we should have to order something,' said the Military Attaché. 'It would hardly do if a great big British Embassy car drew up outside one of these miserable little inns, and three full-grown men, in their best clothes, jumped out and asked for three glasses of cold water for the good of the house. Remember, these people are neutrals, and we want 'em to remain so, and not to drive the whole country into the arms of the enemy. Use your imagination, Padre, if you've got any.'

The Assistant Military Attaché felt that he could accept the argument as qualified assent. 'May I tell the chauffeur to stop at the next likely place, sir? I've got a flask of whisky in my pocket, if you'd care for a whisky-and-soda. We can easily get soda-water, and personally I like the wine of the country.'

Now, a whisky-and-soda was the one thing on earth that the Military Attaché most wanted, but all he said was: 'Very well, you can do as you wish.'

A few minutes later the three of them were sitting in the cool shade of a great tree with two bottles before them, a jug of water and a bowl of ice. The Assistant Military Attaché, who knew more of the language than either of the others, had slipped into the rôle of master of ceremonies. He first half filled the Military Attaché's glass with whisky from his flask and then poured in the mineral water. The Military Attaché saw that it was strong, but felt he needed it. He was in pain, but determined not to show it. He could sleep during the rest of the journey, and all he had to do at the end of it was to stand to attention.

The Assistant Military Attaché helped himself to wine and then, seeing that the Chaplain was gazing rather dejectedly at his glass of cold water, he leant over and poured some whisky into it, saying in reply to the feeble protest, 'Come on, Padre, you know you like it, and it will kill those awful typhoid germs that Colonel Hamilton was talking about.'

The Chaplain allowed himself to be persuaded. The Assistant Military Attaché looked at his watch.

'We're well up to time,' he said, 'and can afford to relax for at least a quarter of an hour.'

Peace came to them as they sat there, stillness after speed, shadow after sunlight. Irritation and animosity were smoothed away. The Assistant

Military Attaché was sensitive to atmosphere and felt that the moment was favourable for putting questions that he had long been wanting to ask.

'It's a strange business, this funeral that we're attending,' he hazarded. 'It's much stranger than you suppose,' replied Colonel Hamilton, sipping his whisky.

'He was in your regiment, sir, wasn't he?'

'I suppose so. There's nobody else of that name in the Army List.'

'Was he only recently promoted?'

'You're thinking of the telegram I sent two days ago. As they're going to put a stone on his grave, I thought they'd better state his rank correctly. A month ago he was a captain, and one who had been passed over for promotion half a dozen times. He was out of a job, and so far as I could see had little chance of getting one. You saw the reply of the War Office to my telegram. "Rank correctly stated as major".'

'It does seem a bit mysterious.'

'It's as mysterious as be damned.'

'Could it have been that he was employed by the Secret Service?'

'No, it couldn't. I don't know much about the Secret Service, and the less you talk about it, young man, the better. I dare say they trip up occasionally, but I can't believe they could be such fools as to employ this particular fellow.'

'How about that packet that was found on the body? It was pretty decent of these people here to send it along to the Embassy without opening it.'

'How do you know they hadn't opened it?'

'The seals were intact, sir,' answered the Assistant Military Attaché confidently.

'Proves nothing,' grunted the other, 'but they'll know in London.'

'Was he a good officer, sir?'

'I never thought so. He was not a fellow of whom I thought very highly. But I suppose there was no harm in him. *De mortuis nil nisi bunkum*, or whatever the old tag is. I'm talking too much. We ought to be on the road. That damned clergyman has gone to sleep. Wake him up and get a move on.'

CHAPTER I

Nobody ever had fewer relations than Willie Maryngton. Neither his father nor his mother had brothers or sisters, and he himself was an only child. His mother died in giving birth to him on the 1st of January 1900, and his father, a professional soldier, was killed at Villers Cotterets in September, 1914. Willie's childhood was spent at the various military stations to which his father was posted, and his heart was given to the cavalry regiment in which his father served. The little boy could not tell that all the glamour which surrounded that regiment was part of the century he had missed, and that even in the war that was coming the cavalry was destined to play only a secondary rôle.

Willie was at a public school in 1914 when the war broke out, and for a few days he had wild plans of running away and joining the army as a drummer-boy. But news of his father's death, which arrived long after the event, had a sobering as well as a saddening effect, and he determined to concentrate henceforth all his abilities on making himself fit to receive a commission as early as possible. The Officers Training Corps then became for him more attractive than the playing-fields, and, although he had no natural bent for study, the mere name of the Army Class, when he attained to it, inspired him, so that he made up by hard work for what he lacked in ability.

His father had nominated a brother officer to act as the boy's guardian, and when he also fell, without having made any further provision for guardianship, his widow took on the responsibility of looking after Willie during the holidays. The loss of her husband, the care of her children and all the difficulties of war-time had embittered the middle-age of this in many ways admirable woman, leaving her with only one principle in life: the determination to do her duty. She was the daughter as well as the widow of an officer, and the noble ideal of service was the foundation of her character. She had three children; the eldest, Garnet, was three years older than Willie, went to a cheaper public school and was destined for the Royal Army Medical Corps. The youngest was a little girl of two who had been christened Felicity because she was born on the day when her father was promoted to the rank of major.

9

It was an austere household. There was little money to spare, and Mrs. Osborne, like many people by nature disinclined to spend, had enthusiastically accepted the Government's injunction to economise, and felt every time she saved a shilling a private thrill of pleasure as well as the satisfaction of performing a public duty.

Willie was no burden on the household. Both his father and his mother had had incomes of their own, and he would in due time inherit between two and three thousand pounds a year. Lawyers, whom he never saw, paid his school bills and also paid Mrs. Osborne liberally for his board and lodging in the holidays. She would render meticulous accounts of how the money was spent, and this effort at amateur book-keeping added to her cares, deepening the lines across her forehead and draining the colour from her fine eyes. Neither Willie nor the lawyers looked at the accounts she rendered, but she thought it her duty to render them, and whatever was her duty she would do. For duty was the watchword of this small house, situated between Aldershot and Camberley, and the only problem that could ever arise was to know where duty lay. That once known, the rest was simple.

There was, however, one member of the household to whom neither habits of austerity nor the call of duty made any appeal. If it be true that the criminal classes are largely recruited from the children of clergymen, it is equally easy to discover recalcitrants to the military tradition in officers' families, and even to find the sons of generals in the ranks of the pacifists. Horatio, Mrs. Osborne's second son, was nothing so serious, or so foolish, as a pacifist. He was one of those fortunate people to whom this world seems a vast park of amusement, and who dislike nobody except those who are bent on preventing others from enjoying themselves. To this disagreeable category soldiers, it seemed to Horry, evidently belonged. As a child he had hung about the barrack square and had heard the way in which non-commissioned officers spoke to private soldiers, and he hadn't liked it. He had seen the delinquents paraded for appearance before officers, when they must answer for the crimes of idleness, dirty buttons, unpunctuality, insobriety or absence without leave, and he had felt that those were his friends. He had once heard a drill-sergeant shout at a recruit, 'Take that smile off your face,' and the incident had made a deep impression on his childish mind. In later years he used to quote it to justify his hatred of militarism, saying that any system which discouraged smiling ought to be damned. There was nothing revolutionary in Horry's attitude; he only felt that soldiers, like schoolmasters – no doubt very good fellows in their way – were the natural enemies of those who, like himself, wanted to have fun.

Horry was younger than Garnet and older than Willie, who liked and looked up to both of them, with the respect that boys feel for immediate seniors. And they liked him. Everybody did. They were also, although he was quite unaware of it, impressed by the wealth that was coming to him, and the independence that it would bring. Garnet felt vaguely that a rich friend might be useful to him in his career. Horry thought what a good time Willie ought to have with his money, and hoped that he might sometimes be allowed to share in it.

Willie was distressed that Garnet should have chosen to go into the R.A.M.C. What he found difficult to understand was why such a big and powerful fellow as Garnet, bigger and more powerful than he would ever be, one who played football for his school and had won boxing competitions, should join a branch of the Service that was not actually engaged in fighting.

'I must say,' he said one day to Garnet, greatly daring, 'that I shouldn't care for your job – stuck somewhere well behind the lines, cutting people's legs off, with the supply of anaesthetics always running out.'

It was difficult to provoke Garnet. Conscious of his own strength and satisfied with his own wisdom, he could take as much teasing as a large St. Bernard dog. He looked at Willie with mild contempt.

'Stuck well behind the lines!' he echoed. 'That's all you know about it. Perhaps you'll be surprised to learn that the only man in the Army who has won two Victoria Crosses is a Medical Officer.'

This came as news to Willie, but he wouldn't own it, although he felt that the bottom had been knocked out of his argument.

'Yes,' he said, a little flustered, 'but decorations are all a matter of luck,' quoting something he had heard his father say more than once. 'All I meant was' – changing his ground – 'that the medical profession is one thing and the military profession another, and I'd rather go in whole-heartedly for one or the other.'

'Would you indeed?' replied Garnet calmly. 'Well, I prefer to go in whole-heartedly for both.'

This seemed to end the conversation, but Garnet, seeing that Willie had nothing more to say and was feeling snubbed, crushed and crestfallen, went on, out of the kindness of his heart:

'And you see, my boy, one has got to think of the future. A day comes when the Army doesn't want you any more. They turn you out in the cold with a pension which you can't live on if you've got a wife and brats. It'll be all right for you, no doubt, because you've got a bit of money of your own. But lots of chaps find themselves right up against it and don't know where to turn for a living. An officer of the R.A.M.C., on the other hand, is a member of a great profession which he has been practising all his life. He has had lots of experience, tried all sorts of climates and had a jolly good time. Then he buys a practice in some nice part of the country and settles down to a happy old age, while his pals, who've never been taught to do anything but fight the enemy, are trying to become secretaries of golf clubs, and when they succeed they add up the accounts wrong and go to prison for peculation.'

This was a long speech for Garnet, but it was a matter to which he had devoted much thought. While Willie was still considering the new possibility of being obliged to leave the Army before he wanted to – he had hitherto believed that soldiers remained soldiers until they died – Garnet went on:

'And you know, Willie, my grandfather was in the R.A.M.C., which is another reason for joining it – and a jolly good one, too. I've heard tell that he was one of the most popular officers in India. He was known all over the country. They called him the Deliverer of Bengal.'

Garnet laughed.

Willie laughed, too, but he didn't know why. The nickname given to Garnet's grandfather sounded very splendid to Willie – like the title of a novel by G. A. Henty. But it must be funny if Garnet laughed, for he did not laugh easily. Willie wondered whether it were something improper. Things usually were if he didn't understand them, but Garnet, unlike Horry, was not amused by impropriety.

Willie took his problems to the latter for solution. The gynaecological joke was explained, but Willie didn't think it funny, and when he asked what Horry meant to do if he had to leave the Army before he was a very old man, Horry answered:

'See here, little Willie' (an unkind nickname in those days, for it meant to the British public the German Crown Prince), 'the Army's problem about me is not how long they are going to keep me, but how they are going to get me into their clutches. That's what's worrying the War Office and keeping General French awake at night. They'll have to make this war last as long as the siege of Troy if they hope to get Horry Osborne into the ranks.'

'Into the ranks!' exclaimed Willie. 'But don't you want to be an officer?'

'No, I do not,' said Horry.

'But what else can one be,' asked Willie, 'except a barrister, or go into the Diplomatic Service? Surely you wouldn't be a doctor or a clergyman?'

'There are more professions in heaven and earth, little Willie,' said Horry, looking very profound, 'than are dreamt of in your philosophy.'

So Willie's conversation with Horry ended, as had his conversation with Garnet, with a remark that he couldn't understand.

CHAPTER II

The war went on and the boys grew up. Willie passed into Sandhurst at the earliest opportunity. His arrival there in August 1917 coincided with a prolongation of the course, which had formerly lasted nine months, and in future was to last a year. This was a cruel blow to him. It meant three further months away from the front. He had seriously thought of going through a course in a temporary officers' training corps, which would have lasted only four or six months. But it might have prevented him from getting a regular commission after the war, and the thought that his father had been at Sandhurst had clinched his decision, which he now regretted.

He did not distinguish himself at Sandhurst except by hard work and devotion to duty. He had hitherto had very little opportunity of riding, which he now took to with enthusiasm. He was not, and never became, a fine horseman, but he knew no fear, and the frequency of his falls became a legend. These, combined with his keen enjoyment of work and play, his easy good-nature and his guileless modesty, made him one of the most popular cadets of his year. The fact that he had plenty of money and no hesitation in spending it may have added a little gilding to his genuine charm.

He enjoyed that year. There are few more precious moments than those in which a boy feels for the first time the independence of manhood, when he can take decisions for himself, has no longer to ask permission or account for every action.

One anxiety only marred his happiness, and even made it difficult for him sometimes to share sincerely in the alternate rejoicing and gloom of his companions. When, in the autumn of 1917, orders were given for the church-bells to be rung in celebration of a British victory they brought no message of cheerfulness to Willie's heart, and when, in the following spring, the French and British armies were driven back, until it seemed that the retreat might turn into a rout, he could not suppress a secret thrill of satisfaction. That England could lose the war was not a possibility that ever entered into his calculations. When one of his companions suggested that this might happen he was not even angry, but looked upon that cadet ever after with indulgent pity, as someone who was not in possession of all his wits.

What Willie feared was not defeat but that the war should end before he crossed the Channel. It was not unnatural. During the four most formative years of his life he had had only one ambition. To go into battle with his regiment had been for him the summit of human desire. That regiment had seen comparatively little active service during the previous half-century. Willie had read its history again and again. Perhaps another fifty years would pass without a great war. He had seen somewhere a book called *The War to End War*. The title had sent a shiver of horror down his spine. And he had heard with deep dismay people talking about a League of Nations, which would make war impossible. So all the news that seemed good to others seemed bad to him, and whatever brought hope to most of the world brought him despair.

At the end of the following summer Willie left Sandhurst. He had acquitted himself with credit there, if without distinction, and he had made many friends. It was a proud day when he received his commission, and an anxious one when he presented himself to his regiment. Friends of his father ensured him a good reception among the senior officers; and among the junior ones he already had friends of his own.

The regiment had suffered casualties during the enemy offensive in the spring. There was a shortage of officers in France and every reason to suppose that Willie would find his way there within two or three months. Such leisure as he had from training was therefore devoted to the purchase of kit. No bride ever selected her trousseau with greater care and delight than Willie devoted to the buying of the drab little articles that compose an officer's kit. He never tired of consulting those with experience of such matters concerning the latest gadgets, and he was interested in the smallest details of such objects, from periscopes to writingpads.

If only the news from the front had been less favourable he would have been the happiest of men. But he consoled himself with the thought – a thought which depressed so many others that it was only the swing of the pendulum, that pendulum which had swung so often and so far since August 1914. There had been similar waves of optimism, like that which had followed the Battle of Cambrai only a year ago, when many had prophesied that the war would be over by Christmas, only to find that six months later the Allies were seriously thinking of abandoning Paris, and pessimists whispered that the war was lost.

These hopes and fears were for a while expelled by the exultation with which he received orders to be ready to go to France with the next draft. Earlier in the war officers had been granted a week or more 'draft leave' before going overseas. This had now been abolished, but there were few if any duties imposed on those who were awaiting departure. Farewells to relatives – a tiresome obligation or a trying ordeal

– filled the time of most young men in these circumstances. But no such obligation or ordeal awaited Willie. So that these were idle, happy and proud days for him. He frequented the military club to which he now belonged, and could not suppress a little swagger when he informed his acquaintances that he might be off 'any day now'. The departure of the draft was twice postponed, to his extreme annoyance, but at last the day was fixed, and Willie, who had promised to spend his last Saturday to Monday at Mrs. Osborne's, travelled down to Camberley on November 9th.

Horry was there on his arrival and greeted him with a cheer.

'Hail, little Willie. Come and kiss me. The war's over, and we're both safe.'

'What rot you talk!' said Willie angrily. 'I rang up barracks before I left. They had heard nothing. Everything was proceeding according to plan, and the draft is leaving on Wednesday. Instructions from the War Office were to carry on.'

'Oh, I don't suppose your rotten old barracks has heard anything, nor the War Office either. It took them about a year to know the war had started, and they'll go on fighting it for a year after it's over, but everybody outside the War Office has heard that the Kaiser's chucked his hand in.'

'You think you're very clever, Horry,' said Willie, who was now flushed and heated, 'but there was an officer at the club this morning, an old officer of my regiment, who did frightfully well in the Matabele war, and he's always been right about this war – Colonel Wright his name is, and he says the Kaiser's abdication will only make the Germans fight more doggedly, and he can speak German, and he thinks the Kaiser had only been a hindrance to Ludendorff and it's probably the German General Staff that have made him get out.'

'All right, Willie,' said Horry, seeing how deeply the other was feeling. 'Three cheers for Colonel Wright, but I hope the old bastard's wrong this time. We'll drink his health in a glass of sherry, if Mum's got one, and hope for the worst.'

Willie's wrath, which always went as quickly as it came, evaporated before Horry's smile, and at that moment Mrs. Osborne came into the room. She kissed the two boys with unusual warmth, and Willie noticed with surprise that there was colour in her cheeks and that her eyes were shining as they had not shone for four long years.

When Horry asked if there was any sherry in the house, she said that she had bought a bottle that afternoon and two bottles of claret.

'You'll be surprised,' she added, for she saw they were, neither of them ever having seen her drink anything but water, or spend a shilling on the smallest luxury – 'but Garnet may be coming tonight or tomorrow, and it will be the first family reunion we've had for so long.'

Willie felt that he was not to be the hero of the evening, as he had expected, and he vaguely resented it. Knowing Mrs. Osborne's economy, he had taken his precautions, and he said, as gaily as he could:

'It's not only a family reunion, it's also the orphan's good-bye. I'm off to the war on Wednesday, and I've brought some champagne for you all to drink my health.'

Mrs. Osborne gave him a quick look, and the light in her eyes went out for a moment.

'It was very sweet of you, Willie, to think of it,' she said quietly. 'We shall be very happy to drink your health, and happier still to think that the war is probably not going on much longer.'

'Don't be too sure of that,' said Willie, adding rather pompously, 'There are, if I may say so, two schools of thought on the subject.'

'One headed by Colonel Wright and the other by Colonel Wrong,' sang Horry as he poured out the sherry.

Sunday was a day of rumours. There was nothing definite in the one newspaper which came to the house. Horry walked into Camberley while Willie played with Felicity, a beautiful, large-eyed, quiet child. Garnet arrived in the afternoon. He was careful not to commit himself, but said that there was no doubt at all that the Kaiser had abdicated and that the German delegates had gone to meet Foch in order to discuss the terms of an armistice.

'After all,' said Willie, 'an armistice doesn't necessarily mean peace. It's only a kind of an *entr'acte*.'

'Quite,' said Garnet, 'but once the troops have stopped fighting I think it'll be very difficult to persuade them to begin again.'

They drank champagne that evening, to which none of them was accustomed, and under its reassuring influence Mrs. Osborne lost her last fears that the war might continue, and Willie forgot his anxiety lest it should stop. Horry was in wonderful form, or at least they all thought he was, and they sat up later than they had ever done in that house.

Willie overslept the next morning, and when he came down found the dining-room empty. Mrs. Osborne was attending to household duties. Garnet and Horry had walked into the village to collect the news. Willie felt deeply depressed. Disconsolately he consumed the tepid remains of breakfast and strolled into the sitting-room, where he found Felicity engrossed in some obscure game with two battered dolls. She took no notice of him. He walked up and down for a minute or two and then he cried out:

'Oh, Felicity, I'm so unhappy.'

She turned and looked at him very gravely. Then she nodded her head slowly and said:

'Yes, and I'm unhappy because you are.'

The front door was opened and slammed to with a bang. The two young men dashed into the room. Mrs. Osborne followed them, breathless.

'It's all over!' shouted Horry. 'No more doubts or rumours. Official announcement. The armistice will be signed this morning at 11 a.m.'

'That is to say,' added Garnet, looking at his wrist-watch, 'in exactly forty-three minutes from now.'

Mrs. Osborne's eyes were damp as she stretched out her hands and caught both her sons by an arm. Then she looked at Willie, and saw that his face was white and his lips were quivering.

'Run upstairs, Willie dear,' she said quickly, 'and see if I left my spectacles in your room.'

Willie was through the door, up the stabs and into his room in a flash. He locked the door, threw himself on the bed and burst into tears.

As he lay there sobbing, two superficial sentiments almost made him forget his deeper sorrow. The first of these was shame that he, a grown man, holding the King's Commission, should have broken down and cried as he had never cried since he could remember. The other sentiment was one of profound gratitude to Mrs. Osborne, gratitude that made him love her, for having saved him from disgracing himself before the others. One could see that she was a soldier's daughter, he thought, by the rapidity with which she had appreciated the situation and given the right word of command. That was how he must act if ever he found himself in a critical situation in the war, and then he remembered again, with a fresh pang, that the war was over. But he could not lie there all day blubbing like a baby. It was nearly eleven o'clock. He must go downstairs and show a brave face, not a tear-stained one, if he could help it.

Having bathed his eyes and brushed his hair, he went downstairs, hearing the hall clock strike eleven as he went. He found them in the dining-room, where Horry was too busy struggling with the recalcitrant cork of a champagne bottle to pay any undue attention to his entry. The cork came out, followed by some of the contents of the bottle, which flowed over the table-cloth. Horry mopped up the spilt wine with his fingers, which he then rubbed behind his ears, explaining to his surprised companions that this was for luck. Then he filled the four glasses.

'Here, Willie,' he said, 'have a glass of your own champagne, and as you won't like to drink to peace, let's drink to the next war.'

'No,' said Mrs. Osborne; 'that would be wicked. Let us drink to the British Army,' which they did, she adding softly to herself as the glass touched her lips, 'Alive and dead.'

'We've forgotten Felicity,' cried Horry. 'If she never drinks champagne again in her life she must have some to-day.'

They found her in the next room, still absorbed in her play. Horry filled a liqueur glass and told her she must drink it all for luck. She obeyed solemnly, and when asked if she liked it, she felt that the occasion called for something special, so she brought out an expression of Horry's.

'Yes,' she said, 'damned good.'

When the young men shouted with laughter, her large dark eyes spar-
kled with success and mischief.

That afternoon Horry accompanied Willie to London. The sorrows
of youth, like the sorrows of childhood, although they may leave deep
wounds and lasting scars, can be quickly, if only temporarily, banished by
other distractions. Among the crowds that thronged the streets that day,
waving flags and cheering vociferously, there were few who waved more
enthusiastically or cheered louder than Willie, who had felt a few hours
earlier that there was nothing left to live for on earth.

By dinner-time they were both exhausted, and Horry said that if Willie
would pay the bill he would take him to the best restaurant in London.
Willie didn't mind what he paid, so they dined at Ornano's, which did
seem to Willie a very wonderful place indeed, and he was glad to notice
that even some of Horry's self-assurance deserted him when the urbane
head-waiter of historic fame approached them with the menu. His atten-
tions were mainly owing to the fact that the restaurant was almost empty,
for they were dining at an unfashionably early hour, and this was also
why, Horry explained, none of the famous men and beautiful women,
whose presence he had promised, had yet arrived. Food was bad in those
days and insufficient; sugar and butter were almost unobtainable, but
what was served to the young men, seated on one of the corner sofas in a
dim pink light, with music gently playing, seemed to them delectable. The
champagne was really good, and so was the brandy, though it had not, as
they imagined, been bottled in the reign of Napoleon I.

They had had a long day and a great experience. They felt tired, but
very pleasantly so. The sophisticated atmosphere of the restaurant made
them feel suddenly older. The wine was able to have its soft, mellowing
effect. Self-consciousness, the curse of English youth, fell from them, and
they found words coming to them easily. Willie was able to pour forth all
his sorrows, and the burden of them grew lighter for the telling. He even
confessed that he had wept in his room that morning.

'I knew you had, old boy,' said Horry. 'We all knew, and we all thought
the more of you. But don't you worry. You're not nineteen yet, and you'll
be young for another twelve years. I'll bet there's another war in less time
than that. You don't insist on a European war, do you? They're a damned
sight too dangerous, in my opinion. You'd have much more fun smashing
up the old Zulus or leading a cavalry charge against a pack of dancing
Dervishes, like the 21st Lancers did at Omdurman. You see, you've got
a vocation, Willie. I've always felt you had. You're a born soldier. You've
never dreamt of being anything else – have you? Admit it!'

Willie, who was now enjoying himself enormously, gladly admitted it,
and Horry went on:

'Now, if a man's got a vocation he always makes good. Somehow, some-
time, his opportunity comes, and because it's the one thing he's been wait-

ing for all his life, he's ready when it comes and he takes it. Your chance will come all right – and you'll take it – don't worry.'

He paused a moment and lit a cigarette, while Willie, profoundly believing all that he had said, felt as though he had already distinguished himself in a war, and tried to look modest.

'You may not believe it,' Horry went on, 'but I've got a vocation too. But mine's a secret. I don't think I can tell you because, if you have a fault, it is that you're a bit old-fashioned, and you might be shocked.'

'Oh, do tell me about your vocation, Horry,' said Willie. 'I long to hear, and I swear not to tell anybody.'

'Let's have two more brandies first,' said Horry, 'one for you, to help you bear the shock, and one for me, because I like it.'

The brandies were ordered, and they took some time to come, while Horry smoked reflectively and Willie wondered what Horry's vocation could possibly be.

'Well,' said Horry at last, speaking with deliberation as he sipped his brandy, 'it may surprise you, Willie, to learn that ever since I was ten years old I have had only one ambition in life, and that is to go on the stage.'

Willie was shocked. Had he been in a less receptive mood the shock would have been greater, but tonight everything seemed strange and new; the world had changed since yesterday. His first thought was that Horry was making fun of him, as he had so often done before.

'You're pulling my leg?' he asked hopefully.

'I never was more serious in my life,' was the reply.

'But, but,' Willie stammered, 'chaps like us can't be actors.'

'What do you mean by chaps like us?' asked Horry scornfully.

'Damn it, Horry, I mean gentlemen.' He could not have said it if he had been quite sober.

'There you are,' exclaimed Horry. 'I said you were old-fashioned. I might say you were a snob, but I know you're not. You're living in the past. Times have changed. They had changed even before the war, and they're going to change a jolly sight quicker after it. Not gentlemen, indeed! How about Sir Henry Irving and Sir Herbert Tree? And Charles Hawtrey was at Eton! And there's Gerald du Maurier, just got a commission in the Irish Guards. Since when have the Irish Guards given commissions to chaps who weren't gentlemen?'

This last argument, although the fact on which it was based was not strictly accurate, carried most weight with Willie. But he remembered hearing his father say that an officer, in a good regiment, who married an actress, would have to send in his papers. Yet it seemed to him easier for an actress to be a lady than for an actor to be a gentleman. He had heard of people's daughters going on the stage, not without parental protest, but never of their sons doing so. However, he didn't want to quarrel tonight, or even to argue. He had always been fond of Horry, but never so fond as now, so that he allowed himself to be easily converted, and soon he was discussing with animation the kind of parts in which Horry would do best.

When they left the restaurant the Strand was quiet, although sounds of revelry came from the Mall, where the mob were burning a German cannon. The two young men walked home arm in arm, feeling happy and very superior to the roisterers. Horry was taking his call at the end of a triumphant first night, and Willie was galloping across the veld, at the head of his regiment, under a hail of assegais.

CHAPTER III

The twenty-one years that passed between the two great wars seemed to many who lived through them to go quickly. The passage of time is measured by events, and when there are few events time passes unnoticed. It certainly flowed smoothly for Willie Maryngton. When he came to look back on it all, on the eve of the second world war, he was surprised to find how few events there were that stuck out in his memory.

He remembered very well leaving for the Continent two days after the Armistice. It was the journey to which he had been looking forward for years. How different it was from all that he had imagined! The thrill of war had been taken out of it, and there was nothing left but confusion, delay and discomfort. Inaccurate information awaited him at every turn. The troops were moving forward as fast as he was, and much faster than correct news of their movements travelled back.

He caught them up at last, and spent some months with the army of occupation. It was a depressing and disillusioning experience. Depressing because once again he found that the happiest hours spent by his brother officers were the least happy ones for him. These would occur at evening, in the mess, when the port was going round. Then would begin the endless discussions and reminiscences of the fighting. Sometimes these conversations were serious and even melancholy, but more often they were full of gaiety, for men remember more easily, and prefer to remember, the pleasanter incidents in their lives. The war was the great subject that they had in common, and it was inevitable that they should revert to it whenever good cheer and good-fellowship encouraged conversation. Nor could they be expected to know, or, if they had known, to care that the youngest and latest joined officer should suffer from their conversation. How often he felt that if only he had been present at one action all would have been different.

He was disappointed also in the enemy. All his youth he had pictured these formidable people as very fierce, very brutal, very evil, very brave. What he found was a herd of lumbering louts, subservient and clumsy, sometimes sullen and surly, but more often too anxious to please. Were these the same men, or any relation to those who had swept through

Belgium almost to the gates of Paris in a few weeks, held up the Russian steam-roller, smashed the empire of the Czars and come near to defeating the Royal Navy in the North Sea? He could hardly believe it.

Nor was he satisfied with the spirit of his own men. He had thought to find in the regiment abroad a little less discipline, perhaps, but more enthusiasm and keenness than at home. So he had been led to expect by returning officers. But this, if it ever had been, was no longer the case. The men were restless and discontented, talking only of the return to civilian life, speculating on how soon it would come, and complaining of the delay. How could Willie at the age of nineteen understand that the morale of troops is better on the eve of battle than on the eve of demobilisation?

This first experience of being abroad with his regiment was not one upon which he looked back with any pleasure, and he was glad to return to England and to find himself quartered in a part of the country where good hunting was easily available. Horses henceforward filled his life. When he was not in the saddle he was talking or thinking about them. Those who do not know would be surprised to learn how large a part horses can come to play in the existence of a man, particularly of a young man, and above all of a young cavalry officer. In the days when horse cavalry still existed, the horse represented for such a one the centre both of his profession and of his recreation. It combined work and play. It could fill every hour of his activities during daylight, and prove an inexhaustible topic of conversation at night. Every day during the winter months, that his military duties permitted, he would hunt, his season beginning, indeed, long before winter with the first morning's cub-hunting. Point-to-points and steeplechases were the only other amusements in which he indulged. He bought a few jumpers and rode them in races with varying success but with unvarying enthusiasm, and he shocked himself once by saying in the heat of an argument that he would rather win the Grand National on his own horse than be awarded the Victoria Cross. He retracted this wild statement immediately, apologised and said that he must be drunk. But he wasn't, and there were those among his audience who agreed with him, to such a point can hippolatry stir the imaginations of young men.

The coming of spring meant for Willie the opening of flat racing, which in his opinion was an inferior sport. It meant also polo and the London season.

In the nineteen-twenties London was a gay city and England was a happy land. Those who had lived before the war made unfavourable comparisons with the past, but to the new generation, without previous experience, life as it was seemed agreeable enough. There had been a redistribution of wealth, but there was still plenty of it, and there was a boom of prosperity. The number of war casualties had been greater than ever before, but they were soon forgotten by the majority of the survivors, and the spectre of war was banished from men's minds.

All that the country had to offer in the way of enjoyment was laid before a young subaltern in a good regiment with an agreeable appearance and ample means. Willie helped himself generously to the good things that were offered him, but he did not fall into excess. Although he had no parents to guide him, their place was taken by the regiment, which he loved and honoured more than anything else in the world, and which therefore exercised over his conduct as strong an influence as any parents could have done. There were certain things which officers in that regiment did not do, and those things would never be done by Willie Maryngton.

He danced, he rode, he went racing and indulged in all the pleasures that became his age and circumstances. He was fond of dancing, but, out of the ballroom, he spent little of his time with girls. He found them difficult to talk to, and the regiment disapproved of men who were always hanging round women's petticoats.

He took a flat in Jermyn Street and joined another club, to which his father had belonged, and where the atmosphere was very different from that of the military club to which he belonged already. Most of the members were older men, but, although at first he was intimidated, he soon made many friends among them, for towards his elders he bore himself with a frank, unassuming manliness that quickly won for him sympathy and goodwill.

During these years, although it may be said that he had found his place in the world and was occupying it with confidence, he never forgot what he had missed, or ceased to regret it. A chance question from a neighbour at a dinner-party, 'Where were you in the war?' a chance remark from an old member in the club, 'You young fellows who've been through the war,' would bring back a pang of the anguish he had felt when he was first told of the Armistice. And now that he was beginning to meet, as grown men, those who had been still at school on that day, he felt that they also had an advantage over him.

Hunting in the winter, polo in the summer and racing all the year round demanded an income larger than Willie's, and although he was not extravagant he came gradually to understand, as the years went on, that he was living beyond his means. It therefore came to him as a relief rather than a blow when he learnt that the regiment was to go to India. He was at the time facing a financial crisis. The prospect of cutting down his hunters, and perhaps having to give up polo altogether, was not a pleasant one. The news brought down upon him his creditors like a swarm of locusts. He was horrified to discover how much he owed. London tradesmen are very patient with rich young officers in good regiments, but their patience comes abruptly to an end when there is any question of the young gentlemen proceeding overseas for an indefinite period. Willie had to sell out capital in order to meet his liabilities, and discovered, as so many have before and since, that it is always the very worst moment to sell. Looking back on it all, Willie remembered only some very dull conversations with solicitors which had depressed him more than the knowledge that he had to face life in future on a reduced though still adequate income.

He almost lost sight of the Osbornes during these years. Mrs. Osborne wrote to him at regular intervals, giving him full information about each member of the family. Garnet was working in one of the large military hospitals; Horry, having done well at the Academy of Dramatic Art, was usually with some touring company in the provinces; Felicity was at school in Brussels. They all seemed very far away from the life that Willie was leading.

He saw Horry once before he left for India. He was having supper at the Savoy Grill with some brother officers after the theatre. Horry was there with a very pretty girl. Neither Horry nor his companion was in evening clothes, which slightly distressed Willie. But the girl was lovely, and one of his companions suggested that he should invite them both to join their party. Guilelessly Willie approached them and asked:

'Hallo, Horry! won't you both come over and sit with us?'

'No, we certainly won't,' said Horry gruffly.

Willie was taken aback.

'Why not?' he asked.

'Because we think you'd bore us to death,' said Horry.

The girl saw the hurt look on Willie's innocent face, and gave him a charming smile of compassion, which softened the blow.

Later, when he saw the two of them leaving the restaurant, he ran after them and asked Horry to lunch with him on the following day.

'No, I won't,' said Horry, who seemed still unaccountably annoyed.

'Oh,' said Willie, 'that's too bad. I'm off to India at the end of the week, and you may never see me again.'

'You're going to India?' cried Horry. 'How was I to know? Of course I'll lunch with you to-morrow, bless you. Sorry I was cross. Name the time and place.'

Willie suggested his club. Horry demurred.

'Wouldn't a restaurant be more fun? I tell you what, let's go to Ornano's, where we dined together on Armistice night.'

And so it was agreed.

It was with mixed feelings that Willie remembered the luncheon that took place on the following day. His first impression was that Ornano's had changed. It was no longer the magic haunt where illustrious beings consumed rare dishes and precious wines. It was a distinctly second-rate restaurant frequented by the riff-raff of Fleet Street and the Strand. The head-waiter of international renown had long ago soared to higher spheres, and the clientele had deteriorated. Willie noticed a couple of bookmakers, whom he knew, drinking champagne with two buxom blondes. He obscurely felt, although it would have been impossible for him to express the feeling in words, and he would have protested had he been charged with it, that this was a place to which he did not belong. What was worse, he felt that Horry did belong to it. Horry ordered a 'gin and it' as though he were at home, and Willie felt he was being pompous when he said he would prefer a glass of sherry.

Horry was not unaware of the impression that Willie was receiving.

'This place has gone down a bit, but I still like it. You meet all sorts here, and the grub's good; but of course it's not the place it was in the days of Luigi.'

'Why were you so cross with me last night?' asked Willie.

'It wasn't you, old boy; it was your friends. I know the type – more money than brains – stroll into the Savoy Grill half-tight and think they can pick up any girl they see there.'

'No, no,' Willie protested indignantly, 'they're not like that at all. They're very good chaps; all in my regiment. I told them I knew you, and they said couldn't we all get together and have a jolly evening.'

'Yes, and you probably told them I was on the stage, and they assumed she was, too, and they thought because she was an actress one of them might go home with her.'

Willie indignantly denied the accusation.

'Look here,' said Horry. 'Supposing they'd met another fellow in the regiment, one of their own sort, out with his sister, and supposing she'd been a pretty girl, do you think they'd have suggested joining up?'

'Yes,' said Willie, candidly, 'I think they would.'

'Well, I don't,' retorted Horry, 'and that's what made me so damned angry. Perhaps I was wrong, but you know what *esprit de corps* is – honour of the regiment and all that sort of twaddle. Well, we people on the stage feel about our profession as you do about yours, and however it may have been in the past, our morality in these days is just as good as anyone else's – better, perhaps, because we work harder. So it makes me mad with rage when people treat actresses as though they were all no better than they should be. And that was what I felt was happening last night. The girl I was with is an actress, as a matter of fact, and she happens to be an angel – happily married: her husband's playing lead in a first-rate show on tour, and she may be getting a West End job. I adore her, but I'm not in love with her. I've never even held her hand in the taxi. I kiss her on the cheek, you know, when we meet or say good-night, just as I would Mum or Felicity. So you can imagine what I feel when I think people are treating her like a tart.'

'Yes, I think I can,' said Willie, 'but really you're wrong about the brutal and licentious soldiery. None of us were tight last night, and if you had come over to our table you would have had nothing to complain of; everybody would have treated her just like a lady.'

'Just like a lady,' echoed Horry, 'but she is a lady, damn you! and much more of a lady than lots of the melancholy sisters of second-rate Army officers that I've met.'

'Oh, for heaven's sake don't get angry again,' said Willie. 'You know jolly well that I didn't mean it that way. I meant they would treat her just the same as anybody else.'

Horry recovered his good temper without difficulty, and they talked of other matters. There was no more quarrelling, but the conversation was not what it should have been between two fosterbrothers on the eve of a long separation. They clung rather desperately to family matters, both feeling conscious of the lack of other topics. There were jokes about old Garnet, speculations on Felicity's future, slight anxieties about Mrs. Osborne's health. But when these subjects were exhausted and they tried to talk of themselves, they were both conscious that there was a mutual lack of interest. They had no friends in common. Horry cared nothing about the Army and as little about horses. Willie tried valiantly to discuss the theatre, but his interest in it was limited to musical comedy and revue. He hadn't seen the plays that Horry talked of, nor even heard the names which he mentioned with the greatest respect. So that they were both secretly glad when the meal was over, although they were both sincerely sorry to say good-bye.

CHAPTER IV

The happiest years of Willie's life were those that he spent in India. He had no doubt about it, when he reviewed the past. There he was able to recapture the nineteenth century, and enjoy life as he would have enjoyed it had he been born fifty years earlier. The days of the British Raj were already numbered, but a British cavalry officer could still be gloriously unconscious of the fact. On little more than his Army pay he could live like a prince, obedient servants at his beck and call, the best of everything the country could provide at his command, a string of polo ponies in the stable, and even an occasional shot at a tiger. Willie's reduced income was wealth in India, and although sometimes, sweltering in the sunshine, he would have given much for a cold, grey day in the shires, he was on the whole as happy as it is given to mankind to be.

But, because men can never be quite happy for long, he suffered during these years from one continual source of irritation and experienced one great sorrow. The irritation came from a brother officer, who was a few years senior to him and whom he had never liked. Hamilton was his name. He was not popular in the regiment, but he was indifferent to popularity. He was extremely efficient, and he was working for the Staff College examination. His efficiency was reluctantly admired, but his professional ambitions were regarded with suspicion. The general feeling was that a man who prepared himself for the Staff College would be obliged to waste in study precious hours that might be spent in playing or practising polo.

During their stay in India Hamilton became adjutant, a position which enabled him to inflict many minor annoyances on junior officers whom he didn't like. For some reason that would be hard to discover he had never liked Willie. Perhaps it was because everybody else liked him. Perhaps he secretly envied the popularity he affected to despise.

One of the reasons why Hamilton was not liked was that he had the courage to speak openly in favour of mechanisation, that fearful fate which hung like a shadow of doom over all cavalry regiments at this period.

'I'd as soon be a chauffeur,' exclaimed Willie passionately one evening, 'as have to drive a dirty tank about and dress like a navvy.'

'Of course,' replied Hamilton blandly, 'if all you care about is wearing fancy dress, playing games on horseback, and occasionally showing off at the Military Tournament, you're perfectly right to take that view; but if you were interested in war, or ever hoped to take part in one, you'd be praying that your regiment might be mechanised before the next war comes.'

This was a cruel thing to say to Willie, and only Hamilton knew how cruel it was. Willie grew very red, then very white. He longed to throw something or to strike a blow. With difficulty he controlled himself, muttered a monosyllabic expletive and stalked from the room.

The wound that had been inflicted took long to heal. Hamilton had won a Military Cross in the war and was no doubt entitled to sneer at Willie, who had seen no fighting. But Willie would wake up in the night and recall the incident. He would think of clever answers that he might have made, and groan with rage. He knew all the arguments that had ever been put forward for the retention of horse cavalry, but he had forgotten them when he needed them. Hamilton had had the best of it. He always did, he always would, because he was clever. He was a good soldier too, there was no denying it, but he couldn't really love the regiment, or be loyal to it, if he could speak of uniform as fancy dress, and if he wanted to see their horses taken away.

The misfortune that befell Willie in India was his first love affair. The opening act of this little drama was all that it should have been, and fitted perfectly into the nineteenth-century pattern of life. The heroine's father was the Colonel of an Indian Cavalry regiment – an old regiment with honourable traditions – and the father and grandfather of Colonel Summers had served in it. Daisy was a pretty girl of a very English type, who looked prettier in India than she would have done at home. She was fair and fluffy, with large blue eyes and a complexion like a wild rose, the delicacy of which had not yet been dimmed by the Indian sun, for she had only recently arrived from Europe. She had finished her education at the same school in Brussels as Felicity Osborne, and it was the discovery of this fact that first brought her together with Willie. It gave them a subject of conversation, and Willie never found it easy to discover such subjects when he was brought into contact with young ladies.

Daisy spoke with enthusiasm of Felicity. She had been the beauty of the school and the favourite of the headmistress. Some of the girls found her proud and reserved, but she and Daisy had always got on well together, and had been the closest of friends. She was glad to talk of her school life, for with her also subjects of conversation were not always easy to find. So, at the various entertainments that the station offered – polo-matches, picnics, cocktail parties and dances – Willie came to be on the look out for Daisy and to spend with her the greater part of his time. It was a happy day when he discovered that, not only was she a friend of Felicity, but also that she took an interest in racing, and was quite well informed about the branch of that sport which he himself preferred. Endless vistas of conversation now lay before them, for the beauty of the turf as a conversational subject is that in racing, unlike art or philosophy, some important event has always just happened, or is just about to happen, and the daily Press is full of reports and speculations, which can be read and quoted.

Willie's admiration for Daisy increased rapidly and, being a simple soul, he found it difficult not to talk of what was occupying his thoughts. One evening before dinner, when the officers were smoking on the veranda and the conversation was about horses, he remarked:

'That young Miss Summers knows an awful lot about racing, both out here and at home.'

'I suppose she gets her information from Coper Caffin,' said Captain Hamilton, and there was something in his tone that Willie didn't like.

'Why, is he a pal of hers?' he asked casually.

'They're inseparable,' replied the other.

'Oh,' said Willie, 'I've never seen them together.'

Then dinner was announced.

Caffin was a captain in the regiment which Daisy's father commanded. To Willie he seemed an old man. In fact, he was barely forty. Willie was respectful to his seniors, and grateful if they were kind to him, which Caffin had always been. He had an attractive Irish brogue, and a full share of all those charming qualities that make Irishmen popular. Hamilton said of him that he was more like a stage Irishman than the genuine article. He was good looking, with light eyes and dark curly hair beginning to go grey, and he was a superb horseman.

Not only could he ride a horse, but he could sell one; and there were those who said that he was even more skilful in the latter activity than the former. Buying and selling horses certainly occupied a great deal of his time, and had earned him the nickname by which he was generally known. In the horse market honourable men accept a lower standard of integrity than elsewhere, but whether Coper Caffin always conformed even to that low standard was sometimes questioned; and there were young officers who long remembered with bitterness the deals they had done with him. Willie was not one of them. He had once bought a horse from Coper and he had paid a high price for it, but it had proved a good horse, and Willie was not one to complain of the price if he were satisfied with the purchase.

'Do you know Coper Caffin?' he asked Daisy the next time he met her.

'Oh yes,' she answered. 'He's sweet, don't you think so?'

'Sweet' was not the adjective that Willie would have chosen. 'He's not a bad chap,' he said, and added with greater conviction, 'He's jolly good on a horse.'

'Yes, he rides beautifully, doesn't he?' she agreed, and added, 'And he's always been ever so sweet to me.'

'You've known him some time, have you?'

'Oh yes, ever since I was a flapper. And he came to Brussels when I was at school there and took me out to lunch.'

'What was he doing in Brussels?' Willie asked.

'Selling horses, I suppose. He's always selling horses. He's going to leave the Army soon and set up on his own in Ireland. He's got a lovely place there.'

'Oh,' said Willie dubiously. Nothing that he had heard of him previously had led him to believe that Coper Caffin belonged to the landed gentry.

Not long after this there was a dance to which Willie got permission from Daisy's mother to escort her, together with another young lady who was staying with them. The party was well planned, it was a beautiful evening, the heat was not excessive and dancing went on until late. When they at last decided to leave, the other young lady could not be found, and after a search which caused further delay they were informed that she had left earlier with somebody else. So they drove home together, Willie at the wheel and Daisy's pretty, tired head resting gently on his shoulder. When they reached the Colonel's bungalow they got out of the car and without a word fell into one another's arms. There was a broad seat upon the veranda, on which they prolonged their embrace. Those were moments Willie never forgot. It was the first time that he had held the yielding body of a young girl in his arms and felt soft lips pressed passionately to his.

'I think I've been in love with you for a long time,' he said, 'but I never really knew it until this evening. When did you know you were in love with me? It seems so wonderful.'

That she was in love with him he had no doubt, else she would not have kissed him.

'You are so very sweet,' was her answer, and her arms stretched out to him again.

When next they spoke he put another question.

'When shall we be married?'

Even in the dim light of very early dawn he could see she was surprised, but surely she would never have allowed him to kiss her so passionately unless she were prepared to marry him, and surely she would not have suspected him of being the kind of man who would treat a girl, a Colonel's daughter, in that way, unless he meant to make her his wife.

'Marry, marry, marry – oh, my sweet, it's very late at night to talk of marriage.' She laughed a little indulgent laugh, as though she were talking to a child. 'How do you know that you'll feel the same in the morning?'

'I'm not tight, if that's what you mean,' said Willie. 'You could see I wasn't by the way I drove the car. And as for to-morrow morning, it's that already. Look, the dawn is breaking. Could there be a better time of day to get engaged?'

Daisy was still bewildered. She was a child of her epoch, gay and shallow, not mercenary or scheming. She knew that she must get married. There were two younger sisters coming along, and two brothers at school, who were a heavy drain on the family resources, even while her father still drew full pay and lived in India. Willie, as she put it to herself, was very sweet – she had never met anyone sweeter. He was attractive, too; and yet she hesitated. He was so simple and so good – she had a curious unaccountable feeling that it would be rather a shame to marry him. She fell back on the excuse that one child gives to another.

'But what would our people say?'

'I haven't got any people,' answered Willie – 'not even an aunt or an uncle. I'll come and see your father to-morrow morning – this morning, I mean. Perhaps I should have done so before I asked you. I don't see why he should object' – and he added with some embarrassment, 'I've got a little money, you know, as well as my pay.'

'Oh, Daddy won't object. He'll be thankful to get rid of me, bless his heart. But are you sure, Willie, that you really want to marry me? You haven't known me very long, and one always hears about boys who marry the Colonel's daughter in India and spend the rest of their lives regretting it. Don't you think you might come to regret it, Willie?'

But as she asked the question she moved closer into his arms, thereby dissolving any doubts that he might have had. It was almost daylight when they separated, and they were engaged to be married.

Willie remembered vividly the interview he had with Colonel Summers on the following day. Military duties occupied the earlier hours of the morning, and midday is not a suitable time in India for paying calls, so that it was about sundown when he arrived, by appointment, at the Colonel's bungalow and was ushered into his presence. He had been feeling nervous, and had vaguely wondered whether he should not stand at attention, as in the orderly-room, and apply in official terms for permission to marry the Colonel's daughter. But he was immediately put at his ease.

'Help yourself to a glass of sherry, my dear fellow, and sit you down. It's been damned hot all day, hasn't it? But there's a breeze this evening. Now tell me what I can do for you.'

Haltingly Willie told his story, confessing that he had already put the question to the young lady, and excusing himself for not having first obtained her father's consent. The Colonel did not pretend to be surprised. He had known well enough that there could be but one subject on which Lieutenant Maryngton would ask for a private talk with him. Nor did he pretend to hesitate. His wife had already given him all the information which a prudent father might demand of a prospective son-in-law.

'Well, my dear boy,' he said, 'I'll tell you frankly that, although I don't know you very well, you seem to be just the sort of young fellow whom I'd like my daughter to marry. You have my consent and my blessing, and I hope she'll make you a good wife. Let us shake hands on it, Willie.'

They shook hands and finished their sherry, half bowing towards each other and half muttering something about good luck. Lighting his pipe and leaning back in his chair, the Colonel continued:

'It's a funny thing, but you probably know Daisy better than I do. I've hardly seen her, because I've been out here most of her life. Girls are very different from what they used to be. I suppose every father has said that – especially stuffy old colonels in the Indian Army. But tell me now, does Daisy ever talk to you about anything except balldancing and the moving pictures?'

Willie laughed. 'Oh yes, sir; about hundreds of things. I think she's very clever. She's not highbrow, of course, but then I'm not quite what you'd call one of the intellectuals. She's awfully interested in horses, for one thing, and so am I.'

'Yes,' said the Colonel meditatively. 'I've noticed that. I've noticed that.' But he didn't seem particularly pleased about it.

That was a great evening for Willie. He was not sure afterwards whether it was he or Daisy who had let out the news. They agreed between them that it must have been her father. By dinner-time it was all over the station. Wherever he went he was congratulated, and the little bungalow which he shared with a brother officer was crowded with friends who dropped in to drink his health.

One of the earliest callers was Coper Caffin.

'It's you that have broken my heart,' he said, 'for I would have married the girl myself. But let the best man win has always been my motto. Would you not like to give your bride a lovely hack as a wedding present, for I think I know the animal?'

Willie laughed, and said he would be glad to inspect it. He thought to himself that Coper was joking. He could not really have hoped to marry Daisy. He was old enough to be her father.

Of the months that followed Willie's recollection was faint and hazy. He was very happy, and the days slipped quickly away. He wrote his good news to Mrs. Osborne and asked her to tell the others whose addresses he no longer knew, and he also wrote to Felicity to tell her that he was going to marry one of her school friends, and that they often talked of her together and looked forward to seeing her when they came home. Mrs. Osborne sent him her congratulations, together with much family news, and a silver flask that had belonged to her husband. He received no reply from Felicity.

To buy a suitable engagement ring he made a journey to Calcutta, which he thought the most horrible place he had ever seen. Yet many of his friends said they had great fun there, and arranged short visits as often as they could. Daisy was pleased with the ring, and she seemed pleased with him. They saw each other very often, and they never quarrelled. Perhaps true lovers would have warned them that this was a bad sign, for those are wrong who believe that there are more quarrels after than before marriage. It was only when he looked back upon it all afterwards that he understood there had been something missing. They danced together, and rode together, and talked about dances and horses. She refused to accept the mare that Caffin had wanted to sell him as a wedding present, although she could give no good reason for doing so. She said she had heard of a better one, and that in any case there was no hurry. In spite of this continual companionship, Willie saw afterwards that they came no closer together. They knew no more of one another's heart and mind, and even the rapturous caresses that had led to their engagement were not repeated. There never seemed to be any opportunity, or was it, as Willie sometimes thought, that Daisy deliberately avoided one? If it were so, he did not blame her, attributing reluctance, if it existed, to maiden modesty.

Of all the conversations that they had at this period he remembered only one distinctly. He had accompanied her home from a party, as on the other occasion, but this time it was in her father's car and there was a chauffeur in the front seat. None the less when they reached the bungalow she drew him into the dark shadow of the veranda, and laid her hands on his shoulders.

'Willie,' she said, 'I am very fond of you. I want you to believe that, and I want you to promise me something.'

'Of course you're fond of me, or you wouldn't be marrying me, and of course I'll promise you anything in the world,' he said lightly, pressing forward to kiss her. But she still held him back.

'No, this is something serious. I want you to promise me, because I know that if you make a promise you will keep it always.'

'Fire away,' he said.

'I want you to promise that whatever I do you will always forgive me, and will believe that even if I hurt you I was sad to do it.'

'Of course,' he answered, 'and you must promise me, too. I'm sure I'll be a rotten husband.'

'No,' she persisted. 'You have got to say "I promise that I will always forgive you, Daisy, and that even if you hurt me, I will believe that you were sad to do it."'

Solemnly he said the words, she repeating them under her breath, her hands still resting on his shoulders. When he had finished she drew him close to her and held him in a long embrace.

A few days later she ran away with Coper Caffin.

CHAPTER V

The elopement gave military circles in India something to talk about for many days. Willie was at first more astonished than hurt. Men who have been seriously wounded are often unaware of the fact at the time, being conscious merely that they have received a blow. He was not proud, and therefore his pride did not suffer, as it would have with most young men. He felt vaguely sorry for Daisy, and he felt very sorry for her father, after he had seen him.

Their interview was one that he remembered. The Colonel, who had sent for him, was standing when he came into the room.

'Mr. Maryngton,' he began almost sternly, 'I have to apologise to you for the behaviour of my daughter and of an officer under my command. It is a hard thing for a man to feel ashamed both of his family and of his regiment.'

'Oh, sir,' interrupted Willie, who was moved by the older man's suffering, and who remembered the promise that he had made, 'don't blame Daisy. She may have behaved foolishly, even wrongly, but I've forgiven her, for I know she's a good girl at heart. Captain Caffin's a rotter, but there are rotters in every regiment, and everyone knows that yours is one of the best in the Indian Army.'

'Maryngton,' said the Colonel, 'you're a good fellow, a damned good fellow. I wish you'd married her. I fear you were too good for her.' He blew his nose noisily. 'Sit down for a minute and let's have a talk.'

Willie sat down, feeling curiously at ease despite the other's embarrassment, and began to talk of how he had first heard the news and of the surprise he had felt.

'I can't blame Daisy,' he went on, 'for not marrying me if she didn't want to. In fact I think she was perfectly right. It must be wrong to marry someone you don't love. But what I can't understand is why she didn't tell me all about it. I should, of course, have agreed to call the engagement off. She knew me well enough to be sure that I wouldn't make any difficulties; and then – after an interval, of course – she could have got engaged to Caffin.'

'My poor boy!' groaned the Colonel. 'You don't understand the matter at all, nor all the wickedness of it. Caffin is a married man. He's been separated from his wife for many years, but they're not divorced and they can't be, because they're both Roman Catholics, or pretend to be.'

Willie was horrified. 'Do you mean to say they are going to live together without being married?'

The Colonel nodded.

'My God! what a swine the fellow must be,' Willie exclaimed. 'I bet Daisy never knew he was married.'

But the Colonel could not allow him even this cold comfort. 'Her mother tells me,' he said, 'that she knew perfectly well.'

Willie was neither strait-laced nor narrow-minded. Although he had lived a more chaste life than most of his contemporaries, it was due rather to lack of temperament than to high principles. He knew that many of his friends were the lovers of married women, and he thought none the worse of them, although he imagined they must feel very uncomfortable in the husband's presence. He knew that the marriage tie was looser than it used to be, and that conjugal infidelity was more easily condoned than in the past. He accepted the standards of his companions, and never worried his head about them; but young unmarried girls of his acquaintance still belonged, in his eyes, to a category set apart. Married women could do what they pleased, but that a young girl should commit adultery with a married man and bring shame on her family seemed to him an abominable thing.

It took him long to get over the shock. Perhaps it would be truer to say that he never got over it. Often he had to remind himself of the promise that he had made to Daisy. Sometimes he felt that she had obtained it under false pretences. She must have known then what she was meaning to do. He could still say to himself that he forgave her, but he could no longer have the same warm feeling towards her that he had had when he told her father so. He was afraid she must be a bad girl, after all, for she had run away with a married man, who was not only a terrible scoundrel but was also not quite a gentleman.

Willie felt that he must inform Mrs. Osborne of his misfortune and return the flask she had sent him as a wedding present. It was a difficult letter to write. Self-expression had never come easily to him, and to express himself on paper was far more difficult than to do so by word of mouth. He wrestled with his task for many days and nights, but when at last he had completed it, he felt a great relief, and in retrospect he always believed that the writing of this letter had helped him to understand his own feelings and to bear his sorrow. Too easily had he at first accepted the conventional opinion that a young man who has been jilted must be broken-hearted. Too tempting had he at moments found the obvious consolation that he had had a lucky escape. He had no desire to adopt an attitude, for he was naturally sincere, but the people who surrounded him, both men and women, were inclined to approach him on the one assumption or the other. The romantic pressed his hand and looked at him silently with sad eyes, while the worldly-wise almost gave him a congratulatory tap on the shoulder. And because he was not quite sure of his own feelings he found himself meeting the sad gaze with one equally melancholy, and responding to the congratulations by an intimation that he knew himself to be well out of a bad business.

He succeeded in telling Mrs. Osborne very simply that he was not broken-hearted, but that he was disappointed and unhappy; that he did not feel that he had had a lucky escape, but that he doubted whether his marriage to Daisy would have been a success. He had looked forward to being married and having a home of his own. He had thought it wonderful that a beautiful girl should love him, and for the first time he had had an interest in life outside horses and the regiment. But now, although he had forgiven Daisy, and was determined to retain no harsh feelings towards her, he felt sure that it was better for both of them that they had not married. This assurance comforted him, but did not make him happy. She had given him something that he had not possessed before, and now that it was gone, he missed it. He had come to look forward to life with a companion. Now the companion had vanished and he was feeling lonelier than he had felt before.

All this he succeeded in setting down in the letter which he eventually sent to Mrs. Osborne, but it took him a long time to do and, almost before the letter was despatched, he received one from England in a handwriting that was unknown to him.

Dearest Willie,

I'm so glad you didn't marry Daisy Summers. She was not the girl for you. I never liked her.

Best love,
Felicity.

Willie had not seen Felicity since she was a child and he found it hard to believe that she was now the same age as, or perhaps a little older than, Daisy. The latter had always spoken of her as though they were great friends. This letter seemed hardly to confirm it. But Willie had noticed among Daisy's weaknesses a tendency to claim intimacy with people with whom it appeared, on closer enquiry, that she was barely acquainted. Willie had accumulated a good deal of leave by now. Curiosity aroused by this letter, the desire to see some of his foster-family again, and the growing sensation of loneliness, almost decided him to spend his leave in England, but the prospect of an extensive big-game shooting expedition, including invitations from ruling princes, proved more attractive.

He regretted this decision later. Before he set out on his expedition he received a long letter from Mrs. Osborne. It was kind and sympathetic, and Willie thought she seemed to understand him better now than she had done before. She gave him news of Garnet, whose duties had taken him to Malaya, and of Horry, who had made a success in a small but important part in the West End. Felicity was living with her in the old home, but went frequently to London, where she saw much of Horry. Mrs. Osborne was sending him back the flask and she hoped he would keep it always in memory of her. When he returned to his regiment three months later he found a letter from Horry informing him that she was dead.

CHAPTER VI

When the regiment's tour of duty in India was over and they were expecting to return home, orders came that they were to proceed to Egypt, which caused much disappointment and discontent. The general rule was that regiments spent three years in Egypt, followed by five in India, and when, owing to political complications, the regiment had been ordered direct to India, they had innocently supposed that they had escaped the first part of their exile. The War Office may overlook but it does not forget, nor was there any reason why one regiment should have more favourable treatment than others, so in the normal course of trooping the regiment went to Egypt, and spent three years there, following upon the five they had spent in India.

Willie remembered very little of what happened during his time in Egypt. He knew that he enjoyed it much less than he had enjoyed India. There was plenty of polo and plenty of racing, but both were of a more professional character. In India, or the parts of it that he had visited, the Army had seemed the centre of life, but here in Egypt it was only an adjunct. In India the subject of politics was never mentioned in the mess. Everybody knew that there was a steady move towards the diminution of British power and prestige, and everybody regretted it. But there was little to be said and nothing to be done about it. These things were controlled by politicians, who, it appeared, were all determined to destroy the British Empire and to ruin the Army. But here in Egypt politics were a common subject of conversation, and everybody seemed to know something about them. It appeared also that Lord Allenby, who was a great soldier, had been weak and had given in to the natives, whereas Lord Lloyd, who was a politician, had been strong and refused to give in. All this was very puzzling to Willie. In India he had been able to feel separated by time as well as by space from the modern world. In Egypt he was in the heart of it, and he could not feel at home there.

He thought once or twice of returning to England on leave, but always some more attractive alternative presented itself. He visited the Sudan and went on hunting trips into Kenya and Abyssinia. These he enjoyed, but he disliked Cairo and Alexandria.

It was while he was in Egypt that he completed his thirtieth year, and was promoted to the rank of captain. Neither event gave him much satisfaction. To him thirty meant middle age, and although he was pleased to be promoted, he knew that in other regiments there were still to be found subalterns who had taken part in the fighting. There were also thousands of civilians – he had often met them – who had splendid war records, and had even temporarily commanded battalions, and who now had abandoned their Army rank altogether. In the presence of such people he felt needlessly ashamed, as though he were assuming a rank to which he was not entitled.

When the time came for him to return to England he had an exaggerated idea in his own mind of the length of time he had been away. He felt that he had left as a boy and that he was coming back as an old man. He even wondered whether his friends would recognise him. It was therefore a great surprise when, on the morning after his arrival, the hall porter gave him a familiar nod when he walked into his club, and he had been there only a few minutes before an acquaintance greeted him casually with 'Hallo, Willie! Haven't seen you about for quite a while. Been abroad or something?'

A club provides a wonderful home for the lonely, and an equally convenient escape from home for those who occasionally feel the need of it. There are the faithful old servants, who are always pleased to see members and who, unlike the servants at home, have neither complaints of their conditions, nor quarrels between themselves; or, if they have, the ordinary members never hear of them. There are all the daily newspapers, and the weekly ones, which are hardly worth purchase but merit a glance. The chairs are comfortable, there is never a crowd, and refreshment is easily and instantly obtainable. But above all there is the ease of intercourse – the conversation lightly begun and as lightly broken off the moment it becomes a burden, or even threatens to become one, to either party. Nor are subjects of conversation ever lacking. The news provides them, and, for such as Willie, the racing news, above all. They are varied by those very funny stories, which spring from an inexhaustible anonymous source, and which, for some mysterious reason, are very much funnier when told in the club than anywhere else.

Willie was happy in the society of men, especially men of his own sort, and he had been in the club hardly half an hour before he felt that he had never left it. After lunching there he spent much of the afternoon trying to discover at what theatre Horry was acting and, with the help of the hall-porter, he was at last successful. He bought a ticket and went there alone. The play proved to be an excellent comedy, and Willie, who had seen nothing of the sort for so long, thoroughly enjoyed it. It seemed to him that Horry, who had a good part, acted wonderfully well, and also that he had become younger and taller than Willie remembered him; but when they met afterwards he proved to have altered very little.

40

Willie had sent him a message saying that he would await him at the stage-door and inviting him to supper. Horry, as gay and enthusiastic as ever, threw his arms round Willie when they met, and was obviously delighted to see him.

'It couldn't be more fortunate,' he exclaimed. 'I promised to meet Felicity after the show; we shall find her at Rules, and you'll be able to swallow the majority of the family at one gulp. It's a pity Garnet's not here. He was home last year on leave, but he's gone back to the Far East, and I don't know when we shall see him again. Rules is quite close – we can walk there.'

As they walked to the restaurant Willie talked of the play and was able, in all sincerity, to say how very much he had enjoyed it and how impressed he had been by Horry's performance. Horry was very pleased. All actors, indeed all artists, are made happy by praise, and Willie's praise was so genuine and so unqualified that it would have given pleasure to one much older and more hardened than Horry.

They were therefore both happy and smiling when they arrived. A tall, dark girl got up from a corner table and came towards them. She looked from Horry to his companion at first with curiosity and then with almost instant recognition. 'It's Willie,' she said, and taking his hand kissed him on the cheek, so gracefully and so naturally that he felt no embarrassment, but a thrill of happiness.

'How clever of you to recognise me,' he said.

'You haven't changed a bit,' she answered.

'Well, you certainly have,' he told her. 'You were a little girl with a pig-tail when I saw you last. And then you were always away at school. I don't think I saw you at all during the last five or six years I was in England.'

There followed, while they gave their orders, a discussion as to when exactly he had seen her last and how old she was at the time, and whether she had ever had a pigtail. Like all historical facts, these were curiously hard to establish, and Horry entered into the argument, holding strongly a view which differed from those of both the others.

'Anyhow,' said Felicity, getting bored with the discussion, 'all that matters is that I was a little child then and now I'm a grown-up woman – and you were a young man then and you're a young man still.'

'How long does one remain a young man?' asked Willie.

'Until about sixty in my profession,' said Horry, 'and then they're middle-aged for an indefinite period until they suddenly turn into grand old men.'

Felicity laughed. 'I wish the girls could do the same.'

'They damned well try to,' said Horry, and then an argument started about the ages of actresses, into which Willie could not have entered even if he had known who the people were about whom they were talking, which he could not do, as all the ladies were referred to by their christian or more intimate names. It gave him an opportunity to look at Felicity. He had felt dazzled at first. He remembered suddenly that Daisy Summers had said she was beautiful, and yet, for some reason, he had not been prepared for her to be so. He had simply not thought about it. She seemed to him more beautiful than anyone he had ever seen. Her large dark eyes, her short curling hair, the grace of her gestures, the animation of her conversation, and the simplicity of her manner, the complete lack of any coquetry or apparent eagerness to please – all that she was made an impression upon him that he found difficult to understand. He felt for a moment that he wanted to laugh out loud, and then that he wanted to go away with Horry and drink a bottle of champagne, and then again all that he desired was to remain forever where he was, watching and listening and not having to talk. For a moment he wondered whether he was drunk. It was not till afterwards, when he was alone, that he knew he had fallen in love for the first time in his life.

One cause of his happiness that evening was the way in which they both treated him as one of the family. They were plainly pleased to see him, but showed him none of the consideration that is shown to a stranger. They talked without restraint about matters of which he was ignorant and people whom he didn't know. They felt no obligation to draw him into the conversation. This gave Willie a sensation that was new to him – the sensation of being at home.

He liked Rules. It was bohemian, but there was nothing modern about it. From there they took him on to a place in Covent Garden called the Late Joys or the Players Club. Here they drank beer and ate hot sausages and watched a variety entertainment. Most of the actors and the audience seemed acquainted with one another, and everybody joined in the choruses. The songs came from the music-halls of the last century, and to Willie, who had never seen anything of the kind before, everything seemed perfect. It was late when the brother and sister dropped him at Jermyn Street, where he had luckily found vacant the flat he had lived in before. They were both bound towards Chelsea.

'How about lunch to-morrow?' he asked Felicity.

'I can't to-morrow, Willie dear.'

'May I ring you up in the morning?'

'There's no telephone where I'm staying, but we'll meet soon.'

'And you, Horry?'

'I've got a matinée to-morrow, but you've got my telephone number. Give me a ring whenever you like and we'll fix up something. Good night, old Willie.'

'Good night.'

Willie felt a little sad that nothing had been arranged for the next day, but it was such a small regret that it could not cast a shadow over the great happiness in which he fell asleep that night.

CHAPTER VII

In spite of many efforts, Willie failed to see Felicity again before he left London. He heard that she had gone to Brighton, and he was obliged to join his regiment in a remote part of the country. On the next occasion that he came to London she was still away, but he saw as much as he could of Horry, and turned the conversation in her direction as often as possible. He felt that, although he had known her so long, he knew her so little. He had no idea of who her friends might be, or how her life was spent, and he wanted most eagerly to find out.

He found Horry surprisingly unhelpful. He was, like many in his profession, extremely self-centred. Warm-hearted, sociable and very generous, he was always glad – unaffectedly glad – to see his friends, but never thought of them when he did not see them. He felt the same with regard to his sister. He was perhaps fonder of her than he was of anyone. There was nothing that he would not have done for her had she asked him. But when she was absent he never thought of her, and even when she was present he never questioned her about her plans or prospects.

'But what is her life?' asked Willie. 'Who looks after her and takes her to parties?'

Horry could not have looked vaguer if he had been asked to solve a problem in algebra. These were questions that he had never asked himself.

'Well, you see,' he said with much hesitation, 'she was grown up before Mum died, and I think she used to go to gloomy parties in Aldershot and round about. Then people, friends of Mum, would ask her to stay in London. Then she got keen on acting and went to the Academy of Dramatic Art. Then she got a small part in some half-amateur, highbrow show, which led nowhere. She's got lots of friends, and she always seems perfectly happy.' This he said almost defensively.

'But how about money?'

Horry's face cleared. Here was a question he could answer.

'Oh, she's all right for money. Mum left her everything that she could. Garnet was here at the time, and went into the whole thing very thoroughly. When everything was paid up and sold up and probated and executed and all the rest of it, he and I got a thousand quid each in ready, and young Felicity would have about five hundred a year safe for life in gilt-rimmed securities or whatever they're called. It's not the earth, but she won't starve, bless her heart, and if ever she wants a bit extra she's only got to ask her rich brother, the West End favourite with the big future in Hollywood.'

It was true that Horry was making a name for himself on the stage and had already appeared successfully in pictures, but it was not the financial prospects of the Osborne family in which Willie was really interested.

'How about young men and all that?' he asked, trying very hard to make the question sound casual.

'Oh, she's got plenty,' Horry answered. 'I'm always seeing her with them at restaurants. Nobody I know, though, and she doesn't introduce them.'

'What do they look like?' asked Willie.

'Not like you, Willie,' Horry laughed. 'No, not a bit. Flabby and floppy, coloured shirts and long hair, and I always hope they're going to pay the bill. Girls seem to like that sort nowadays. It puzzles me sometimes.'

Willie's feelings were mixed. Relief predominated.

'Where does she live?' was the next question.

'She's sharing rooms at present with a girl friend, while she tries to find a flat. They're devilish hard to get these days. I've just seen one that I think will do for me, in Bloomsbury, very handy for the theatre,' and then followed a long account of Horry's own future movements which interested him very much more than those of Felicity.

Before they separated, Willie made Horry promise to make a plan for his next visit to London, the date of which he already knew. Horry would get seats for a play, a popular success, which he knew that Felicity wanted to see, and Willie would take her. They would all meet for supper afterwards, when Horry would bring another girl to complete the party.

So Willie travelled north with the comfortable sensation of looking forward to a certain day. He needed comfort when he got there, for he learnt that the blow had fallen, and that the regiment was to be mechanised forthwith. To make the blow yet harder to bear there came the news that Hamilton, who had been away for two or three years, was returning as second-in-command.

It was at this time that the thought of leaving the Army first presented itself to Willie's mind, as a course that ought to be considered, and not as the abandonment of all that made life desirable. He had never taken any interest in machinery. He had never shared the interest which most of his contemporaries took in motor cars. He had found them useful for getting about and he had learnt to drive them, badly, but he had never tried to tinker with them when they went wrong. Even the little musketry and knowledge of machine-guns that a cavalry officer was obliged to master had proved a hard task for him, and he would not have liked to have had his knowledge tested.

Many of his friends who had joined when he had, and later, were now leaving the Army, and the news of mechanisation speeded up the dispersal. 'You can't teach an old dog new tricks,' one of them said to him, and the proverb, for some reason, stuck in his mind, and recurred to him as often as the possibility of leaving came up for review. But still he kept in his heart the ambition that he had had as a schoolboy and which had always remained with him. He was still young and active, and there were beginning to be rumours of war. The day might yet come when that ambition would be fulfilled and he would go into battle with his regiment.

The evening to which Willie had been looking forward arrived. Felicity came in her small car to pick him up at his club. He was standing in the window waiting for her. He felt proud to be called for by such a beautiful girl. They had a box at the theatre, which gave a sensation of comfort and intimacy. Between the acts Felicity took him to the bar, where she drank gin-and-orange, while he drank whisky-and-soda. He might not have approved of this in another girl, but she could do no wrong. He found no difficulty in talking to her. Conversation flowed easily. She told him that when she was a child he had been her hero. He trembled with pleasure, and asked her why.

'Oh, I don't know,' she said. 'I suppose because the others were brothers, and apart from them I didn't know anyone else.'

His heart sank. He asked her whom Horry would be bringing to supper.

'I expect it will be Miriam Love,' she answered. 'They've been friends for a very long time. Horry does go off the rails occasionally – and so does she, if it comes to that – but they always come together again.'

'What is she like, and what does she do?' asked Willie.

'She's very pretty. She's on the stage, but she hasn't got a part just now. She's married to a second-rate actor who does Shakespeare in the provinces.'

'Does Horry love her?'

'Yes, I think he really does.'

'Will they get married?'

'I don't think it has ever occurred to either of them. She's not divorced, so it wouldn't be possible at present. Oh, Willie, tell me about Daisy Summers. I'm so glad you didn't marry her. What happened?'

Willie told the little there was to tell, and Felicity listened sympathetically. He ended by saying how glad he had been to get her letter, and asked why she had written it.

'Oh, I don't know,' she said. 'I used often to think of you, and I was so sorry when I heard you were engaged to a girl of that sort.'

'Did you think she was a bad girl?'

'Oh no, no – only silly, ordinary, and pointless.' They went on to the Savoy Grill, where they met Horry with Miriam Love. Willie recognised her at once as the girl who had been with Horry on that night, so many years ago, when he had invited them both to join him and his brother officers at supper. Ten years had made very little difference to her. He thought her better-looking than ever. He recalled that evening which they both remembered, and they laughed about how angry Horry had been.

'He still gets very angry about things that don't matter,' said Miriam. 'We had a terrible argument the other day about conscientious objectors. I said they ought to be shot, and that if they knew they were going to be there wouldn't be any. There aren't any in France or Germany. Horry got wild, said they were the bravest people in the country, and finally swore that if there were another war he'd be a conscientious objector himself.'

'Oh, Horry!' said Willie. 'How could you?'

'It was Miriam's fault,' said Horry. 'She's got a most irritating way of arguing. She can never keep anything in the abstract. If you say that the Chinese are very fine people, she says, "Would you like to sleep with one?" If you say no, she says, "There you are, you see," and thinks she's won the argument. If you say yes, she says, "Dirty beast!"'

It was a gay party. Everybody had plenty to say; Willie less than the others, but he did not feel out of it. When he suggested that they should go on to the Players Club it was already too late. Horry and Miriam went off together, and Willie was left with Felicity.

'Can't we go on somewhere else?' he asked.

'No,' she answered decisively. 'I'm tired. Jump into my car. I'll drop you. It's on my way.'

He knew it would be useless to argue, but although he had enjoyed every minute of the evening, he was left with a feeling of failure. He thought it a pity that girls should own cars and should drive them. Especially at night. What were taxis for, anyway? He said good night almost crossly when she left him at his flat.

During the remainder of that summer Willie saw Felicity as often as he could. She seemed to have many engagements and never told him what they were. She never introduced him to her friends and, when he asked her to, said she did not think they would amuse him.

'You mean I shouldn't amuse them,' he said.

'No,' she answered, 'but they wouldn't see your point, and you wouldn't see theirs.'

She seemed always very pleased to see him, and although he did not tell her he was in love with her, she must have known it. When the holiday season came she disappeared without warning, and he heard that she had gone to Brittany. He himself paid visits in Scotland and Ireland, shooting and fishing, and thinking as little about Felicity or about the future as he could. He had been hurt by her going away without telling him, and he thought he would be wise to forget her. He began to hope that he had succeeded in doing so.

During the winter it happened that he had to spend a Sunday evening in London. He rang up Horry, and they arranged to dine together at a little restaurant in Soho. When he arrived there Horry was waiting for him at a table for three.

'Felicity's coming,' he explained. 'I told her she hadn't been asked, but she insisted.'

While they waited Willie asked after Miriam and enquired, with assumed innocence, whether Horry still treated her only as his sister, reminding him of what he had said years ago. He was not in the least embarrassed, but answered frankly.

'No, that platonic, pedestal stuff didn't last long. It can't between normal people. Her husband, about the worst ham-actor on the stage, was unfaithful to her first, so she saw no reason why she should go on being faithful to him. She's a grand girl, and has a heart of gold. I love her.'

'Why don't you get married?' asked Willie.

'The ham-actor, who's as nasty a piece of work off the stage as on it, won't agree to a divorce. He's glad of a good excuse for not making honest women of the girls he seduces. We're very happy as we are.'

'Don't you want to have children?'

'I'm not at all sure that I do,' said Horry, and became more serious. 'I have a good time myself and I enjoy life. I'm one of the lucky ones; but I've no great admiration for this world, and I shouldn't think that I was doing anybody a very good turn by bringing them into it.'

Felicity arrived late. When the door of the restaurant was flung open Willie knew it was her, and when she walked quickly in and sat down without explanation or apology, he knew that he was more in love with her than ever. How happy he felt to be with her, and with Horry once again! How different their conversation was from that of his other friends! And how infinitely more amusing! They drank Chianti and talked until all the other diners had left, and most of the waiters. Then they drank liqueurs, until the proprietor was obliged, very reluctantly, to tell them that it was long past closing time. They took a taxi, and they dropped Horry first, and Willie insisted upon driving Felicity back to Chelsea. He threw his arms round her and kissed her passionately. She made no resistance. And when he told her that he loved her better than the whole world, and that he had never loved anyone else, she answered 'Darling.'

It was not a word that she used often. Too many of her contemporaries had robbed it of its beauty, and reduced it to the gutter by making it the commonest word in their vocabulary. But in her soft, deep voice it retained its own dark tenderness and sounded to him like a magic spell. It conveyed love and sympathy, and promised surrender.

'I've been so angry with you,' he whispered – 'I've tried so hard to forget you.'

'Yes, I was afraid you were,' she answered, very low.

'Why did you make no sign?' he asked, but she answered only 'Darling.'

When they came to the house where she was staying he asked whether he might come in. 'No, my love,' she laughed gently, 'of course not. There are people there.'

'Then you must have lunch with me to-morrow, for I have to leave in the afternoon.'

'I can't to-morrow,' she said, 'but next time you're here.'

They arranged when they would meet.

'I love you so,' he said.

'I love you, too,' she answered, and then firmly slipped out of his embrace and was gone.

CHAPTER VIII

In Willie's mind marriage remained the natural and logical sequel to love. If Felicity loved him she should be prepared to marry him, and yet he could hardly believe that she would. She had ideas on every subject that were so different from the ideas of other people. Under her influence his own views had broadened and undergone a far greater development than he suspected; yet, even so, she often said things that surprised him and expressed opinions that he could not accept. But she never shocked him. Sometimes he wondered why. The true reason probably was that she was always sincere and was incapable of indecency or vulgarity.

When he asked himself why he had not mentioned marriage during that memorable drive, he knew that it would have spoilt everything, but why it would have done so he found more difficult to explain.

He thought of little else during the days that followed. Out of his deep cogitations one conclusion emerged. He was sure that she would not marry him so long as he remained in the Army. He could not ask her to follow the drum. He could not picture her passing her life with the wives of his brother officers. They were nice women, whom he liked very much, and they were just like the women she had known as a child in her mother's house, but their ideas were not her ideas, nor their world her world. So he had to choose between his love and his regiment. It was a hard choice for him to make.

One evening he found himself alone with Hamilton. He had not come to like him, but long acquaintance had induced a certain intimacy, and his advice on any matter was worth having.

'I'm thinking of chucking the Army,' Willie said suddenly. 'Would you advise me to?'

Hamilton usually addressed Willie in a tone of superficially good-natured, but occasionally malicious, banter. Asked a serious question, however, about a serious and partly military subject, he immediately became serious himself, and sought to answer it to the best of his ability.

'There's a good deal to be said on both sides,' he answered. 'I know that you don't like mechanical warfare and you are finding it difficult to adapt yourself. It has robbed you of half your interest in soldiering. Much of your duty has now become a burden to you; once it was all a pleasure.

And because you don't like it you are not going to be much good at it. At the same time, you are very fond of the regiment. I know that. I think you might miss it very much if you gave it up.'

Touched by such good sense and such sympathy, Willie blurted out:

'I'm thinking of getting married.'

'Bravo!' said Hamilton. 'That solves the problem,' and then returning to his lighter tone, 'Paterfamilias has no time for regimental duties.'

'But is there going to be another war?' asked Willie. 'I just missed the last one, you know, and I couldn't bear to miss the next one.'

'I don't know whether there's going to be a war,' said Hamilton, 'but this I do know: if you leave the regiment now you'll go on the reserve of officers, and if a war comes along while you can still bear arms, you'll return to the regiment on the day of mobilisation – or a few days earlier.'

'Can I count on that?' asked Willie. 'Can I be quite certain that I shouldn't be pushed off into some other awful show, be made a Colonel of Pioneers or something?'

'You may be quite certain,' said Hamilton gravely, 'that you would rejoin the regiment as soon as war broke out. We should need every trained officer we could lay our hands on.'

'That's a great relief to me,' said Willie. 'In fact it removes the chief obstacle that stood in my way. The only other thing is that I should have liked to have got my majority before I left.'

Hamilton was silent. He had his own opinions as to Willie's qualifications for the rank of major. So after a moment or two Willie added:

'Well, I shall go on thinking it over. You won't tell anybody, will you?'

'I won't,' said Hamilton, and he didn't.

When Willie next met Felicity he told her that he intended to leave the Army. She was very surprised.

'Oh, Willie,' she said, 'would you be wise to do that? It seems hard to imagine you out of the Army. It's so much a part of you. Would you be happy if you gave it up?'

'I should be happy if you would marry me,' he said.

She gave him a quick look, uncertain if he were serious. She saw that he was.

'Oh, my poor love,' she cried in deep concern, 'I hope you will not think of that. I have no wish to marry. Whether I ever shall I cannot say, but certainly not now, not now. If that was why you wanted to leave the Army, pray do nothing of the sort.'

'But why should you refuse to marry me?' he persisted obstinately. 'You said you loved me a few nights ago.'

'I do love you, I do indeed. But I can never see that that has much to do with it. So few married people love each other, and so many people who aren't married do.'

'That's all cynical rot,' said Willie. 'Would you do away with marriage altogether?'

'Oh no, of course not, but I feel that it is not for me – not at present, anyway. I sometimes think that life is like a play – not a very original idea, because Shakespeare had it; but he said that each man in his time played many parts. I think most of them play only one. You're the soldier, just as Horry is the actor. I can't imagine either of you as anything else. I don't think I've been cast yet. I'm not the *jeune fille* – not the kind the audience expects, anyway – and, frankly, can you imagine me playing the married woman?'

'I don't know what I can imagine,' said Willie ruefully. 'I'm not imaginative – but I know that I'm madly in love with you and can never be happy unless you marry me.'

'Please don't say that. Never is such a terrible word. You make me feel wicked and unhappy.'

'Well what am I to do?' asked Willie.

'I suppose that if I were a nice girl I should say 'Forget me,' but that's the last thing I want you to do. So go on loving me, my darling Willie, and I will go on loving you. And we'll have great fun, and not be too serious, and who knows what may happen in the end?'

Willie took these last, vague words as a kind of promise. He would say to himself afterwards, 'She told me not to give up hope, but to wait.' This was not quite what Felicity had meant.

CHAPTER IX

Time passed. Willie, hoping for promotion and lacking encouragement from Felicity, continually postponed a decision about leaving the Army. But his duties grew more irksome, and his desire to be in London whenever he wished increased. The regiment had lost its place in his mind, if not in his heart. He seldom thought of it. His first thoughts were of Felicity, his second of racing, so that he lived in two worlds and, together, they sufficed to fill his time. The regiment interfered with both. So that when he received yet another disappointment with regard to promotion, and when Felicity, to console him, said that captain was a more romantic rank than major, he decided to take the plunge and, not without many final searchings of heart, sent in his papers and became his own master for the first time in his life.

He went into partnership with a friend, and set up a small training-stable under National Hunt rules, partly in order to have something to answer when people asked him what he was doing, for in those days young Englishmen were ashamed to admit that they were doing nothing, and partly in order that when he went racing he might feel that he was attending to business and not wasting his time.

Felicity was sorry when he left the Army, although she had not tried to influence him in either direction. She had been brought up in the military tradition, and although she had moved into another sphere, she retained her respect and affection for the Army. Her opinions were not influenced in any way by the people who surrounded her.

Willie met Felicity by chance one day when she was with a tall young man, whose good looks were of a kind that he found particularly irritating. In the first place they were undeniable, and in the second place the young man, although his appearance and his clothes were unconventional, was not effeminate. His hair was long, and he wore a red sweater instead of a waistcoat, but there was something in his bearing that commanded respect. Felicity introduced them and said that her friend had just come back from Spain, and was returning there shortly.

'Have you been fighting in the civil war?' asked Willie.

'One mustn't say so, but as a matter of fact I have,' the other answered.

Willie looked at him with envy. Here was a man, ten years younger than himself, perhaps, who had already taken part in war, and was continuing to do so. He surprised his friends at the club that evening by informing them that he was going off to Spain to take part in the fighting.

'On which side, Willie?' somebody asked him.

'Oh, I don't much mind about that,' he said.

'Well, you see,' it was explained to him, 'either you have to join up with the Reds, burn down the churches and rape the nuns, or else you have to fight for Hitler and Mussolini and probably take your orders from a German officer.'

'Is it as bad as that?' he asked.

'Worse, old boy. You're committing a legal offence by going there at all. Of course you'd assume a false name, but if you were caught, you being an officer on the reserve, you'd probably be cashiered. There would be headlines in the papers, and, oh golly, what a disgrace for the dear old regiment!'

Everybody knew Willie's weakness, and the theme was too good to be dropped.

'It wouldn't look well in the papers, I must say. "Cavalry Captain caught in Convent," "British officer in crack regiment wins Order of Lenin," "Captain Maryngton embraced by Hitler." It would break the poor old Colonel's heart.'

Willie thought such jokes were not amusing, but they sufficed to destroy any intention he might have had of going to Spain. For the first time it was impressed upon him that it was far more difficult for a regular soldier than for a civilian to take part in a war.

Apart from the feeling of frustration that never altogether left him, these were not unhappy years for Willie. He was always occupied. His training-stable had ups and downs, and although over a long period the downs predominated, the ups were numerous and frequent enough to make life agreeable. He loved his club. He played all games of chance and enjoyed them, and the place where he had found so warm a welcome when he came back from India seemed likely to become his home for life.

What was lacking in this very masculine existence was provided by Felicity. His devotion to her never faltered, and she provided for him all that he demanded in the region of beauty and romance. She made no demands upon him. It was he who had always to arrange their meetings, and they were not as frequent as he would have liked. Often he felt that she was treating him badly, but he had only to be with her for five minutes to forget his grievance. Sometimes weeks or even months passed without their being alone together for a moment, and she seemed to be unaware of the fact. Sometimes she seemed to welcome and give back all his passion, at others she hardly allowed him to touch her hand. When he asked her to explain, or to give any reason for such strange alterations in her behaviour, she would say that she was sorry, she knew herself to be very tiresome, but he must take her as she was.

Willie went on living in Jermyn Street, where Felicity never visited him. It was one of her own unwritten laws. Nor did he invite her. There were still matters that he could not discuss with her, and favours that he could not ask. But despite the restrictions set upon their love-making, she made him happy. Her companionship was an unending pleasure, intensified by the thrill of desire. Sometimes, in the summer, they would take picnics into the country, spreading a cloth in some green, secluded spot and sleeping afterwards under the trees. Sometimes they would go to the coast and bathe in the sea. Best of all, he thought, were the autumn and winter evenings when, having spent the day in the open air, hunting or racing, he would return to London and go to the club, where he would remain until the hall-porter came and murmured to him, confidentially, that there was a lady waiting for him outside. Then they would perhaps, if it were not too late, have something to eat and drink before going to the theatre, and afterwards they would have supper either alone or with Horry, and Horry would usually bring a fourth. It was not always Miriam, and when there was a change Willie and Felicity would enjoy, afterwards, criticising the new favourite and speculating on Horry's degree of intimacy with her. Horry was earning a large salary now, his services were always in demand and he could pick and choose his parts. He had taken his flat in Bloomsbury, of which Willie approved, because it lay in the opposite direction to Chelsea, and there could therefore never be any occasion for Horry to drive Felicity home. She, on the other hand, after all these years, was still looking for a flat, and still sharing rooms with a friend, which Willie deplored, because it disposed of any argument that he could use for crossing the threshold. It was a strange love affair, but Willie was beginning to become reconciled to it, as he was beginning to become reconciled to his existence. It seemed to be his fate, he sometimes thought, to be a soldier who never went to war, and a lover who never lay with his mistress.

CHAPTER X

While his life was thus jogging easily along there happened the great political event that was known as the Munich crisis. It made a disturbance in many people's lives. In Willie's it made a vast upheaval. Once again he felt as he had felt twenty years before and, while nearly all the world was hoping for peace, he prayed for war. Naturally he resented the settlement with great bitterness, and he was glad to find that there were others who felt as he did. His reasons were not their reasons, but this did not prevent him from applauding their denunciation of the shameful surrender. But when they said that the worst part of the policy was that it only meant we should have to fight the war later under less favourable conditions, he secretly hoped that they were right, and that it would come as soon as possible.

He was disappointed in the attitude of Felicity, who was for peace at any price, and they nearly quarrelled about it, as at that time so many good friends did. But he found an unexpected and fervent ally in Horry. It was unexpected, because he had always thought of Horry as a man who was opposed to any form of violence. He was, however, one who behind an easy-going, humorous approach to life hid a profound hatred of injustice and cruelty. He knew of the fate that had befallen some Jewish members of the German theatrical world, and he could not bear to think of Englishmen shaking the hand of the man who was responsible for such enormities. He was much more violent than Willie, and what he had to say about the paper signed by Hitler, which the Prime Minister waved triumphantly in the face of the applauding populace, was very savage.

In the days before the settlement, while Willie was eagerly awaiting his mobilisation orders, he had travelled up to where his regiment was stationed in order to be on the spot. The Colonel was abroad on leave, which shocked him, and Hamilton was in command. Hamilton refused to believe there would be a war, and told Willie not to get over-excited. He had been in Germany himself last summer and had talked to some German officers – very good chaps. He thought that if our politicians knew their business they could arrange for Germany to fight Russia. The officers he had met were pro-British, but very keen to have a go at the Reds. We ought to encourage them to do so and kill two birds with one stone.

Willie had asked whether the winner would not then turn on us, but Hamilton had replied that both sides would be exhausted.

'And then the looker-on, who will be us, and who, as usual, will have seen most of the game, who will have learnt a lot about modern warfare, without fighting, and will have built up his own armaments while the belligerents are destroying theirs, will be in a position to dictate to both sides. That's what's called statesmanship.'

'I don't care what it's called,' said Willie, 'it sounds to me a dirty, tricky, cowardly business – the sort of thing that politicians would invent – and, what's more, I don't believe that any good will come of it. Well, you will know where I am if you want me.'

'We shan't forget, Willie, and you may be sure that we shall send for you in the hour of danger.'

Willie had felt that Hamilton was laughing at him, and hated him for it, but henceforth he had a very definite object in life and a great hope in his heart.

During the months that followed he thought of nothing but the coming war. He was now thirty-nine, and he had never bothered to take care of his health. Riding had kept him active, and he had detected in himself no symptoms of growing old. But he consulted a doctor and insisted upon a thorough examination. The doctor found little wrong with him, but suggested fewer cocktails and plainer food, and Willie followed his directions as scrupulously as though they were military orders.

He saw less of Felicity during this year. She refused to take life as seriously as he did, and preferred to accept the assurances given by Ministers and newspapers that there was nothing to worry about.

CHAPTER XI

Being on the reserve of officers, Willie did a short period of training with his regiment every year, and it so happened that he was actually with the regiment and under canvas in the month of September when the war broke out. Once again he experienced the same thrill of exultation that he had known just twenty-one years before when he was warned that he was to go with the next draft to France. He felt no older than he had done then, and on his knees he thanked heaven that his chance had not come too late. In the camp during those first days everything was in a state of feverish activity, for it was known that the regiment would be among the first to go.

Then came the shattering blow. One morning the Colonel sent for him. 'I've bad news, I fear, for you, Willie, but it's bad news for me, too. We're both in the same boat, or rather we're both out of it; neither of us is to go with the first contingent. Hamilton is taking the regiment abroad, and you and I have got to stay behind, look after what's left of it, and train on the young officers.'

Willie's mouth went dry, he was unable to speak, and for one terrible moment he feared he was going to cry.

'Don't take it too hard,' the Colonel went on. 'It's worse for me than for you. In my case, if they don't let me go now it's a hundred to one they won't let me go at all. It means I'm on the shelf, finished for life.'

Willie longed to say that the Colonel had fought in the last war, as the row of ribbons on his chest bore witness, that he was over fifty, a married man with children, and that he had much to console him for staying at home. He wanted to fall on his knees and beg to be allowed to go, but he knew that the decision did not rest with the Colonel, so that he could only stand there, still unable to speak.

'Don't take it too hard, Willie,' the Colonel repeated, seeing that he was taking it very hard indeed. 'I remember so well at the beginning of the last war, when some fool in high places had said, or was reported to have said, that it would all be over by Christmas, and lots of us were in despair because we thought we should never get out in time. But we all went in the long run, and it will be just the same again – heavy casualties in the first scrap, more officers wanted, none of the new boys ready to go. They'll be grateful enough for the old 'uns then, and there won't be too many of them. Meanwhile there will be plenty of work for us to do at home, and very important work too, and there's a job or two I want you to get on with immediately.'

Willie was thankful that the Colonel then went on to explain to him a number of things that he wanted done which would necessitate a visit to the War Office and several days in London. He was, in fact, to act as second-in-command of the training unit that would remain behind. Although he found it difficult to follow all that the Colonel said, and was obliged to ask a number of questions, he was thankful to have these matters to discuss and not to be obliged to refer to the fearful blow which he had just received. If only he had been prepared for it, he felt that he could have borne it better. But in his crass stupidity, he told himself, it was the one thing that had never occurred to him. He knew perfectly well that when a regiment went abroad on active service some officers and men were left behind. But he had never thought that he would be among those officers. Some people, he told himself, were struck by lightning, some were eaten by sharks, some won the Calcutta sweepstake, but he had never believed that any of those fates would befall such an ordinary chap as him, Willie Maryington. And he would never have thought that he would be the officer who was left behind. The Colonel had talked about the first scrap, but that was just the scrap that he wanted to be in. He had said something about heavy casualties. Willie minded little how heavy they were if he was in it, but how could he bear to sit at home hoping that his brother officers would be killed, so that he could take their place?

No reference was made in the mess that evening to the regiment's forthcoming departure, but Willie felt that it was generally known that he was not to go. Everybody was polite and kind to him as though he had just suffered some domestic tragedy, and, when he said that he was going to London next morning, nobody asked why.

When Willie went into his club on the following day he was surprised to find how many of the civilian members were already in uniform, and how many were expecting to go overseas almost immediately. At the time this made his position more painful, although subsequent experience taught him that these hopes of active service, if genuine, were too optimistic, and many of the most confident remained in uniform, and in the club, for the rest of the war.

He spent the greater part of the next day at the War Office, and was very far from having completed his mission at the end of it. The light was failing as he turned up Whitehall towards Trafalgar Square. He had almost bumped into a man who was walking rapidly in the opposite direction, when he saw that he was Horry, and they greeted one another.

'You're a bit off your beat here, Horry,' he said. 'Turn back with me and we'll have a drink at the Carlton bar.'

'I'm sorry, old chap,' said Horry, 'but I'm in a hurry. Walk along with me in my direction for a bit.'

Willie turned. As he did so he glanced curiously at Horry. There was something unusual in his appearance. Could he be sunburnt? No – he looked again, and then he saw what it was.

'Horry,' he said quietly, 'have you been playing in a matinée?'

'No, indeed. My show came off last week – and who ever heard of a matinée on a Friday?'

'Then, by God, Horry, I don't understand it,' said Willie rather fiercely. 'I thought perhaps you'd forgotten to take off your make-up. Are you aware, man, that your face is painted?'

He asked the question as though it were an accusation, and in order to add solemnity to it, he stopped, laid his hand on Horry's arm and looked straight into his eyes.

Horry threw back his head with his old gay laugh. 'Oh, my beloved Willie,' he said. 'Scotland Yard's just round the corner. Would you care to run me in for accosting? Come on, you old silly. I've got no time to lose.'

'But explain, for God's sake explain,' said Willie, as they walked on.

'It's very simple,' said Horry. 'I'm over forty, you know. I never thought I looked it, but it seems I do. They've turned me down at two of these damned recruiting places already, but there's one down here near Westminster Bridge. They haven't got the electricity working in it yet, but they keep it open till six, and by then the light's pretty bad. The chaps will be tired, they don't know me as you do, so they won't suspect anything, and I believe with this make-up I'll pull it off.'

'Oh, Horry, how splendid! I thought that you'd be the last person to do a thing like this.'

'I know.' Horry looked almost ashamed of himself. 'I'm not so keen on King and Country and all that stuff, but when I think about those blasted Nazis I just feel that I can't walk on to the stage and make an ass of myself as long as one of the bastards is left alive.'

Willie was deeply moved, but all he could mutter was 'Damned good show,' and as they had reached the end of Whitehall he turned, rather abruptly, towards Storey's Gate and began walking back to his club across the park. His mind was full of admiration for Horry and of pity for himself. Here was a man two years older than he was, who, since leaving school, had never done a day's military training, and who might now be going to the war, while he, whose whole life had been devoted to the Army, who had made every possible effort to render himself an efficient officer, was forced to stay at home. The injustice of it rankled deeply.

He had broken off his conversation with Horry so suddenly that he had forgotten to ask him to telephone the result of his visit to the recruiting station. When he reached his club, therefore, he rang up and heard the jubilant-voice of Horry at the other end of the line. All had gone well. The only doubt in the minds of the officials, so he assured Willie, was whether he was old enough to join the Army. He was to report on the following day.

Willie suggested that they should dine together, but Horry, after a moment's hesitation, feared it was impossible. Willie concluded that he was having a farewell dinner with Miriam, and keenly envied him. He asked for news of Felicity. He had tried to find her by telephone without success. Horry gave him a number. When he succeeded in getting it, after some difficulty, and asked for Miss Osborne, he was informed in a harsh female voice that 'Osborne would be coming on duty at 10 p.m.' He enquired who it was that he had the honour of speaking to, and learnt that it was the Superintendent of the Chelsea Branch of the Auxiliary Fire Service. He asked that Osborne might be requested to ring up his number when she arrived, and a grudging assent was given.

He was in the middle of a rubber of bridge after dinner when the call came through. Felicity's voice sounded tired on the telephone and not very friendly. After the usual greetings she said:

'I hope you're enjoying the war that you've been looking forward to for so long.'

'Oh no, Felicity,' he answered. 'I am not enjoying it at all.'

Her voice changed at once, and the warmth he loved so much came back into it.

'My poor Willie. I hate you to be unhappy. We'll lunch together tomorrow, and you shall tell me all about it.'

She gave him the name of a restaurant in Chelsea, and told him the hour at which she would be there, warning him that her time was limited and that he must be punctual.

On the following day he waited for her at the restaurant for half an hour. Thinking there had been a mistake, he was about to leave, for it was not a restaurant which tempted him to have luncheon alone, and he was standing at the entrance, when she came running down the street. Breathlessly she explained that she had been unable to get away earlier, that her hours of duty were always being changed, that she would never have forgiven him if he hadn't waited, but that now all was well, as she was free for the afternoon.

He thought that she had never looked so lovely. The uniform – dark blue tunic and trousers and a small blue hat that could not contain her thick curling hair – became her admirably. She carried her gas mask slung over her shoulder and somehow conveyed a curious impression of efficiency. He was delighted with her.

'Tell me quickly,' he said, 'all about this Army you have joined, what your duties are and how you like it.'

'It seemed,' she said, 'the best thing to do. One can't get into the Wrens, the Ats all hate it, and I can't bear the uniform of the Waafs, so here I am.

I've got some friends in the same show. We can't have much to do until the bombing starts, then we shall have to go round putting out the fires and carting away the corpses. I'm only a driver. The one thing I can do is to drive a car, but I've only just learnt to clean one. Look!' She held out to him her beautiful hands, already dirtied and roughened by labour.

He took one of them in his, pointed to the scratches on it, saying, 'Honourable scars, honourable scars,' then turned it over tenderly and kissed the palm.

'Even you,' he murmured, 'wounded already!' He asked her whether she had heard about Horry. She had heard nothing, and when he told her she was not surprised.

'I thought he'd do something like that,' she said, 'but I wish he could have had a commission. He loves his comforts, and he has been used to them for so long.'

'Perhaps he'll get one,' said Willie. 'Serve him right if he does, for then they won't let him go near the fighting.'

He poured forth all his own unhappiness, and Felicity listened with large-eyed sympathy. She offered him such consolation as she could, but found little to say that he had not said to himself already. There was, of course, the very likely possibility of heavy casualties, against which Willie argued that young officers were being rapidly trained to fill the gaps.

Felicity maintained, rather feebly, the view that this war was not going to be like the last. Not only was there just as much important work to be done at home, but the people who stayed at home would be in as great danger as those at the front.

'Not the soldiers,' said Willie bitterly. 'You ought to see our air-raid shelters; we've been digging them all the summer, although the C.O. didn't believe in war. They're the best in the country and, what's more, it's an order to go down into them at the first alert. It's an offence to risk the life of one of His Majesty's valuable soldiers, even those who are too old to go out and fight for him. And what do you suppose we're spending our time doing now?' he added. 'Camouflaging our barracks!'

'Well, you won't be safe when you come to London, anyhow, and I hope you'll come often because I see that I'm going to be terribly bored.'

'I'll come as often as I can; you can count on that. But if you think that a bomb falling on my head in a London street is going to make up to me for not fighting with the regiment in France, you're wrong.'

'My poor Willie,' said Felicity sadly. 'It seems to me that wars don't make people happy – not even the people who wanted them' – and she stretched her hand the table and held his for a minute.

CHAPTER XII

Willie was kept very busy that winter and the time passed quickly. If there were few casualties it was some consolation to him to know that there was so little fighting, and therefore that he was not missing much. He seldom came to London, and when he did he found it difficult to see Felicity, whose time also was occupied with small, tiresome duties, and who was intensely disliking her apparently unnecessary job, which increased the dreariness of the hard winter, the black-out and the uneventful war.

The only casualty that occurred in Willie's regiment was one that he least desired. The Colonel greeted him one morning in high spirits with the information that Hamilton had suffered some injury and was coming home.

'It seems,' he said, 'that he had a fall out riding. It has lamed him, and he's coming home for a bit, and I am to take his place. He'll take over here for the time being. He's fit for light duty.'

'What was he riding a horse for?' grumbled Willie. 'Why doesn't he stick to his dirty old tank? He can't fall off that.'

That the Colonel should go out and that Hamilton should come home was a double-barrelled disaster for Willie, and made a bad beginning to the second six months of the war. Events of so much greater importance, however, followed that for a while Willie forgot his own grievances while the German armies swept through Denmark, Norway, Holland, Belgium and France. His reaction to these tremendous events was that of many Englishmen. After the dim frustration of the first eight months he felt a new enthusiasm and a kind of spiritual exaltation. For the first time in his life it occurred to him that defeat was possible, but it was a possibility that did not appal him. There could be no defeat unless the enemy landed, and if they landed there could be no defeat so long as there was one true Englishman alive. Then at last he would have the opportunity of fighting for his country and of dying for it, if need be.

On one of his visits to London at about the time of the fall of France he spent an evening with Felicity. She greeted him with the news that Horry had been killed in Boulogne. She had only just heard, but she was quite calm about it, although Willie knew that it meant even more to her than it did to him.

'Garnet told me this morning,' she said. 'He had had the telegram as being next of kin.'

'It's too bad,' said Willie.

'Too bad,' she said.

'I sometimes think,' he went on, 'that we shall all be killed. I'd sooner be, if we're going to lose the War.'

'Of course,' she said quietly. 'But it won't be so easy for women.'

'Will they let you fight?' he asked.

'Can they stop us?' she answered. 'We had a lecture yesterday about Molotov bombs. You throw them out of the window at a tank, and if you hit it the tank goes up in smoke. It sounds fun, but nobody has seen one yet.'

Then they went on to talk of Horry, of how much they had loved him and how deeply they would miss him for the rest of their lives. It was a calm, sad evening. When they parted and Willie took her in his arms and kissed her cheek, he felt they had never been so close to one another before.

The important thing for Willie at this time was that the regiment, having suffered very lightly, was home again, and that he was with it. The Colonel was no longer there. He had had the final satisfaction of commanding during the retreat to Dunkirk, and had been transferred to some non-combatant job. Hamilton had been cured of his disability, promoted to the substantive rank of lieutenant-colonel and was in command. This slightly, but only slightly, mitigated Willie's happiness in being with his comrades again. He felt that the greater part of what was left of the Army was now in England, so that he was happy to be there too, and he secretly hoped that the enemy would invade.

The Battle of Britain damped his hopes, but he was uplifted by the glory of it, and cursed his fate that he had never learned to fly. His friends consoled him with the assurance that, judging by his prowess at the wheel of a car, he would certainly have destroyed any aeroplane he was in charge of, and himself with it. And even if he had survived he would have been permanently grounded long ago.

He still had his flat in London, and he went there as often as he could. He was there on the Sunday evening in September when the first serious bombing attack took place. Felicity was on duty that night. He was able to have only a few words with her on the telephone the following morning before he travelled back. When he pressed her for some account of her experiences she was reticent.

'Come on,' he urged, 'tell me more about it. What sort of time did you have?'

'Pretty bloody,' she said, and he could get nothing more out of her, but he felt as he returned to the country that she had come closer to the war than he had.

As the days shortened and the frequency of bombing raids increased, the rumours of invasion began to be discredited, and in Willie's regiment they were replaced by whispers that the regiment would shortly be moving to the Middle East. Now, so it seemed to Willie, the great crisis of his life must come. When they had crossed the Channel without him, the blow had been severe, but they had been distant only a day's journey, or a few hours in the air, and he had always hugged to his heart the hope that any morning the summons to join them might arrive. But if they went to the Middle East, and it was said that troops now travelled round the Cape to get there – if they went to the Middle East without him, he felt that his fate would be sealed. Speculation on this subject occupied his mind day and night. Here at home he was treated like any other officer. He was senior captain and performed all the duties and received all the respect belonging to his rank. His health was excellent. He had worked conscientiously to make himself efficient. Conceit was the least of his failings, but he quite honestly believed that he was as good an officer as the majority. *But*, that terrible word which came at the end of all his optimistic reasonings, *but* he had been left behind a year ago when he was thirty-nine, he was now forty and soon he would be forty-one. The next youngest captain in the regiment was thirty-four. This captain was married with children, as so many of these young men were, while he himself was single, with no dependants in the world. That was a consideration that ought surely to be taken into account.

The men liked him – that he knew – and so did his brother officers. He was not brilliantly clever, but nor were they. He knew his job as well as they did, and had more experience. It was true that he had been away from the regiment for some years, but he had worked hard to catch up, and thought he had succeeded. Did they think that because he was a little older he was more likely to go sick? A doctor had assured him that a healthy man of forty was in every way as sound a proposition as a man of thirty. He had passed his medical examination with flying colours. Since he had rejoined he had not had a day's illness, which was more than most of them could say. *But, but* they had left him behind a year ago, why should they take him with them now?

Willie became so haunted by this obsession that he finally decided that he had better take some action that would put himself out of his agony. Between the decision and the action many days passed. At last one night, which was selected for no better reason than that he had had an extra glass of port after dinner, and that he found himself alone with Hamilton, the others having gone to the cinema, he boldly broached the subject.

'They say we may be going overseas again,' he began.

'Do they?' said Hamilton, stretching for a newspaper.

'Oh, I'm not trying to extract confidential information about the movement of troops. I'm only interested in the movements of Captain

Maryngton. I don't want to know whether the regiment is going or not, but what I do want to know – pretty damned desperately bad I want to know – is whether, if the regiment does go, I am likely to go with it.'

Hamilton was silent.

'Look here, Colonel,' Willie went on. 'You've known me for a long time, and you must know what this thing means to me. I missed the last war by a few weeks, and all I have hoped for all my life is to see some fighting with the regiment. I had given up hope some years ago, when I left the Army. I thought there wouldn't be another war in my time, and then I thought I might get married. You were the only fellow I told, and I don't believe you ever repeated it, for which I'm damned grateful. Well, it didn't come off, and now I don't expect it ever will. I'm alone in the world, hale and hearty, just the sort of cannon-fodder they ought to be looking for – and, and, oh Hamilton, for God's sake tell me – have I got a chance?'

Hamilton replied, 'Not an earthly.'

Willie put his face in his hands, and Hamilton went on calmly:

'As you have asked me, it is better that you should know the truth. No officers, under field rank, of your age, or anything like your age, are being sent abroad. You may have heard of exceptions. There are exceptions to every rule, but I can see no chance of your being one. It's bad luck, but that's how it is.'

'I see,' said Willie, 'I see.'

He got up slowly, left the room and walked upstairs to bed. As he went he thought he might have asked whether he had any chance of promotion. But he knew what the answer would have been.

The final calamity comes often almost as a relief after long anxiety, and Willie, although he assured himself that life no longer held any interest for him, slept better that night than he had done for some time. Next morning he felt very miserable, but told himself that he must bear sorrow with fortitude, and that at such a moment in the world's history there were more important things to think about than the fate of Willie Maryngton. There was still the regiment and there was still Felicity.

In a few days came confirmation of the rumours about the regiment's movements, and it was followed by definite orders to sail. Henceforth they all lived in a turmoil of preparation, where there was as much work for Willie to do as for anyone else. His heart was in the work and he threw himself into it with passion, resisting firmly any inclination to pause and think. Like a discarded suitor employed on the preparations for the wedding of his beloved, he tried to think only of the task in hand, and to forget what must be the end of it. But too soon the end arrived. There could be none of those festivities or farewell parties that used to celebrate the departure of troops. The demands of security insisted that to the public eye the regiment should be there one day, carrying on their normal functions and giving no sign of departure, and on the morrow they should have disappeared, leaving no trace behind. Willie travelled with them to the port of embarkation, and actually went on board the ship in which they were sailing. When he had shaken hands with some of his friends, and came over the side for the last time, he had a curious and most uncomfortable feeling in his chest, and he found himself foolishly wondering whether people's hearts really do break, whether it might not be more than a mere figure of speech.

CHAPTER XIII

When he got back to London that evening an air-raid was in progress. There seemed to be one every night now. It was December 1940. There was no hope of getting a taxi at the station, so he left his kit there and walked through the deserted streets to his club. There were sounds of distant explosions, but the streets through which he walked were as quiet as they were empty. A gentle drizzle was falling. When he reached his destination he was damp and very tired. It was too late for dinner. He ordered some biscuits and a drink. Some members were playing billiards, others were watching them, and making unfavourable comments on their play. A friend came to sit by Willie and talked to him about racing. They had a drink together and then another one. Willie began to feel warm and at ease. The physical well-being spread from his senses to his mind. The regiment had gone but there were still good chaps in the club. The hall-porter dame in to warn them that it was nearly closing time. He could not bear the thought of his lonely flat. Was there nowhere they could go on to? he asked. Somebody knew of somewhere – an underground night club, which was sure to be open. They had another drink, and three of them went on. It was far from being a first-class establishment. The jangling music, the tawdry decorations, the tired faces of the girls, brought back to Willie the mood of acute depression from which he had been escaping. Another drink only intensified his gloom. Two of the girls were sitting with them. They knew his companions and they had mutual friends of whom they talked. Willie tried to take part in the conversation, but whatever he said sounded stilted and dull. He wished that Horry were there. Horry always got on with everybody. He knew how to break the ice. Did either of these girls know Horry? Or had they known him, rather, because he was dead, killed in the war. He was an actor but he got killed in the war. Funny thing. He would order another bottle so that they could all drink Horry's health – drink to his memory, rather – no good drinking his health now. Too late. How curious it was that even talking of Horry had helped to break the ice. He was getting on well with the girls now. They were nice girls too, and seemed sympathetic. He had no wish to go home with them, but he needed friends. Why shouldn't a man be friends with girls of that sort? He thought of Felicity and wondered where she was. He knew. She was driving round London, serving her country wherever the bombs were falling thickest. And the regiment was now at sea, going out to the war, hunted by submarines and enemy aircraft. And here was he, sitting half tight in a night club, talking to tarts. 'But it is not my fault,' he muttered to himself, 'God knows it is not my fault.'

Willie had eaten little all that day and, although he had forgotten it, he was very tired, so that the wine was too much for him, and he had to be helped to bed.

When he awoke next morning to a dark December day and found himself in his bleak, ill-kept bachelor flat, with no very clear recollection as to how he had got there, he felt that he had reached the lowest rung on the ladder of depression. There was even a moment when he contemplated putting an end to his life, but he remembered having once heard his father say that to commit suicide was the act of a coward, and therefore, whatever fate might befall him, he knew he must face it rather than run away.

He was disturbed about his behaviour on the previous evening. He was not in the least ashamed of having been drunk, but he remembered talking about Horry, and he was afraid that he might have been maudlin and lachrymose, which he would have considered contemptible. For some time he lay on his back contemplating the misery of human life. Then he rang for breakfast and telephoned to Felicity.

'Willie speaking. Have I woken you up?'

'No, dear idiot, it's just struck eleven.'

'What sort of a night did you have?'

'Pretty foul.'

'Were you up very late?'

'No, the all clear went at 2.30. What were you doing?'

'Well, I stayed up pretty late, and I don't remember hearing the all clear.'

'Tight again, I suppose.'

'I don't see why you need say "again". It happens very seldom. And if it did happen last night, there was good cause for it.'

'Why, what's the matter?'

'You know those chaps I was staying with, up in the north. They have all gone away and they've left me behind again.'

'Oh, my darling!' she cried. 'No wonder, no wonder. What can I do for you?'

'Can you dine with me to-night?'

'I can and will. I have two nights off. I get them every fortnight, you know. I had thought of going to rest in the country, but I hate the country at this time of year. So we'll dine together in that deep underground place in Berkeley Square where you can't hear the bombs, and we'll forget all about the war for once.'

'You're an angel,' said Willie. 'I had just sent out for a pistol to shoot myself. I'll countermand the order and meet you there at eight. I shall be waiting with the largest and coldest martini ever manufactured.'

Having eaten his breakfast and dressed, Willie set forth for his club, fortified in body and soul. He found one of his last night's companions, and eagerly asked him:

'Did I make a fool of myself last night?'

'Not more than usual, old boy.'

'I was feeling a bit depressed and I was afraid I might have got maudlin.'

'I think you asked one of those girls to be a sister to you, and you told the other she reminded you of your mother.'

'I can't have said that,' protested Willie, 'because I never saw my mother.'

'Oh, it may have been your grandmother, but you didn't make any suggestion to either of them that really interested them.'

'No, I know I didn't. I was very tired and I hadn't had any dinner, so I got a bit muzzy, but I remember everything really. It was very good of you to see me home.'

'Oh, I'm glad you remember that,' said his friend – 'but it happened to be George who saw you home, and he put you to bed. I felt it my duty to look after those poor girls.'

The chaff that followed made no impression on Willie. His volatile spirit had risen at the thought of dining with Felicity, and looking forward to it made him happy for the rest of the day.

He was first at the rendezvous that evening. He usually was. He ordered double martinis, poured them both into one glass, and ordered another. Then he sat down to wait.

'Hullo Willie,' he heard a voice say. He sprang up gladly to welcome Felicity, and found himself looking at someone whom for a moment he failed to recognise. Then he saw that it was Daisy Summers. They had not met since her elopement. She had changed so much that Willie forgave himself for his delay in recognising her. She had lost her prettiness, but she was still good looking, although her face was hard and lined.

'I am so glad to see you again, Daisy,' he said. 'I'm waiting for someone, but she's always late. Won't you sit down for a minute and have a drink?'

'That's very sweet of you, Willie,' she said. 'You always were very sweet.' She sat down. 'Your girl friend seems to have a healthy thirst, judging from your preparations. I'll have a whisky sour if I may.'

'What's your life now, Daisy? Are you happy?'

'Yes, I'm pretty happy, thanks. I don't think anybody's very happy, do you? I've been working in the postal censorship since the beginning of the war. One feels one's doing something, but it isn't much.'

'And er – your husband?'

'Oh,' she laughed, 'I suppose you mean the Coper. That didn't last long. I've been married since then. I heard from the old skunk the other day. He's living in Ireland, and says it's very nice to be a neutral.'

'He's much too old to fight,' said Willie. 'They tell me that I am, and they won't let me go out.'

'Poor old Willie! You always get the dirty end of the stick; I ought to have married you if I hadn't been a silly little fool, and a bitch. And you never have married, have you? Well, I expect you're wise.' She looked at him reflectively for a moment – 'We might go out together one evening.'

'I'd love to,' said Willie, but he didn't sound as though he meant it, so she shrugged her shoulders and said, 'There's my boy. So long, Willie,' and walked over to an overdressed young gentleman who was waiting impatiently at the door.

Willie sat down again and finished his cocktail. 'Poor old Daisy!' he thought. 'She was never a bad sort at heart. She was just fascinated by the Coper. I wonder how it would have turned out if we had married. She seemed to regret it just now. We might have had a lot of children. It would make one feel less useless if one had brought some decent people into the world. It would be interesting to discuss it with her. I might have been more welcoming about her suggestion that we should go out together. I'll go over and speak to her, if only to irritate that young puppy who's with her. Why isn't he in uniform?'

Willie strolled across to where Daisy and her friend were sitting.

'Daisy dear,' he said, 'you suggested our going out together but gave me no address except the postal censorship. What do I do? Ring up the Postmaster-General and say "Please put me through to Daisy" – because I don't know your surname?'

'Silly Willie,' she laughed, while the over-dressed young man glared furiously. 'We're not under the Postmaster-General but the Minister of Information. Here, give me your pencil,' she said to the young man, who sulkily produced a gold one. She scribbled on the back of the menu. 'Here you are,' she said. 'Name, address and telephone number. Mind you don't lose them, and mind you make use of them.'

As Willie returned to his seat, Felicity arrived. 'Who were you talking to?' she asked him.

'An old school friend of yours, Daisy Summers. Do you ever see her now?'

'Never, and I didn't see much of her then. She's made rather a hash of her life, I'm afraid.'

'What has she done?'

'She didn't stay long with that Irishman she ran away with. I doubt if they were ever married, but they pretended to be. Then she did marry somebody quite nice, but it didn't go well, and they separated. Now they say she's being kept by that little Argentine.'

'How dreadful!'

'Oh, I don't know. I dare say she's quite happy.'

'I've promised to go out with her one night.'

'Don't let her seduce you.'

'Would you mind, Felicity, if she did?'

'Not if you promise to tell me all about it.' This hurt Willie. She often hurt him without knowing it.

'Well,' he said, 'if you've quite finished that enormous cocktail and can still walk, we might go over to our table and have some dinner before closing time.'

She had made no comment on the cocktail. This also had disappointed him. He would prepare things to amuse or please her and she would fail to notice them.

As they sat down at their table she said, 'I think it's going to be a bad night. The moon's nearly full and there are no clouds. I'm glad I'm not on duty. By the way, have I seen you since the bombing of London started?'

This was the third unintended blow she dealt him. The dates on which he saw her were engraven on his heart, and the days between impatiently counted.

'Of course you have. We had luncheon together in October, and I saw you for a few minutes when I passed through London last month.'

'Of course,' she said absently, and he knew that she had no memory of those meetings. Then, as though recollecting herself, she turned to him impulsively. 'But tell me about you. They've left you behind. Aren't they devils! I'm sure it's all the fault of that evil Hamilton. But I'm glad I've got you still here – darling. I know I'm selfish.'

All Willie's irritation vanished, forgotten for ever, and he was the happy lover again. So he was able to talk about his disappointment calmly and to discuss the possibilities of invasion, which he had to admit were diminishing. He found that her sympathy really comforted him.

They heard faintly the sound of explosions from time to time, and the head-waiter whispered to Willie that a popular restaurant with a dancing-floor had been struck. He told Felicity, who said, 'Lucky we didn't go there to-night.'

'I wish you could get some more reasonable job,' he said.

'By "more reasonable" you mean safer. I'm beginning to wish so, too. I'm not very brave, you know. And I don't find that I get any braver. It's rather the other way round. I suppose nerves, like everything else, wear out.'

'I heard of a job in the country, near where the regiment was, which might interest you.'

'Oh no,' she said at once, 'I can't leave London. That would be running away. You may think it silly, but that's how I feel – and I think one's own feelings are the best guides one has as to what is right or wrong. I do lots of things that people think wrong, and I don't feel guilty, but if I left London I should be ashamed for the rest of my life.'

'I don't believe you could do wrong,' protested Willie, but she went on without listening to him.

'And I love London so. I think I love it more than England. If you had seen the people of London as I have this month – the ordinary, little, common, heroic people – so brave, so cheerful and so funny – with all their small treasures that they loved blown to smithereens, and making jokes about it, and sticking up their pathetic Union Jacks on heaps of rubble. And the great city itself, with its poor wounded face, so gaunt and ugly and grand and glorious – and old.'

'Yes,' said Willie doubtfully, 'but I like the country better.'

She looked at him, startled, as though she had forgotten he were there. Then she said, slowly:

'My darling Willie. I would not have you any different.'

'Thank you,' he said. 'I so often wish I were different.'

'In what way?' she asked.

'Oh, I should like to be witty and brilliant, as I suppose your other friends are, whom you won't let me see.'

'Talking of brilliance,' she said, 'old Garnet is home again. He's back from North Africa, where he had quite an exciting time. There's nothing brilliant about him. And, oh, Willie, he's grown so old. I can't bear people to grow old, can you? Of course he's more than fifteen years older than me, but he is my brother. I suppose it's the climate of the Far East. He wants so much to see you. I'll give you his telephone number. Write it down, don't lose it and don't get it mixed up with Daisy's, or there might be trouble.'

She gave him the number, which he recorded in his pocket-book, and shortly afterwards they left. As they went up the stairs which led to the street she turned suddenly from the higher step and, bending down, kissed him on the lips.

The streets were quiet now and the moon was bright, but when they came to Jermyn Street they found policemen and firemen guarding the approach. Willie explained that he lived there and was going home. The policeman asked at which number he lived, and on being told said, 'I fear you won't find much of that left, but you can go and have a look. You can't take the car through.' Where had stood the substantial building in which he lived there was an empty space through which the moon, that should have cast a shadow on to the other side of the street, shone without hindrance. From what had been the basement smoke and dust were rising, together with the noise of men at work. Ambulances and fire-engines were standing by.

'Can I be of any help?' asked Willie of somebody who seemed to be in authority.

'No, thanks. The bomb fell an hour and a half ago. We have all the help we need.'

'I lived there,' said Willie, pointing to the void.

'You might very easily have died there to-night,' said the stranger, and Willie, feeling there was no more to be said, returned to the car.

He explained to Felicity what had happened. He had lost everything he possessed in the world, for what he had left in the barracks, that the regiment had recently quitted, had arrived at his flat that day.

'And what are you going to do now, poor Willie?' she asked, smiling at him with amusement and love.

'I've got nowhere to sleep,' he said weakly, standing by the door of the car.

'You had better come and sleep with me,' she said. 'Jump in.'

Half dazed by the sudden event, and still further bewildered by her words, he obeyed her and sat silent by her side while the car sped westwards. It stopped at the entrance that he knew so well.

'Come in,' she said. 'There's nobody here to-night. I'll leave the car here. You can take it in the morning – but you must go early and send it back.'

Willie hardly closed his eyes that night. He had no wish to sleep. He did not want to forget, even for a moment, that Felicity was lying in his arms, and that after all these years she had suddenly given herself to him with the sweetest simplicity and grace. But what did it mean? She had always said she loved him. Did she love him more now, and in a different way? She had always refused to marry him. Surely she would now consent? But what mattered most were the precious moments that were passing. Her head was resting lightly on his shoulder. She slept as silently as a child. He must not wake her. How tenderly he loved her now! Surely this precious night made up for all that he had lost in life.

Long before dawn he left her, very quietly. She turned with a little sigh on to her other side and was still asleep. He was glad that she had not woken. He would not have known what to say. He decided not to take the car, but to walk. He had plenty of time and plenty to think about. As he went down the King's Road, the lurid lamps of night became innocent primroses against the faint morning sky. He felt like a poor man who had suddenly inherited a vast fortune, in which he could hardly believe.

He went first to the site of his flat, in the vague hope of recovering some of his belongings. Any such hope was extinguished by one glance at the scene of devastation. He had then thought to go to his club, having forgotten that it would not be open at that hour. Nor did he like the prospect of arriving in an empty hotel bedroom with nothing but the clothes he wore. Suddenly he remembered that Felicity had given him Garnet's telephone number. Garnet was the type that would not mind being woken before his time. He turned into a telephone booth and rang the number. A voice answered immediately, 'Colonel Osborne speaking.'

'How like Garnet,' thought Willie, 'not to waste time saying "hello".'

'This is Willie Maryngton,' he said. 'Did I wake you up?'

'No, I'm cooking my breakfast.'

'Well, cook some more for me. I've been bombed out, and I'll come along as quick as legs or a taxi can take me.'

'Very well.'

CHAPTER XIV

Garnet's faded eyes shone with pleasure as he opened the door of the flat to Willie.

'Right glad I am to see you,' he said. 'I suppose you got my number from Felicity. I feared she would forget to give it you.'

Then Willie remembered that Garnet was Felicity's brother, and the thought made him feel a little wicked, but very grand.

'I never knew you were such an early bird,' he said, for Garnet was fully dressed, and was laying tea and eggs, toast and marmalade, on the table, all of which he had plainly prepared himself, for there was no sign of a servant.

'I have to be,' he answered – 'I'm due at the hospital at nine, and I've patients to see before I go there. I was never so busy in my life.'

'Everyone is except me,' said Willie sadly. 'How right you were to join the R.A.M.C. You've already been to the war, and now you're as useful as you ever were, serving the country every hour of the day, while I, younger than you, am no good for anything.'

He was very hungry, and while they ate their breakfast he recounted to Garnet all his misfortunes.

Garnet listened sympathetically, and at the end said, 'You're looking very tired. I'll prescribe for you. I have a small spare room. You're welcome to live in it as long as you like. Go there now and lie down on the bed and sleep. An old woman comes in the course of the morning to wash up and dust and break the crockery. She won't interfere with you. I'll leave her a note. When you wake the shops will be open. You can go and buy the things you most need. Except breakfast I have no meals here, and never know when or where I may get them, but I shall come back to sleep, and shall look forward to seeing you. Now I must hurry away.'

It was too early, Willie thought, to telephone to Felicity, so he obediently lay down on the bed and slept until past midday. Then it was too late.

He was busy all day buying the things he needed. Every hour he telephoned to Felicity, but there was no reply. He came back to the flat soon after dinner to unpack his purchases, and having done so, was telephoning for the last time when Garnet returned.

'I was ringing up Felicity,' he said, 'but I can get no answer from her flat.'

'She gets a couple of nights off now and then and usually goes away for a rest. She needs it. That work is a high strain on a girl.'

'I am sure it is,' said Willie. 'I wish we could find her something less tiring and nerve-racking.'

'Her health seems satisfactory. You look more tired than she does. What have you been doing all day?'

'Buying my trousseau. I thought it would be fun, but I didn't enjoy it. I suppose I should have made a list before I started. I seem to have got all the wrong things. Look at this beautiful dressing-gown, and I forgot to buy pyjamas and a brush and comb.'

Garnet thought that Willie looked pathetic, helpless and strangely young.

'Come on now,' he said. 'We'll sit down and make a sensible list. I'm used to this sort of thing.'

The next day was Saturday. Willie was due to stay with friends in the country, but he felt he could not leave London without having spoken to Felicity. He believed that she must be wanting to speak to him. She could not know that he was staying with Garnet, but she could have left him a message at the club. It was late in the afternoon when at last he heard her voice on the telephone. He had somehow vaguely expected that it would be altered, fraught with a new intensity, a more intimate affection, but she sounded as she had always done – cheerful and hurried. He told her that he was staying with Garnet, and she approved of the arrangement. He said he had been going away but would stay if she wanted to see him.

'Oh no,' she answered. 'I'll see you when you come back.'

'Which day?'

'You'd better telephone next week.'

He could not leave her so lightly.

'Felicity——' he said.

'What?'

'I'm so glad my flat was bombed.'

'Yes, it must be fun to have the chance of buying everything new. I suppose the government will give you the money. Mind you buy some pretty new suits. I'm in a great hurry, have to go on duty, good-bye.'

'Good-bye, my darling Felicity.' She rang off.

Willie felt disappointed, but he did not know why. He had expected something different, but he could not say what. There were moments when he wondered whether the bomb that destroyed his flat had not also scattered his wits, and whether all that had happened afterwards had not been a dream.

It was many days before he saw Felicity again. Small things prevented them from meeting. When they did he came as soon as possible to the point.

'Now will you marry me?' he asked.

'No, my darling,' she answered, 'I won't.'

'But surely what happened the other night has made a difference?'

'I see no reason why it should.'

'But what is it that prevents you from marrying me?'

'It is too difficult to explain.'

'Do you love somebody else more than me?'

She made no reply.

'Do you behave with lots of other people as you have behaved with me?'

'Willie, I refuse to be cross-questioned. You might make me angry, which I have no wish to be. You ought to know me better by now. You love me and you must try to understand me. I know it's hard. I am unreliable. I am wanton. I am ruled by my moods. I suppose that I am very selfish, and that alone would make me a bad wife. But I can't change and I don't want to. You must take me or leave me as I am.'

'But have you no morals?'

'I suppose not. I know that some things are right and some are wrong. Sometimes I do wrong things and I am very sorry, but sometimes I do things which other people think are wrong and which don't seem wrong to me. I thought what we did the other night was not wrong. What did you think?'

'I don't know,' said Willie, which was the truth. He had never asked himself the question, and now he wondered how he could have failed to do so.

'I haven't any religion,' Felicity went on. 'Perhaps I should be better if I had. Mother had none, you know. It was very curious that somebody so conscientious, so conventional and so very good should have been without it.'

They went on to talk about the late Mrs. Osborne, and Willie got no farther in his quest, no nearer to his goal. Despairing of his hopes for marriage, he longed to enquire whether he could expect again what she had given him once. But he dared not ask her, for she still retained some quality – cold, remote and virginal which he trembled to offend.

They separated on that occasion without anything else of importance being said and with the briefest of caresses. The next time they dined he asked her whether her flat was occupied by others that evening. She said that it was. He asked her when it was likely to be empty again. She laughed.

'My poor darling,' she said, 'I know what you mean. But I can't arrange to make love as one fixes dates with dentists. Something will happen – all will be well.'

Their relationship continued with little change. Willie took a furnished flat from a friend for the summer months. Sometimes his evenings with Felicity would end there, but not often. He never knew how it was to be.

In the autumn he was appointed to the post of instructor in an O.C.T.U. He was jubilant when he got the job, but it proved, in the end, another disappointment. The commandant was only a few years older than Willie, but those few precious years had enabled him to distinguish himself in the first war and earn a row of medals. Willie, on grounds of seniority, was second-in-command, and it just so happened that every one of the junior officers had been out to the war, and had either been wounded or become medically unfit. There was one who had been taken prisoner and had escaped.

Willie was determined not to be sensitive. He fought against it, but he was like a man with some physical blemish at which he feels that others must always be looking. He felt that these young officers must despise him – a dreary old dug-out who had never seen a shot fired in battle. And feeling so, he began to imagine things and to detect sneers where none were intended. He became suspicious and distrustful. He took unreasonable dislikes and began to find pleasure in exerting his authority and snubbing his juniors. He lost the happy gift of inspiring affection which he had unconsciously enjoyed all his life. He was no longer popular, and he knew it.

He came to look forward more and more to his visits to London. There at least he could find at the club the old companions, whom he knew so well, and upon whose good-fellowship he could rely. It never occurred to him that even here the standard had deteriorated; that the worthier members were either serving abroad or working too hard at home to have time for lounging.

Leave was difficult to come by. Although the work was not hard, not nearly so hard as Willie would have liked it to be, he was expected to be always on the spot and to take a sort of schoolmaster's interest in the welfare of the cadets. To go away, even when he had no duties to perform, was frowned upon as showing lack of enthusiasm.

Therefore he saw less of Felicity during this year, and the meetings he had with her were less satisfactory. The friend who had leased him the flat had now reoccupied it, so that he was obliged to stay at hotels, where she would seldom visit him. She also had found some new employment about the nature of which she was extremely reticent. It seemed to occupy more of her time than the previous one, and she was less certain as to when she would be free. Her reticence, combined with her obvious absorption in her work, irritated Willie. He was more easily irritated than he used to be.

Then came a break between two courses at the O.C.T.U. and it brought him a few days' leave, to which he had been looking forward very eagerly. He had made all the preparations for it that men do make when they have time to plan anticipated pleasure. He had made sure of having the rooms he wanted in the hotel he liked best, he had taken tickets for the theatre, he had hired a car for the night, and he had, of course, arranged with Felicity that she should go out with him. When he strode triumphant into his club at midday the hall-porter handed him a folded slip of paper on which was written: 'Miss Osborne telephoned that she was very sorry she would be unable to dine with Captain Maryngton tonight.'

Willie crumpled up the message and, tossing it aside, strode gloomily into the club. He felt that everybody must know, the hall-porter at least must, that he had been let down by a girl, and that he looked like a man waiting with a bunch of violets for someone who never comes. He wondered what he should do with the theatre-tickets as he scanned the welcoming faces of his club-mates, and found none with whom he would care to go to the play. Then he remembered Daisy Summers, and was glad to find that he still had her telephone number. He was pleased and surprised when she answered the call.

'It's Willie speaking,' he said.

'Willie Maryngton?' she asked. 'Come to life again after all these years?'

'It's not so long as you think, Daisy, only about a year. I'm up in London on leave. How about coming out with me, or would it wreck the work of the postal censorship?'

'Silly boy,' she said, 'the postal censorship wrecked me long ago, and now they try to do it without me – and a pretty good mess, I hear, they make of it.'

'But will you come out tonight?'

'Of course I will.'

'Shall we go to a play?'

'If there's anything worth seeing.'

He mentioned the name of the play for which he had got seats.

'You'll never get in there,' she said.

'I'll try – and I'm not so stupid as I used to be, so I'll pick you up at 6.30 and we'll have a good time.'

Daisy was looking very pretty that evening, prettier than Willie remembered, and she was smartly dressed. She was impressed by Willie's efficiency in getting good seats for the most successful play in London, and he saw no need to tell her that he had got them three weeks before. After the theatre they went for dinner to a gay restaurant, where there was music and dancing and where Willie saw several of his friends. Felicity would never go to fashionable places of this kind, but Willie really preferred them. He and Daisy danced together, and drank champagne and he told himself he was having a very good time. They went on to a night club and it was late when he drove her home.

'Come in for a minute and have a drink,' she said.

And he, knowing that it was not to have a drink, accepted the invitation.

He saw Felicity before his leave expired. She made no reference to having thrown him over, until he did. Then she said that she was very sorry, but that it had been quite impossible for her to go out with him that evening. She gave no reason.

'It was of no consequence,' he said. 'I got hold of Daisy Summers and we had quite a good time.' He told her of the play, the restaurant and the night club.

'Did she seduce you?'

'That's a particularly catty way of putting it,' he said.

'You know what I mean.'

'Why should I tell you?'

'Because I want to know, and you know you can trust me.'

'You said you wouldn't mind if she did, so long as I told you.'

'I was wrong. I do mind. I am very sorry.'

'But how do you know what happened?'

'I can't explain how I know,' she answered with a tired sigh, 'but I do. I think you will never be able to deceive me, Willie, and I hope you will never try.'

Willie felt unhappy, not like Lothario, but like a little boy who has been caught doing something of which he is ashamed. He was also full of resentment.

'Why should you make such a fuss?' he protested. 'I thought you attached little importance to such things and didn't think them wrong.'

'Am I making a fuss?' she asked. 'I'm sorry. I know very little about right and wrong, as I've always told you. And I can't see that right and wrong, good and evil, have anything to do with it. I just feel, as I have always felt, that Daisy is not the girl for you. You were very young when you got engaged to her, and you couldn't tell the difference, but you ought to be able to tell the difference now.'

'You hate her, don't you?'

'Good heavens, no! How can you think so? I want her to be happy with her own friends, in her own way.'

'I suppose you think I'm too good for her.'

'No, not that either. She may be better than you, or me, for all I care. But she doesn't suit you, she doesn't become you, and I hate you to do what is unbecoming.'

'I believe you are jealous of her,' said Willie sullenly.

She smiled sadly. 'Perhaps I am; you can think so if you like.'

They parted coldly, as they had never parted before. At the last moment Willie felt inclined to throw himself on his knees and implore her forgiveness. But he was too angry to do so, and he felt strongly that there was no reason why he should. He could not live for ever on the scant charity that Felicity dispensed to him according to her unpredictable moods. Daisy was a jolly good sort. He had no idea what Felicity meant by saying that she didn't become him. He had no wish to understand. Could it be that she was jealous? He would have liked to think it, but he knew that it was not so.

CHAPTER XV

After this the relationship between Willie and Felicity grew less happy. He would still try to see her whenever he came to London, but their evenings together were not as they once had been. The subjects of conversation were no longer the same. Felicity had taken an interest in the regiment, about which Willie had loved to talk. She had come to know intimately the lives and characters of men whom she had never seen, and would often surprise Willie by the accuracy with which she remembered details. She would enquire with real interest about the major's growing family or the subaltern's love affairs. But Willie did not care to talk about the men he was serving with now, or if he did, it was only to recount some remark by one of them, which he had interpreted as a hidden insult. His stories about his brother officers had in the past been full of fun and affection. Now they were laden with malice and dislike.

'Do you know who I met in the street this morning?' he said one evening to Felicity – 'that dirty cad Hamilton.'

'I know you don't like him,' she answered, 'but isn't "dirty cad" a bit strong?'

'It's the luck some fellows have that maddens me. I heard he'd been wounded in Africa. It seems to have been pretty bad – his shoulder shattered to pieces, only a few months ago – and here I meet him swanking down Bond Street with his arm in a sling, quite the wounded hero, having just been appointed Military Attaché to one of the few neutral countries where life would be interesting in these days. Why can't they make me a Military Attaché?'

'Perhaps the fact that you can't speak a single word of any foreign language may have something to do with it.'

'I'm told that that doesn't matter a bit. Foreigners respect you all the more if you can't speak their beastly language. I agree with the chap who said that anybody can understand English if spoken loud enough.'

'Really, Willie, you do talk the most terrible nonsense at times.'

Their evenings together seldom ended happily now. Felicity would gently loosen his arms when he threw them around her, and would turn away her face when he wanted to kiss her.

Because he was not happy in his work he was not good at it. He had no gift for teaching and no genuine interest in the progress of those he taught. One autumn evening when the talk had turned on to the fattening of turkeys for the Christmas market, he said, 'That's what our work here is – grooming a lot of silly boys until we think they're fit to be sent out and get killed.' It pleased him to watch the disapproval on the faces of the others, and he did not mind the silence that followed his remark.

He was not surprised therefore when, at the end of the year, his appointment was not renewed, and he found himself once more on the list of elderly officers awaiting employment.

It was now that Willie's friends began to notice a change in him. They found him less good company than he used to be. He had never been a wit or a brilliant conversationalist, but his good manners, his interest in whatever was being said and his happy smile, which came so easily, had made him someone who was welcome wherever he went. His manners were no longer so good, for the fountain from which they sprang, a kind heart, was drying up. He was losing his interest in his fellow beings and finding greater difficulty in smiling. Some thought it was due to an unhappy love affair, others that he was ill, or that he was drinking too much. In fact he was suffering from despair.

He went back to living with Garnet. It saved him the trouble of looking for something else. He disliked taking trouble about anything, and he argued that he might get a new appointment at any moment, so that it was wiser to incur no liabilities. Every morning he would wander to the club and spend most of the day there, doing nothing in particular. Sometimes he would go to a race meeting. More often he would follow the racing results on the tape. Garnet, who watched him with a professional eye, was unhappy about him. He detected symptoms that escaped the eyes of laymen.

'I'm worried about Willie,' he said to Felicity. 'He's letting himself go to pieces.'

'What do you mean?' she asked.

'It is hard to explain, and still harder to understand, unless you have lived in the Far East, as I have. There they say it is the climate which has got you down. There, you know, the retiring age is fifty, and many a man is finished before he reaches it. A moment comes when something happens like the mainspring of a watch breaking. The façade remains the same, perhaps for a long time, and most people can see no difference. I used rather to fancy myself at being able to diagnose this particular disease, and Willie shows symptoms recently that have made me think of it.'

'Oh, Garnet, what can we do to help him?'

'His state may of course be partly due to physical causes. I wanted him to go into hospital for a few days to be overhauled, but he wouldn't hear of it. He said the hospitals were now for fighting soldiers, and he would be ashamed to occupy one minute of a doctor's or a nurse's time.'

'But what can we do to help him?' she repeated.

'A new job that would really interest him, or anything that would take him out of himself would be the best thing.'

'Yes', she said; 'but he is so hard to place. He isn't very clever, bless his heart, and he has no experience of anything except soldiering.'

'We must think about it,' said Garnet, as he left her. He was, as usual, in a hurry.

There is a district in London, near the heart of it, which has acquired, perhaps undeservedly, a bad reputation. Willie was walking through it one evening. He was returning from the club before dinner, because he had no appetite, and was thinking of going to bed. To his surprise he saw Felicity come out from a block of flats, to which is attached particular notoriety. He thought she looked taken aback when she saw him, but she only laughed when he asked her if that was where she was working now. Two evenings later he was there again, designedly, at about the same hour. Again she came out of the same building, but this time she was not taken aback. She walked up to him and, standing still, said:

'You came here on purpose to spy on me.'

He answered, 'I came here to see if you were really working in that house.'

'Have you nothing better than that to do?' she asked.

'No, by God, I haven't,' he answered passionately, and all her wrath gave way to pity, for she felt as though she had torn the bandage off a festering wound.

She laid a hand on his arm.

'Come into this pub with me, Willie, and have a glass of beer.'

He followed her meekly, and looking round at the unfamiliar precincts he said:

'I don't think I've ever been in an ordinary public-house in London before.'

There was so much of the old, childish Willie in his naïve wonder that she was touched.

'I brought you in here,' she said, 'to give you a lecture, but you're really so touching that I don't think I can.'

'Thank you, Felicity,' he said.

'But listen to me, all the same. You know you are not as nice as you used to be.'

'I know, I know.'

'Do you really think that I'm running a brothel or working in one?'

'How could I think such a thing?'

'Then why did you come here this evening?'

'Perhaps it was just in the hope that I should see you.'

'No, Willie, you know it wasn't. You suspected me. Perhaps you didn't define to yourself what it was that you suspected, but your mind is full of suspicion, hatred and darkness, and it is destroying your heart.'

'I know, I know.'

'You look ill.'

'I feel it. I've felt rotten for days.'

'You ought to be in bed.'

'I stayed there yesterday, but it's so lonely in that grim little room. Garnet's out all day.'

'Well, I'm going to take you there now, and put you to bed, and give you a hot drink and some aspirin. Old Garnet must have a look at you when he comes in. I think you've some fever,' she said, holding his wrist.

She did as she had said, helping him to undress and to get into bed. He was very docile. Before she left him she bent over him and kissed his hot lips with her cool ones, and whispered to him that she loved him still, and that as soon as he was well all should be between them as it had been in the happiest days of the past. His arms held her close to him for a moment, but all he said was 'Alas, alas!'

She scribbled a note to Garnet before she left the flat. He telephoned to her early next morning.

Willie had passed a bad night. He was suffering from pneumonia and had a high fever. But his constitution was good, his heart was sound, there were no complications, no cause for anxiety. Garnet had arranged for a good nurse to look after him. When Felicity went to see him that evening the nurse dissuaded her from going into his room. He was sleeping, and he needed all the sleep he could get. All efforts to bring down his temperature had failed. His condition was grave. He was no better on the following day. In the evening he fell into a torpor, and early the next morning he died.

CHAPTER XVI

On that day Garnet went to have luncheon at the Service club to which he belonged. He was sad and weary, having sat up half the night. He was overwhelmed with work, and felt that unless he relaxed for an hour and had a quiet meal instead of the glass of milk and sandwiches that he was accustomed to snatch at midday, he would become a casualty himself. That one of the first duties of a soldier was to take care of his own health was a maxim that he frequently impressed on others.

The large club dining-room was nearly full. In a corner he saw an old friend whom he had known in Penang. He was a Scotsman and now, so Garnet noticed, a Brigadier. He sank into the seat opposite, and the two old soldiers began to exchange grievances. Having disposed of the climate, they proceeded to condemn the long hours during which men were expected to work on this side of the world. Garnet explained that this was the first occasion for many months that he had been able to lunch at the club, and that he was only doing so today because he had felt on the verge of a breakdown.

'I was up half the night with a poor fellow who died early this morning, and when I got to the hospital there were a series of operations, so that I haven't even had time to certify his death.'

'Do you have to nurse your patients as well as dose them?' asked the Brigadier.

'No, but this was a dear friend, who had been living in my flat, Willie Maryngton. Did you ever know him?' Garnet mentioned his regiment.

'I think I met him in India – a nice fellow – very sad.'

'Yes indeed, and I suppose I shall have to make all the funeral arrangements.'

'Can't you leave that to his relations?'

'The extraordinary thing is that he hasn't got any. I've known him all my life. His father, who was killed in the last war, made my father his guardian. My father was killed, and Willie was brought up with us from the age of fourteen. He never had a single relation that he knew of.'

The Brigadier seemed interested and began to put questions.

'You say he died this morning? And you have not certified his death? And he had neither kith nor kin?'

Garnet confirmed all these particulars, and the Brigadier went on to make enquiries about Willie's activities during the war, about his age and rank, and ended by asking:

'How many people have you informed of his death?'

'I telephoned to my sister this morning. We were both very fond of him. The nursing sister and the charwoman, who looks after my flat, are of course aware. But why all these questions? It's very kind of you to take so much interest, but I don't quite understand.'

'I am going to ask one more. Did he make a will? If so, where is it? Who benefits by it, and who is the executor?'

'Yes, he made a will. I found it this morning. He left everything to his regimental benevolent fund, and appointed as his executors the firm of lawyers who have always acted for him.'

'Osborne,' said the Scotsman, solemnly, 'do you believe in Providence?'

'No,' said Garnet.

'Well, I do. I was brought up so to believe, and I have never lost my faith. Providence is a great mystery, and I have seen many proofs of it in my life. I am going to make three requests of you. First, that you will not sign that certificate to-day. Second, that you will not mention Maryngton's death to another living soul. Third, that you will call on me at my office this afternoon.'

Garnet protested that he had no time to spare.

'You will have the time you would have given to registering the death and making the funeral arrangements. You have known me for many years and you know that I do not use words lightly. I tell you that this is a matter of the very greatest importance.'

His Scottish r's rolled impressively, and Garnet, although he felt that he was dreaming, agreed to do as he was asked. Five o'clock was the hour decided upon. The Brigadier drew a blank visiting-card from his pocket book, and wrote upon it. 'That is the address,' he said.

Garnet raised his eyebrows as he read it. 'Well,' he said, 'I should have thought that that was the last place you would have chosen for your office.'

'That,' replied the Brigadier, 'is precisely why I chose it.'

They parted, and a few minutes later the Brigadier was entering that ill-famed building outside which Willie had waited a few days before. He took a lift to the third floor, where he let himself into one of the two flats. A slovenly-looking man, sitting in the passage, sprang smartly to attention.

'Fergusson,' said the Brigadier, 'a colonel, R.A.M.C., in uniform, will be calling at five o'clock. Show him straight in. I don't wish to be disturbed while he is with me.'

'Sir,' replied Fergusson.

The Brigadier went into his office, a small room with a large writing-table, sat down and rang the bell. Felicity appeared.

'I shall have a Colonel Osborne coming to see me about five,' he said. 'I don't wish any telephone calls put through while he is here, unless it is a matter of great importance.'

'Colonel Osborne?' she repeated tentatively.

'Colonel Garnet Osborne, R.A.M.C.'

'He is my brother.'

'Is that so, Miss Osborne? Is that so? Another remarkable coincidence. Do you believe in Providence, Miss Osborne?'

'I don't know. I've never thought about it.'

'There are worse things to think about. Your brother is an old friend of mine. We were together in Malaya. Have you all the documents ready and in order for Operation Z?'

'Yes, sir.'

'Have you not thought of any better name for it? Z is a daft sort of a name for an operation.'

'I haven't thought of another.'

'Well, just go on thinking. Thank you.'

She left the room.

When Garnet arrived he was shown straight into the Brigadier, who greeted him with the question:

'Did you know that your sister is my personal assistant?'

'My sister Felicity?' he asked in astonishment.

'She is Miss Osborne to me, but she tells me you are her brother, and I have no reason to doubt her veracity.'

'Well, well! This is a strange day in my life,' said Garnet.

'And you have not got to the end of it yet,' replied the Brigadier. 'Sit down.'

He then proceeded to confirm all the particulars concerning Willie with which Garnet had supplied him at luncheon. He had a paper in his hand on which he had recorded them. He went through them in order to be sure they were correct.

'Thank you,' he concluded when he came to the end of his questions. 'You have given me some information – and now you are going to receive some in return.

'The purpose of this department, in which you find yourself, Colonel Osborne, is to deceive the enemy. Our methods of deception are, at certain times, extremely elaborate. The more important the military operations under contemplation the more elaborate are our preparations to ensure, not so much that the enemy shall be ignorant of what we intend to do, but rather that he shall have good reason to believe that we intend to do something quite different. I need not impress upon you the importance of secrecy, but I would say to you, what I say to all those who work with me, that there is only one way to keep a secret. There are not two ways. That way is not to whisper it to a living soul – neither to the wife of your bosom nor to the man you trust most upon earth. I know you for a loyal, trustworthy and discreet soldier, but for a million pounds I would not tell you what I am about to tell you, if I did not need your help.

'A military operation of immense magnitude is in course of preparation. That is a fact of which the enemy are probably aware. Its success must depend largely upon the enemy's ignorance of when and where it will be launched. Every security precaution has been taken to prevent that knowledge from reaching him. Those security precautions are not, I repeat, the business of this department. It is not our business to stop him getting correct information. It is our business to provide him, through sources which will carry conviction of their reliability, with information that is false.

'In a few days from now, Colonel Osborne, the dead body of a British officer will be washed ashore, on the coast of a neutral country, whose relations with the enemy are not quite so neutral as we might wish them to be. It will be found that he is carrying in a packet that is perfectly waterproof, which will be firmly strapped to his chest, under his jacket, documents of a highly confidential character – documents of such vital importance to the conduct of the war that no one will wonder that they should have been entrusted to a special mission and a special messenger. These documents, including a private letter from the Chief of the Imperial General Staff to the General Officer Commanding North Africa, although couched in the most, apparently, guarded language, will yet make perfectly plain to an intelligent reader exactly what the Allies are intending to do. You will appreciate the importance of such an operation; and you will also appreciate that its success or failure must depend entirely upon the convincing character of the evidence, that will prove the authenticity of these documents and will remove from the minds of those who are to study them any suspicion that a trick has been played upon them. The most important of all the links in that chain of evidence must be the dead body on which the documents are found.

'Now, Osborne, you are a medical man, and you must have discovered in your student days, when you were in need of material to work upon, what I have discovered only lately, the extraordinary importance that people attach to what becomes of the dead bodies of their distant relations. People, who can ill afford it, will travel from the north of Scotland to the south of England to assure themselves that the mortal remains of a distant cousin have been decently committed to the earth. You can hardly imagine the difficulty I have experienced. The old profession of body-snatching has no longer any practitioners, or I would have employed one. I have now secured the services of a gentleman in your line of business, a civilian, and our hopes rest upon what a pauper lunatic asylum may produce. But there must be difficulties. You may have heard, Osborne, that death is the great leveller, but even after death has done his damnedest there is apt to remain a very considerable difference between a pauper lunatic deceased from natural causes and a British officer, in the prime of life, fit to be entrusted with a most important mission.'

'I see what you are getting at,' interrupted Garnet. 'You want me to agree to poor Maryngton's body being used for this purpose.'

'Bide a while, bide a while,' said the Brigadier, who had not completed his thesis. 'You will appreciate the cosmic importance of this operation, upon which the lives of thousands of men must depend, and which may affect even the final issue of the war. This morning I was wrestling desperately with the problem of the pauper lunatic for whom an identity, a name, a background had to be created. Our enemies are extremely painstaking and thorough in their work. You may be quite certain that they have copies of the last published Army List, and I am sure that they have also, easily available, a complete register of all officers who have been killed since that publication, or whose names have appeared in the obituary columns. Their first action on being informed that the body of a dead British officer has been discovered will be to ascertain whether such a British officer was ever alive. If they fail to find the name of such an officer in the Army List their suspicions will be aroused, and those suspicions, once aroused, may easily lead them to the true solution of the mystery. We should be forced to give to our unknown one of those names that are shared by hundreds, and should have to hope that, in despair of satisfying themselves as to the identity of the particular Major Smith or Brown in question, they would abandon the enquiry. But – I say again – we are dealing with a nation whose thoroughness in small matters of detail is unequalled, and it is my belief that within a few days the chief of their intelligence service would be informed that no officer of the name in question has ever served in the British Army. From that moment all the information contained in the documents, about which I told you, would be treated as information of doubtful value and of secondary importance. The result might well be that the whole operation would fail completely.

'While this grave problem is occupying my mind to-day, you sit yourself down before me and tell me of an officer who died this morning, whose death has not been registered, who has no relations, who was of an age and standing entirely suitable for such a mission and over the disposal of whose dead body you have control. Call it the long arm of coincidence, whatever that may mean, if you desire, but to me, Colonel Osborne,' the Brigadier's voice grew hoarse with emotion, 'it is the hand of Providence stretched out to aid His people in their dire need, and I ask you to give me your help, as God has given me His, in the fulfilment of my task.'

He ceased and both sat silent. After a while Garnet said:

'What you are asking me to do is very extraordinary, and although I perfectly understand the terrible urgency, you must allow me to reflect.' He paused – and then continued: 'In the first place I should be acting quite illegally. I have no more right to conceal Maryngton's death than I have to dispose of his body.'

'*Silent leges inter tirma,*' replied the Brigadier. 'I will give you my personal guarantee, written if you wish it, that will cover you from any legal consequences.'

They sat again in silence for two or three minutes. When Garnet next spoke it was to ask:

'What should I actually have to do? And what am I going to say when Maryngton's friends, many of whom must have known that he was living with me, ask me what has become of him?'

The Brigadier was obviously relieved. He felt now that the other's mind was moving in the right direction.

'What you have to do is to lay out by the side of Maryngton's body tonight his uniform, omitting no detail of it. Don't forget his cap or his belt, and above all make sure that the identity disc is there. Put on the table his watch, his cheque-book and any small personal possessions that he always carried. At 2 a.m. some friends of mine will call upon you. There may be two of them, there may be three. You will show them which is Maryngton's room. Then you will go to bed and sleep soundly. You will, however, dream that Maryngton comes to you in the night and tells you that he is leaving England in the early morning. His mission is of a secret nature, and in case anything should go wrong he hands you his will, which you have already told me is in your possession. When you wake in the morning he will certainly have gone, and you will therefore believe your dream was a reality. It will probably be many days before you have to answer any enquiry. During those days you will repeat to yourself continually how he told you one night that he was leaving on a secret mission, how he gave you his will, and how he was gone on the following morning. You will come to believe this yourself, and it will be all that you know, all that you have to say to anyone who asks questions. One day you will read in the paper that Maryngton has died on active service. Then you will send his will to his lawyers; and that will be all.'

Again Garnet sat in silence for several minutes.

'Does my sister know about this affair?' he asked. 'Miss Osborne is aware,' said the Brigadier, 'that an operation of this nature is in preparation.'

'I would rather,' said Garnet, 'that she did not know that it was – that we were making use of – damn it, respect for the dead bodies of those we love is a very profound instinct in human nature. Willie Maryngton has been like a brother to us all our lives. I am sure it would distress her horribly.'

The Brigadier looked grave and answered:

'You may be sure that I have already given very careful consideration to this part of the problem. Besides ourselves there are three other people, so far as we are aware, who know that Maryngton died of pneumonia this morning. I have decided that the best method of securing the discretion of the nurse and the servant is to say no more to them on the subject. To neither of them will the case present any peculiar or interesting feature. To impose secrecy upon them would merely stimulate their curiosity. If either of them reads the announcement of his death, which is unlikely, the fact that it is described as having taken place on active service will be accepted as part of the incomprehensible vocabulary of Whitehall.

'Now your sister is another matter. I have the greatest confidence in her reliability, but I cannot expect even her to keep a secret if she doesn't know it is a secret. She may have told someone of Maryngton's death already. If not, she is almost sure to do so.'

'She's a strange girl,' said Garnet; 'she keeps her friends in separate compartments, isolated cells as it were. Since my brother was killed she and Willie had no mutual friends. I think it unlikely that she has told anybody. But I can make sure, which I promise to do. What is more, I can pretend to her that my conduct has not been strictly professional in allowing a friend to die in my own fiat without calling in a second opinion, and failing to inform the authorities within twenty-four hours. On that ground I can ask her not to mention the matter, and then we can safely count on her silence.'

'I don't like it, Osborne,' said the Brigadier. 'In affairs of this sort I like to have everything water-tight. The smallest leak may sink the ship – and what a ship it is! Think, man, the whole British Empire is on board!'

An ugly cloud of obstinacy crept into Garnet's eyes.

'I'm sorry,' he said. 'The whole business is hateful to me, and I just can't bear to bring my sister into it. Between ourselves, I once suspected that she was in love with Maryngton. I even hoped that they might marry. Can you imagine telling a girl what it is that you are intending to do with the dead body of a man who might have been her husband? It is a kind of sacrilege.'

The Brigadier looked into Garnet's eyes, and he saw the obstinacy that lay there. He looked at his watch, and then he said,

'I'll not tell her. You have my word for it.'

Garnet sighed.

'In that case I suppose I must consent,' he said. 'I can see no good reason for not doing so – except sentiment, or perhaps sentimentality – and I have never considered myself to be ruled by either. In any case, service must come first. You have given me my instructions. They are simple enough. They shall be carried out. Have you anything further to ask of me?'

'Lay out the uniform,' said the Brigadier, omitting no detail of it. Leave the small personal possessions on the table. Open the door when the bell rings. Dream as I told you, and believe that your dream is true.'

They shook hands and Garnet turned to go.

'One more detail,' said the Brigadier. 'You have not by any chance got some spare major's badges among your equipment?'

'I doubt it,' said Garnet.

'Very well. My friends will provide them. I have been thinking that the rank of captain is just one too low for an officer charged with such a very important mission. He appears as a captain in the last pre-war Army List. If he had been employed on important work since then he would have become a major by now, so I intend to make him one. These small details can prove of vast importance in this sort of work.'

'Oh dear,' said Garnet, 'that was the promotion he was so anxious to obtain. Poor Willie! It is a heartbreaking business.'

'Ay,' said the Brigadier. 'Operation Heartbreak would not be a bad name for it.'

Felicity met Garnet in the passage. 'Come into my room,' she said. 'I've got a cup of tea for you.'

'It will be welcome,' he answered. 'I had a wretched night and I've been hard at it all day. Odd to find you here. You are, I must say, a very secretive girl.'

'Now tell me all there is to tell about Willie. I felt that I couldn't bear to hear more this morning, when you told me he was dead, so I rang off in an abrupt and what must have appeared a callous way. But I can bear it now. Go on.'

Garnet recounted the course of the short illness and explained that it was not uncommon for healthy men in middle-age to be carried off suddenly by a sharp attack of pneumonia.

'But I do think,' he went on, 'that there was something else, another contributory cause as it were, in Willie's case. I told you not long ago that I thought there was something wrong with him. In all illness, and especially in cases of this sort, the will of the patient plays a great part. There comes a moment when an effort is required. In this case that effort wasn't made. I am afraid that one of the reasons why Willie died was that he did not greatly wish to live.'

'Ah!' Felicity gave a little cry, as though in sudden pain, but said no more.

After a pause Garnet went on to ask:

'Do you happen to have mentioned his death to anyone you've seen today, Felicity?'

'No,' she answered. 'I haven't seen anyone, for one thing, and there isn't anyone to whom I talk about Willie, for another.'

'Well, I had rather that you kept it to yourself,' he said, and went on to tell her the story he had invented about his alleged lapse from professional rectitude.

'I promise not to breathe a word,' she said, but she looked at him with curiosity, asking herself whether such conduct was really unprofessional and, if so, whether Garnet could have been guilty of it.

'How about the funeral?' she asked.

'Oh, it seems there are some distant cousins in Yorkshire. The lawyers have communicated with them. They want him to be buried up there. It appears his forbears came from that part of the country. I couldn't object.'

'He always told me he hadn't any cousins anywhere, but I'm glad they've been discovered. I hate funerals, and he would never have expected me to go to Yorkshire to attend one among people whom I don't know.'

Hers was not an inquisitive nature, but it seemed strange to her that cousins who had remained unknown throughout his life should assert themselves within a few hours of his death.

Having finished his tea, Garnet rose to go.

'Good-bye, dear old Garnet,' she said. 'Now that you have found out where I work you might come and see me sometimes. I can always give you tea.'

'I should like to come,' he replied. 'I am very busy, but I feel lonely sometimes.'

'I suppose everybody does.'

'Yes, I suppose so.'

He went, and a few minutes later the bell summoned her to the Brigadier. She picked up her pad and pencil and went into his room.

'I had an interesting conversation with your brother,' he said. 'Did he tell you about it?'

'I told you that I met him in the Far East. We both know something about the pretty ways of the Japanese and we've been having a fine crack about them. Our Government will never resort to bacteriological warfare, you know, but I think it's just the sort of trick the Japs might play on us. So I was thinking that we might get it whispered around that we had something up our sleeve in that line more terrible than anything they would imagine. That might make them think twice before they used it.'

'It might, on the other hand, make them use it immediately so as to be sure of getting their blow in first.'

'Ay, but I think they've held off poison gas so far because they suspect we've got a deadlier brew than they have. Your brother is very knowledgeable in the matter of oriental diseases.'

Felicity wondered why he was telling her all this. She had studied the Brigadier's methods, and she had noticed that when he volunteered information it was usually with a motive, and that the information itself was usually incorrect. Was he trying to deceive her, or had he perhaps some more subtle purpose?

'To change the subject,' he went on, 'to Operation Z, or Operation Heartbreak, as I'm thinking of calling it. I've received information from that doctor of whom I told you. He has to hand exactly what we were looking for. So the matter is now urgent. Time and tide – we depend on both of them, and neither will wait upon the other. There is not an hour to be lost. The Admiralty are standing by. They await only the pressure of a button to go ahead. And I am about to press that button. You have the wallet and the papers. I should like to have another look at them.'

As Felicity went to her room to fetch them it occurred to her that the news which had come to the Brigadier from the doctor could not have been received that afternoon by telephone, for she had had control of all the calls that reached him, and it was strange, if time were precious, that he should have wasted so much of it in discussing remote possibilities with Garnet, and should have attached so much importance to the conversation.

She returned with the carefully constructed waterproof wallet and a thin sheaf of papers. The Brigadier slipped on a pair of gloves before he touched them. She smiled.

'You think, Miss Osborne, my precautions are a wee bit ridiculous. But it is always wiser to err on the side of prudence. I hope that in a few days these papers will be in the hands of a gentleman as prudent as I am, and better equipped. It may be that he will have them tested for finger-prints, and it may be that he has a photograph of my finger-prints on his writing-table. We are dealing with a very thorough people, Miss Osborne, a very thorough people.'

'So this is the letter from the C.I.G.S.,' he went on, carefully taking it out of the envelope. He read it slowly and chuckled. 'He must have enjoyed putting in that joke about the Secretary of State. It just gives the hallmark of authenticity. He has made a very good job of it indeed.'

He laid the papers on the table in front of him, and remained silent for three or four minutes, apparently lost in thought.

'A man setting out on a journey of this sort,' he said at last, speaking very slowly, 'would probably put into his wallet what was most precious and dear to him. A married man might put there the photographs of his wife and children. This is to be a single man.' He paused again. 'Do you think, Miss Osborne,' he asked, 'that you could draft a loveletter?'

'I can try,' she replied, impassively.

'Do that,' he said. 'Meanwhile I must get on to the Admiralty and see the young men in our Operations Branch, who have a full night before them.'

She rose to go.

'Make sure that there's no "G.R." in the corner of the paper you write on, nor "For the service of His Majesty's Government" in the watermark.'

'I will make sure,' she said.

'And there is one more thing.' He hesitated. 'You must try to make that letter the kind a man would think worth keeping.'

'I will try,' she said, and left the room.

The Brigadier continued to look at the door after she had shut it. He had the habit of observing people closely. Was he mistaken or had he detected a light of revelation in her eyes, a kind of exultation in her manner, the air of one who goes with confidence to the performance of a grateful task?

He had no time to waste on speculation. His evening was fully occupied. He first had a long interview with two young men, who were members of his staff but not regular attendants at the office. Then there were a number of telephone conversations with the Admiralty and with other government departments. When he looked at his watch he was surprised to see how late it was. He rang the bell and Felicity came in with a sheet of paper in her hand.

'I am sorry I have detained you so long,' he said – 'all our preparations are now complete. Have you drafted the letter that I suggested?'

She handed him the paper she was carrying and said nothing. He put on his gloves before taking it and held it up to the light, examining it with a magnifying glass, and then, seemingly satisfied with his inspection, adjusted his spectacles and began to read:–

Darling, my darling, you are going away from me and I have never told you how much I love you. How sad, how heartbreaking it would be if you had never known. But this will tell you, and this you must take with you on your dark mission. It brings you my passionate and deathless love. Forgive me all the disappointment that I caused you. Remember now only the hours that I lay in your arms. I cannot have known how much I loved you until I knew that you must go away. I have been weak and wanton, as I warned you once that I should always be, but I have been in my own odd way, believe me, oh believe me, darling, I have been true. When we meet again you will understand everything and perhaps we shall be happy at last.

When he had finished reading it he did not look up.

'This should be signed with a Christian name,' he said.

'Have you any suggestions?' she asked. There was a faint note of bitterness in her voice.

'An unusual one is likely to be more convincing than a common one. Your brother told me yours this afternoon. Have you any objection to making use of it? People show by the way they sign their own names that they are accustomed to doing so. Handwriting experts might be able to tell the difference.'

'I will sign it "Felicity",' she said.

'If the pen you have in your hand is the one with which you wrote the letter,' he said, 'you can sign it here,' and he pointed to the chair on the other side of his table. She sat down and wrote and handed him back the letter. At the end of it she had written in her clear, bold hand "Felicity" and at the beginning "My Willie".

The Brigadier made sure that the ink was dry and then he crumpled the letter between his two hands so that she thought he was going to throw it into the waste-paper basket. He smoothed it out again very carefully, saying as he did so: 'This is a letter which a man would have read many times. It should bear signs of usage.' Then, still looking down at the letter and still smoothing it, he said:

'So you have guessed our secret. I gave your brother my word of honour that I would not tell you. I think I have kept my word.'

'But why did he want me not to know?' she asked.

'He feared that it would cause you pain.'

'He ought to have understood,' she said, 'that it is what Willie would have wished more than anything in all the world.'

CHAPTER XVII

Dawn had not broken, but was about to do so, when the submarine came to the surface. The crew were thankful to breathe the cool, fresh air, and they were still more thankful to be rid of their cargo. The wrappings were removed, and the Lieutenant stood to attention and saluted as they laid the body of the officer in uniform as gently as possible on the face of the waters. A light breeze was blowing shoreward, and the tide was running in the same direction. So Willie went to the war at last, the insignia of field rank on his shoulders, and a letter from his beloved lying close to his quiet heart.

Epilogue

Everything worked as had been intended. The neutral government behaved with the courtesy that is expected of neutral governments. After a certain delay, such as is inevitable in the movements of government departments, they informed the Ambassador, with regret, that the body of a British officer, whose identity appeared to be established, had been washed up by the sea, and that he was bearing a waterproof packet which they had the honour to forward intact. They would be glad to make any arrangements for the funeral that His Excellency might desire. They did not think it necessary to mention that the packet in question had been already opened with infinite care, and that before being closed again with care as infinite, every document in it had been photographed, and that those photographs were now lying under the eyes of the enemy, where the false information that they contained powerfully contributed to the success of one of the greatest surprises ever achieved in military history.

And so it was that the Military Attaché, the Assistant Military Attaché and the Chaplain found themselves travelling from the capital to the coast on that hot morning.

THE MAN WHO NEVER WAS

BY EWEN MONTAGU

To the Team

Contents

Foreword

by

General the Rt. Hon. Lord Ismay,
G.C.B., C.H., D.S.O.

*Secretary-General of the North Atlantic Treaty
Organisation and, from 1940 to 1946,
Chief of Staff to Mr. Winston Churchill,
the Minister of Defence.*

To mystify and mislead the enemy has always been one of the cardinal principles of war. Consequently, *ruses de guerre* of one kind or another have played a part in almost every campaign ever since the episode of the Trojan horse, or perhaps even earlier.

The game has been played for so long that it is not easy to think out new methods of disguising one's strength or one's intentions. Moreover, meticulous care must be exercised in the planning and execution of these schemes. Otherwise, so far from deceiving the enemy, they merely give the show away.

The Allies decided that their next step, after the battle for Tunisia, should be the invasion of Italy through Sicily. We felt sure – one always does on these occasions – that this was such an obvious corollary to the North African campaign, that the enemy would expect it and concentrate to meet it. What could be done to put them off the scent?

I so well remember how I was brought, one evening, the outlines of a cover plan which was ultimately given the somewhat gruesome name of 'Operation Mincemeat'. I was, I confess, a little dubious whether it would work; but I put it up to the Chiefs of Staff, who approved it in principle. Thereafter, Lieut.-Commander Montagu, who originated the idea, and his colleagues went full steam ahead.

The operation succeeded beyond our wildest dreams. To have spread-eagled the German defensive effort right across Europe, even to the extent of sending German vessels away from Sicily itself, was a remarkable achievement. Those who landed in Sicily, as well as their families, have cause to be especially grateful.

It is not often that the whole story of a secret operation can be made public, told by someone who knows every detail. The military student can be grateful that chance has made it possible for him to have a text-book example of a very specialised branch of the art of war: others will enjoy a 'real-life thriller' – which once more illustrates that truth is stranger than fiction.

PARIS.
7th June, 1953.

1. The author.

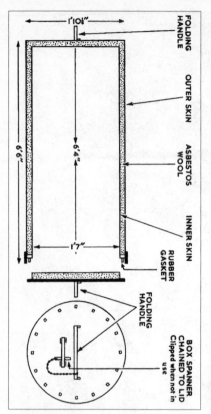

Above: **2.** The design for the canister—not to scale. Inner and outer skins of both 22 gauge steel sheet welded; total empty weight 2 cwt. 12lb (including asbestos wool); weight of wool approximately 1 cwt; probably total operational weight 400lb.

Right: **3.** Major Martin sets out.

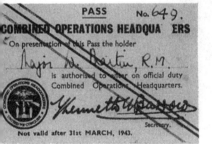

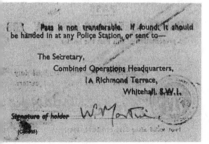

TELEPHONE, WHITEHALL 9400.

WAR OFFICE,
WHITEHALL,
LONDON, S.W.I.

23rd April, 1943

PERSONAL AND MOST SECRET.

My dear Alex,

I am taking advantage of sending you a personal letter by hand of one of Mountbatten's officers, to give you the inside history of our recent exchange of cables about Mediterranean operations and their attendant cover plans. You may have felt our decisions were somewhat ... in fact that the

one particular ... get back ... merely because the Americans happen to be serving there too, we will be faced with a good deal of discontent among those troops fighting elsewhere perhaps just as bitterly - or more so. My own feeling is that we should thank the Americans for their kind offer but say firmly it would cause too many anomalies and we are sorry we can't accept. But it is on the agenda for the next Military Members meeting and I hope you will have a decision very soon.

Best of luck

Yours ever

Archie Nye

Right: **4.** Parts of the letter from General Nye to General Alexander.

Below: **5.** Major Martin's pass to Combined Operations Headquarters.

PASS   No. 649.

COMBINED OPERATIONS HEADQUARTERS

On presentation of this Pass the holder

Major W. Martin, R.M.

is authorised to enter on official duty Combined Operations Headquarters.

Kenneth ....

Secretary.

Not valid after 31st MARCH, 1943.

Pass is not transferable. If found, it should be handed in at any Police Station, or sent to—

The Secretary,
Combined Operations Headquarters,
1A Richmond Terrace,
Whitehall, S.W.I.

Signature of holder   W. Martin.

In reply, quote. S.R. 1924/43.

COMBINED OPERATIONS HEADQUARTERS,
1a, RICHMOND TERRACE,
WHITEHALL, S.W.1.

21st April,
1943.

Dear Admiral of the Fleet,

I promised V.C.I.G.S. that Major Martin would arrange with you for the onward transmission of a letter he had with him for General Alexander. It is very urgent and very "hot" and as there are some remarks in it that could not be seen by others in the War Office, it could not go by signal. I feel sure that you will see that it goes on safely and without delay.

I think you will find Martin the man you want. He is quiet and shy at first, but he really knows his stuff. He was more accurate than some of us about the probable run of events at Dieppe and he has been well in on the experiments with the latest barges, and equipment which took place up in Scotland.

Let me have him back, please, as soon as the assault is over. He might bring some sardines with him – they are "on points" here!

Yours sincerely

Louis Mountbatten

Admiral of the Fleet Sir A.B. Cunningham, G.C.B., D.S.O.,
Commander in Chief Mediterranean,
Allied Force H.Q.,
Algiers.

6. The letter from Lord Louis Mountbatten to Admiral Cunningham.

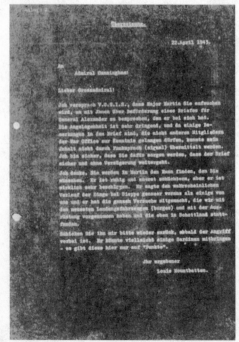

Left: 7. Lieber Grossadmiral! German translation of the letter to Admiral Cunningham.

Opposite above: 8. Some of the "corroborative details".

Opposite below: 9. Pam.

THE MANOR HOUSE
OGBOURNE ST. GEORGE
MARLBOROUGH
WILTSHIRE
TELEPHONE OGBOURNE ST GEORGE 242

Above and opposite: **10.** Pam's first letter.

afraid you'd soon find out. P.S. I am
totally absorbed in this whole place
with Mummy & Dad being so sweet &
understanding this whole time been
beyond words & waiting for Monday so
that I can get back to the situation
again. What an idiotic world!

Bill darling, do let us know
as soon as you get there so can
make some more plans, & don't please
let them send you off into the blue the
horrible way they do now a days —
now that we've found each other
out of this whole world don't think
I could bear it —

all my love,

Paul

11. The bloodhound goes—and comes back.

TELEPHONE Nº MAYFAIR 0261 (2 LINES)
TELEGRAMS EUCLASE WESDO LONDON

113 New Bond Street

London W.1. 19th April 1943.

Major W. Martin R.M.,
Naval & Military Club,
94 Piccadilly - N.1.

To S. J. Phillips,

Silversmith.

Jewels. Antique Plate. Bijouterie.

15th April. 1943	Single diamond ring small die shoulders plat = (pre purchase tax)	52	10	.
	Engraving "P.L. from W.M. 14.4.43"		10	6
	£	53	-	6

12. The bill for the engagement ring.

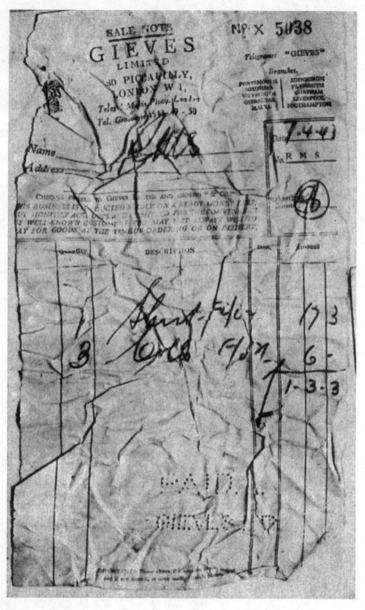

13. The bill from Gieves that was paid!

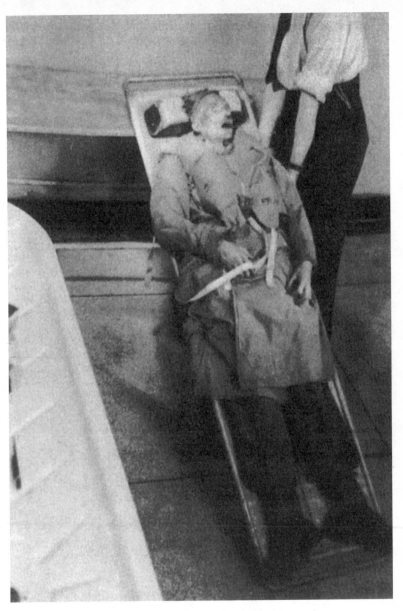

14. Major Martin goes to war.

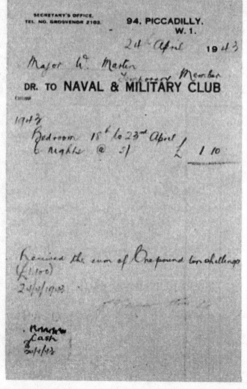

15. The temporary member's bill and the misdirected letter.

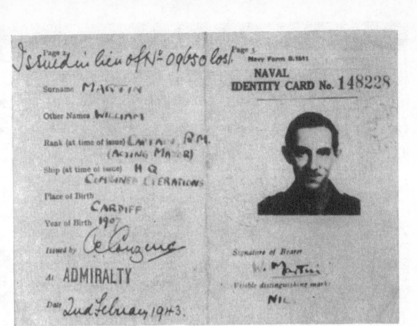

16. Identity card and theatre tickets.

Above: **17.** The journey—the author and Jack Horsfall.

Left: **18.** A very highly magnified photograph of part of the folds in the letter from Sir Archibald Nye to General Alexander. We were very careful to make only one fold—the right one in the photograph. When the Spaniards refolded it they did so in a fold which did not exactly coincide and, from its more pronounced appearance they must have done so before the paper was completely dry again, after they had re-soaked the letter (see paragraph 1 (b) of the German Intelligence Report of 15th May 1943).

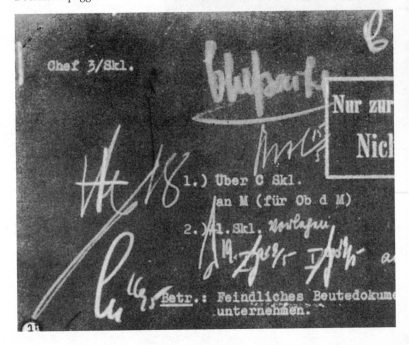

Right: **19.** German Intelligence appreciation.

Below: **20.** Close up of Admiral Doenitz's squiggle.

21. Chief of Staff's squiggle and date, with cross above to indicate distribution to Admiral Doenitz personally.

22. Admiral Doenitz's squiggle over the cross and the date he read the document.

23. Major Martin's resting-place.

Author's Note

This is a true account of an operation carried out in the years 1942–1943. Such facts as are not within my own personal knowledge are derived from contemporary documents and reports, and are neither based on anyone's recollection of what happened ten years ago nor on anyone's attempts to justify his actions or those of his associates.

I naturally could not speak or write about it until a fictional story partially based on this operation, and references in German memoirs to the receipt of the documents which formed the basis of this deception, made it clear that it would no longer be possible to maintain that secrecy which all of us who took part in the operation had preserved. This fact was recognised by the authorities, who doubtless appreciated the possible dangers and disadvantages which might result from publication by partially informed writers, and I was given official permission to publish the full story.

The operation was carried out by a team who must, unfortunately, remain anonymous as some of them are still in Government service. Therefore I have substituted a false Christian name for 'George's' real one. I have also, of course, maintained the secrecy of 'Major Martin's' identity. Where I have referred to other persons I have used the titles and ranks that they held at the time of the operation.

If anyone studies this story, some good may result. Perhaps, when some 'leakage' of a secret document is reported, the public may not be so ready as they have been to blame our security services; they may wonder whether the security services have been stupid – or clever?

I must record my thanks to Lord Ismay for his help in 1942 and 1943 and for writing the Foreword, as well as to Jack Garbutt of the *Sunday Express* for his great kindness and for the wise advice which he gave me on this, my first, excursion into authorship.

I wish to acknowledge my deep indebtedness to all my colleagues, without whose loyal help and brilliant inventiveness there could have been no 'Operation Mincemeat.' And also my indebtedness to Viscount

Norwich, without whose unwitting assistance there could have been no publication of this story.

Ewen Montagu.
Warren Beach, Beaulieu.
1953

CHAPTER I

The Birth of an Idea

In the graveyard of the Spanish town of Huelva there lies a British subject. As he died, alone, in the foggy damp of England in the late autumn of 1942, he little thought that he would lie forever under the sunny skies of Spain after a funeral with full military honours, nor that he would, after death, render a service to the Allies that saved many hundreds of British and American lives. In life he had done little for his country, but in death he did more than most could achieve by a lifetime of service.

It all really started through a wild idea of George's. He and I were members of a small inter-Service and inter-departmental committee which used to meet weekly to deal with questions of the security of intended operations. We exchanged and discussed information that had been obtained from all kinds of sources – from our own Services and other sources at home as well as from neutral countries, together with intelligence reports from enemy countries. With all this and the latest information as to Allied 'intentions' – not only immediate and probable, but also 'long-term possible' – we had to try to detect any leakages that might have occurred and any 'intelligent anticipation' that the enemy might already have made, and also to guard against such leakages and anticipations in the future.

It was not an easy task, but the committee was a good one: it comprised not only regular officers of considerable knowledge and experience, but also temporary officers and civilians with most varied backgrounds. We were a mixed lot, and between us we could view any item of information as it would strike observers from any walk of life. We had a thoroughly variegated fund of knowledge and there were few spheres of activity with which we had no contacts.

George produced his idea during a discussion over a report with which we had been supplied from occupied Europe. As happened from time to time, we were puzzled whether it was genuine or had been planted by the Germans for transmission to the Allies.

George had one of those subtle and ingenious minds which is forever throwing up fantastic ideas – mostly so ingenious as either to be impossible of implementation or so intricate as to render their efficacy problematical, but every now and again quite brilliant in their simplicity. As we puzzled whether this particular report was genuine, or whether the Germans had captured the agent concerned and were sending reports through him or for him, George remembered a recent warning that had been issued reminding officers that it was forbidden for secret documents to be carried in aircraft lest they should be shot down in enemy territory.

Starting from that, George suddenly suggested that as a check on such reports we should try to get the Germans to plant something on us that we knew was planted, so that we could see what their line was and how they put it over: if we could drop a resistance workers' wireless set into France (he suggested) and it started working, it would be difficult to tell whether the Germans or a friendly Frenchman was working it, but if it dropped accompanied by a dead body attached to a badly opened parachute, the task of checking might be easier. A Frenchman would probably tell us what had occurred, whereas the Germans would be more likely to conceal what had happened and work the set as if the agent was still alive. It would not be certain, but it did not involve much effort and might be worth trying. 'Does anyone know whether we can get a body?' asked George.

This was not one of his better inspirations, and we rapidly demolished it. Agents did not carry their codes or their routine and system for sending messages with them for anyone to find, so how would the Germans transmit messages?

Also, if a parachute failed, whatever was hanging from it would be bound to hit the ground with a considerable bump; if it was a body, this would almost certainly result in a broken limb as well as grazes and scratches, and injuries inflicted after death can always be detected. There was therefore no hope of a dead body attached to a partially opened parachute without the finder being able to tell that the body had been dead for some time before it hit the ground. Besides, even if we could get a dead body (and no one knew whether we could), our field of choice would indeed be limited if it had to be that of someone who had died through falling from a height! No, this was one of George's failures, and we quickly turned back to our report: was it genuine or not? But some months later George's wild idea produced results.

By the summer of 1942 our little committee was in the midst of its first big job. 'Operation Torch,' the invasion of North Africa, was being mounted, and the experience that we had gained in trying to guard the security of small-scale operations, involving relatively few units, was receiving its first full test.

In spite of all that could be done in the way of security, it was obviously impossible to prevent the enemy knowing that something was brewing. In the first place, it was apparent to everyone that the Allies would not just sit back indefinitely: there must be an invasion somewhere. Secondly, there could be no restriction on foreign diplomats: they moved around the country and they met and spoke to people, not only people in the know, but also some of the thousands who were bound to see the congregation of ships or of troops before they left this country, and whatever view had to be taken officially, none of us had any illusions as to the neutrality of a number of the diplomats. Besides, even a pro-British diplomat had a job to do: he had to report to his government what was going on over here, and once the report got to his country there could be no doubt that there would be at least one official or minister over there who was either paid, or at any rate ideologically ready, to pass the information on to the Germans. Thirdly, there were neutral businessmen and sailors travelling between this country and the Continent.

Therefore we could not hope to prevent the Germans knowing that there *was* an operation afoot. What we could hope to do was to prevent the vital information of 'When?' and 'Where?' leaking.

Until the invasion of North Africa had taken place the Allies had no foothold on the continent of Europe, and the war in North Africa consisted of a campaign in which we were pushing from east to west with our armies based on the Canal Zone. As a result of this situation there was no reason why the Allies should not make an attack at almost any point. As far as the Germans knew, we might land in Norway, in the Low Countries or in France, or try to push up through Spain; we might seize the Canaries or the Azores to help in the war against U-boats; or we might land in Libya to attack Rommel's army in its rear. Except in Egypt, we were wholly uncommitted, and anywhere in German-held Europe or neutral countries was open to assault.

In these circumstances all that it was necessary for our committee to try to ensure, when we attacked Dieppe or the Lofoten Islands or planned any other assault, was that the actual target and date did not get over to the enemy. That involved nothing more than leaking a false target to the troops concerned, perhaps backing such leaks up with papers about an issue of sun helmets – if they were in fact going to the Lofoten Islands – or something of that kind, and then working really hard to reduce, as much as possible, the bits of information which would inevitably get out of this country. In other words, our principle was to try to make security as complete as possible, and then to try to prevent any leakage that *did* get by our precautions being such as would give away the true target.

When 'Operation Torch' was being launched against North Africa we could still operate on this basis and, as we studied our Intelligence reports and learned of the movements that the Germans made, we realised that this system had worked as the potential targets were so many that the Germans could not get a definite idea even of where we would strike.

But our problem would be entirely different after 'Operation Torch' had been completed. At that stage of the war the Allies would have command of the whole of the North African coast and would be poised ready to strike at what the Prime Minister called 'the soft under-belly of Europe.' Our committee was kept in touch with the strategic thinking of our Chiefs of Staff and also with that of the Americans. We knew that there were some differences of opinion, but there was a definite probability that we would strike there, and our Committee had to be prepared to play our part when the Allies attacked.

With the whole North African coast in Allied hands it was pretty obvious that we would not turn round and transport all those troops back to England for an invasion of France across the Channel, and at least some of them were bound to be used across the Mediterranean. They could form part of an army for the conquest of Italy or they could be used for landing in the South of France or in Greece. Any one of these campaigns was a possibility, and our committee had to be prepared to deal with whatever might eventually be decided upon. We might, perhaps, have been able to cope with this task on the system which had worked so well up till then had that been the whole story, but there was one feature of the strategic situation which created a new problem.

Sicily lay in the middle of the Mediterranean like a football at the toe of Italy, and until it had been captured the passing of a convoy through the Mediterranean was a major operation attended by enormous losses, and this situation would remain even when the airfields in North Africa were finally in our hands. It was made clear to our committee that the reduction of Sicily would almost certainly have to be undertaken before any of the other operations could take place. As we always had to make our preparations long before an operation was launched, we were considering this next job, the security of the invasion of Sicily, even before 'Torch' was finally mounted.

And here we foresaw trouble. If Sicily was a clear probability to us, once North Africa was in Allied hands it would be just as clear a probability to the Germans. Indeed, as the Prime Minister eventually said, when approving this operation of ours, it did not matter taking some risk of revealing Sicily as the target, as 'anybody but a damn' fool would *know* it is Sicily.' How would we be able, when the time came, to prevent the Germans from reinforcing the defences of Sicily to a dangerous extent as the result of the same strategic reasoning which had caused the Allies to attack it?

As we were puzzling over this problem, the penny suddenly dropped, and George's fantastic idea of some time before justified itself. 'Why,' I said, 'shouldn't we get a body, disguise it as a staff officer, and give him really high-level papers which will show clearly that we are going to attack somewhere else. We won't have to drop him on land, as the aircraft might have come down in the sea on the way round to the Med. He would float ashore with the papers either in France or in Spain; it won't matter which. Probably Spain would be best, as the Germans wouldn't have as much chance to examine the body there as if they got it into their own hands, while it's certain that they will get the documents, or at least copies.' So the idea was born. Excitedly, we discussed its potentialities. We would have to check on a number of points. What sort of condition would a body be in after an aircraft crash in the sea? What were the usual causes of death in such cases? What would a *post mortem* reveal? Could we get a suitable body – indeed, could we get any body? Such were the first questions to which we would have to get answers. If those were satisfactory the plan was worth studying with care, for we none of us doubted that, given the chance, the Spaniards would play the part for which we had cast them, and then what a chance we would have given ourselves!

CHAPTER II

Preliminary Enquiries

We had talked glibly of 'getting a body,' but we had realised that there would be difficulties. We had yet to learn how difficult it would actually be. None of us, indeed, entirely liked the idea, for even in the stress of war one's natural respect for the sanctity of the human body remains a powerful instinct. But for us that instinct was overborne by a realisation of the lives that could be saved by the temporary use of a body that we were confident would eventually receive a proper and decent burial. The difficulty with which we were immediately faced was that imposed by security. How could we go to relatives in their hour of sorrow and ask to be allowed to take without explanation the remains of the son or husband or brother whom they mourned? And if we had to explain, what could we say? In fiction one could, perhaps, expect that we would meet a man who happened to be the sole relative of someone who had just died a death suitable for our plan – a man of that rare type who would just agree to our taking the body and would ask no questions as to why we wanted it. In fiction, perhaps, but not in real life!

Before we started our search, we had first to make sure what kind of body we needed. If the Germans were to accept the body as that of the victim of an aircraft crash at sea, we would have to present them with someone whose body did not afford signs of a cause of death inconsistent with that.

It seemed to me that the best approach to this question would be from the point of view of the man who would do the *post mortem*. What would a pathologist expect to find and what would he expect not to find in the body of a man who had drifted ashore after an aircraft had been lost at sea? For, after all, the aircraft need not have actually crashed.

My thoughts at once turned to Sir Bernard Spilsbury. No one had more experience of pathology than he, and I felt that no better security risk existed: one could be certain that he at any rate would not gossip or even pass on what I said to him 'in confidence to someone whom he could trust.' In this respect, there had never been any difference between Sir Bernard and an oyster. And he had one even rarer quality: I felt sure that he would not ask any questions other than those needed for the solution of the problem put to him; *he* would just take the fact that we wanted the Germans and Spaniards to accept a floating body as that of a victim of an aircraft disaster, and would neither ask me why nor seek to find an answer elsewhere.

So I rang up Sir Bernard and we arranged a meeting at his club, the Junior Canton. There, over a glass of sherry, I put our problem to him. After a moment or two of thought, he gave me one of those concise yet complete expositions that had convinced so many juries, and even so many judges. His advice gave me hope. If the body was floating in a 'Mae West' when it was recovered, we could use one of a man who had either drowned or died from any but a few of the 'natural causes'. Victims of an aircraft disaster at sea sometimes died from an injury received in the crash, and some died from drowning, but many died from exposure or even from shock. Our field of search was less narrow than I had feared it might be.

My opinion of Sir Bernard was fully justified. That extraordinary man listened to my questions and gave me his answers without ever for a moment giving vent to the curiosity which he must have felt. He asked me some questions which bore on the pathological problem that I was putting to him, but never once did he ask why I wanted to know or what I was proposing to do.

But even then the quest was not easy. We could not make any open enquiries – at all costs we had to avoid anything which might start talk. We could not risk anyone remembering that someone had been trying to obtain a dead body, and such a search was just the sort of thing that is likely to start gossip: 'Have you heard? It's frightfully odd. So-and-So was asking such-and-such the other day where he could get a dead body.' And so, very quietly, our search went on. There we were, in 1942, surrounded all too often by bodies, but none that we could take. We felt like the Ancient Mariner – bodies, bodies, everywhere, nor any one to take! We felt like Pirandello – 'Six officers in search of a corpse.'

At one time we feared that we might have to do a body-snatch – 'do a Burke and Hare' as one of us put it, but we did not like that idea, if we could possibly avoid it. We managed to make some very guarded enquiries from a few service medical officers whom we could trust, but when we heard of a possibility, either the relatives were unlikely to agree, or we could not trust those whose permission we would need not to mention to other close relatives what had happened – or there were some other snags, such as a complication in the cause of death.

At last, when we had begun to feel that it would have either to be a 'Burke and Hare' after all or we would have to extend our enquiries so widely as to risk suspicion of our motives turning into gossip, we heard of someone who had just died from pneumonia after exposure. Pathologically speaking, it looked as if he might answer our requirements. We made feverish enquiries into his past and about his relatives. We were soon satisfied that these would not talk or pass on such information as we could give them, but there was still the crucial question: could we get permission to use the body without saying what we proposed to do with it and why? All we could possibly tell anyone was that we could guarantee that the purpose would be a really worthwhile one, as anything that was done would be with approval on the highest level, and that the remains would eventually receive proper burial, though under a false name.

Permission, for which our indebtedness is great, was obtained on condition that I should never let it be known whose corpse it was. It must therefore suffice for me to say that the body was that of a young man in his early thirties. He had not been very physically fit for some time before his death, but we could accept that for, as I said to a senior officer who queried the point, 'He does not have to look like an officer – only like a staff officer.'

As a precaution, I had another chat with Sir Bernard Spilsbury. He was quite satisfied: the pneumonia was a help, for there would tend to be some liquid in the lungs, as might well be the case if the man had died while floating in a rough sea. If a *post mortem* examination was made by someone who had formed the preconceived idea that the death was probably due to drowning, there was little likelihood that the difference between this liquid, in lungs that had started to decompose, and sea water would be noticed. Sir Bernard closed our talk with the characteristically confident statement: 'You have nothing to fear from a Spanish *post mortem*; to detect that this young man had not died after an aircraft had been lost at sea would need a pathologist of my experience – and there aren't any in Spain.'

So we arranged for the body to be kept in suitable cold storage until we were ready for it.

CHAPTER III

'Operation Mincemeat'

I now had to get general approval for the principle of the operation. The first step, as always before any operation, was to get a code name. Except in the case of a few major operations for which the Prime Minister himself invented the names, these were always taken from lists issued by us to the Service departments and the various Commands. I therefore went to see what names had been allocated for Admiralty use, and there I found that the word 'Mincemeat' had just been restored after employment in a successful operation some time before. My sense of humour having by this time become somewhat macabre, the word seemed to be one of good omen, and 'Operation Mincemeat' it became.

I had next to decide where we were to send the body, and I chose Huelva as the best destination, if delivery there was possible, for we knew that there was a very active German agent at Huelva who had excellent contacts with certain Spaniards, both officials and others. If the body reached Huelva, the odds were very heavy that this agent would be given any papers or other objects of importance that might be with it. Even if circumstances prevented that happening, there was no doubt whatsoever that he would either get copies or be given detailed information, and we could then be sure that he would alert his superiors in Madrid who would intercept the documents at a higher level. Our only risk was that the body and papers would be handed straight over to the British Vice-Consul so quickly that no one could intercept anything. But the co-operation between the Spaniards and the Germans was so complete that such a proper procedure was most improbable. If there were a Spaniard who proposed to do that, I had little doubt but that there would be several others who would step in and prevent it.

Huelva had a further advantage in that it was not too near to Gibraltar; we did not want the Spaniards to send the body for burial there. The arrival at Gibraltar of the body of an officer who did not really exist might give rise to talk which would be almost certain to be picked up by the many German agents who obtained information through the Spaniards who entered and left that area each day.

So I went to the Hydrographer of the Navy at the Admiralty and made some enquiries about weather and tidal conditions at various points off the coast of Spain at various times of the year. Our luck was holding. Although the tidal stream would not be too helpful and would set along the coast, the south-westerly wind, which would be the prevailing wind in April, would be 'onshore.' Indeed, the hydrographer thought that 'an object' would probably drift in towards the shore, and a body in a 'Mae West' would be comparatively more affected by the wind than would the sort of object which I had led him to envisage.

So Huelva was decided on. There was practically no doubt that the body would float inshore. Then, if the normal procedure was followed, the body would be handed over to the British vice-consul for burial. And, as I have said, we were confident that the efficiency of the local German agent would ensure that any papers, or at least copies of them, would eventually reach the Germans. Our confidence in him was not misplaced.

While we were going into the exact location for 'Mincemeat's' arrival, a means of transportation had to be devised. He could not be dropped for fear of injury, which left three methods of placing him in the sea: submarine, flying boat or a temporary diversion of one of the ships which escorted the convoys up the coast of Spain. Of these a submarine could clearly get much the closest inshore without risk of detection. I therefore asked permission from the Vice-Chief of Naval Staff (Home) to discuss possibilities with Admiral Barry, the flag officer commanding our submarines: it was, of course, on the basis that our planning was purely tentative, so that a complete scheme could be worked out for submission to the chiefs of staff.

Admiral Barry readily saw the possibilities of the idea, and I had a preliminary talk with his chief staff officer. He decided that 'Mincemeat' could be carried in a submarine on passage to Malta, as these quite frequently took important but not too bulky articles to that island. We discussed whether the body should be transported in the casing (that is under what would normally be called the deck) or inside the actual pressure hull of the submarine. In spite of the size of the container, which would have to be some 6 feet 6 inches long and about 2 feet in diameter, he considered that it could be accommodated inside the pressure hull and brought up through the conning tower for launching at sea. This greatly eased our problem as it meant that we would only have to get an airtight canister and not a pressure-proof container, which would have had to be much heavier and more complicated. The question remained whether the body could be kept in a plain canister for the necessary time, after removal from cold storage, without decomposition being too great, or would we have to try to get some form of enormous thermos flask?

So I consulted Sir Bernard Spilsbury once more. He took the view that temperature would be of comparatively minor importance if the body was really cold when it was put into the container. The important thing was to exclude as much oxygen as possible, as it was that which hastened decomposition. He advised that the best method for us to use would be to stand our container on one end and fill it with dry ice, as that, melted into carbon dioxide, would prevent air from entering. We should then lower the body carefully into the canister and pack it round once more with dry ice. If that was done carefully, there should be little oxygen left in the container, and the rate of decomposition would be so slowed down that, if the body was picked up shortly after launching, its condition would be consistent with a few days' immersion floating in from an aircraft crash some distance offshore.

So we arranged for a container to be made of two skins of 22-gauge sheet steel welded together, with asbestos wool between the skins. At the top there was a similar lid which was bedded on to an airtight rubber gasket by sixteen nuts. A box-spanner was chained to the lid to which it was clipped when not in use. A lifting handle was provided at each end, for it would weigh over 400 lb with the body inside.

To complete the account of this part of our preparations, I should record that later on I saw Admiral Barry again and told him that the plan was going ahead and that, if we got final approval, we would want the operation carried out at about the end of April. This would also have the advantage from the submarine's point of view of there being little or no moon, so as to render detection close inshore less likely. He decided that H.M. Submarine *Seraph* might be used, as she could delay her departure for Malta by a fortnight, spending the time 'working up' in home waters. The chance of using *Seraph* was fortunate as she was commanded by Lieutenant Jewell, and he and his ship's company had already had experience of special operations in connection with the North Africa landings. They had picked up General Giraud on his escape from captivity and it was they who had put General Mark Clark ashore on the coast of North Africa when he made secret contact with the French, and then taken him off again.

I had prepared tentative 'operation orders' for the captain of the submarine, and these Admiral Barry approved, but, at his suggestion, Lieutenant Jewell came to the Flag Officer, Submarines Headquarters, where he and I could talk over the whole matter.

I gave him the 'operation orders,' which were as follows:

Operation Mincemeat

1. *Object*

To cause a briefcase containing documents to drift ashore as near as possible to HUELVA in Spain in such circumstances that it will be thought to have been washed ashore from an aircraft which crashed at sea when the case was being taken by an officer from the U.K. to Allied Forces H.Q. in North Africa.

2. *Method*

A dead body dressed in the battle-dress uniform of a Major, Royal Marines, and wearing a 'Mae West,' will be taken out in a submarine, together with the briefcase and a rubber dinghy.

The body will be packed fully clothed and ready (and wrapped in a blanket to prevent friction) in a tubular airtight container (which will be labelled as 'Optical Instruments').

The container is just under 6 feet 6 inches long and just under 2 feet in diameter and has no excrescences of any kind on the sides. The end which opens has a flush-fitting lid which is held tightly in position by a number of nuts and has fitted on its exterior in clips a box-spanner with a permanent tommy-bar which is chained to the lid.

Both ends are fitted with handles which fold down flat. It will be possible to lift the container by using both handles or even by using the handle in the lid alone, but it would be better not to take the whole weight on the handle at the other end, as the steel of which the container is made is of light gauge to keep the weight as low as possible. The approximate total weight when the container is full will be 400 lb.

When the container is closed the body will be packed round with a certain amount of dry ice. The container should therefore be opened on deck, as the dry ice will give off carbon dioxide.

3. *Position*

The body should be put into the water as close inshore as prudently possible and as near to HUELVA as possible, preferably to the north-west of the river mouth.

According to the Hydrographic Department, the tides in that area run mainly up and down the coast, and every effort should therefore be made to choose a period with an onshore wind. South-westerly winds are, in fact, the prevailing winds in that area at this time of year.

The latest information about the tidal streams in that area, as obtained from the Superintendent of Tides, is attached.

4. *Delivery of the Package*

The package will be brought up to the port of departure by road on whatever day is desired, preferably as close to the sailing day as possible. The briefcase will be handed over at the same time to the Captain of the submarine. The rubber dinghy will also be a separate parcel.

5. *Disposal of the Body*

When the body is removed from the container all that will be necessary will be to fasten the chain attached to the briefcase through the belt of the trench-coat, which will be the outer garment on the body. The chain is of the type worn under the coat, round the chest and out through the sleeve. At the end is a 'dog-lead' type of clip for attaching to the handle of the briefcase and a similar clip for forming the loop round the chest. It is this loop that should be made through the belt of the trench-coat as if the officer has slipped the chain off for comfort in the aircraft, but has nevertheless kept it attached to him so that the bag should not either be forgotten or slide away from him in the aircraft.

The body should then be deposited in the water, as should also be the rubber dinghy. As this should drift at a different speed from the body, the exact position at which it is released is unimportant, but it should be near the body, but not too near if that is possible.

6. *Those in the Know at Gibraltar*
Steps have been taken to inform F.O.I.C.[1] Gibraltar and his S.O.(I).[2] No one else there will be in the picture.

7. *Signals*
If the operation is successfully carried out, a signal should be made 'MINCEMEAT completed.' If that is made from Gibraltar the S.O.(I) should be asked to send it addressed to D.N.I.[3] (PERSONAL). If it can be made earlier it should be made in accordance with orders from F.O.S.[4]

8. *Cancellation*
If the operation has to be cancelled a signal will be made 'Cancel MINCEMEAT.' In that case the body and container should be sunk in deep water. As the container may have positive buoyancy, it may either have to be weighted or water may have to be allowed to enter. In the latter case care must be taken that the body does not escape. The briefcase should be handed to the S.O.(I) at Gibraltar, with instructions to burn the contents unopened, if there is no possibility of taking that course earlier. The rubber dinghy should be handed to the S.O.(I) for disposal.

9. *Abandonment*
If the operation has to be abandoned, a signal should be made 'MINCEMEAT abandoned' as soon as possible (see Para. 7 above).

---

[1] Flag Officer in Charge
[2] Staff Officer, Intelligence
[3] Director of Naval Intelligence.
[4] Flag Officer, Submarines (Admiral Barry)

10. *Cover*

This is a matter for consideration. Until the operation actually takes place, it is thought that the labelling of the container 'Optical Instruments' will provide sufficient cover. It is suggested that the cover after the operation has been completed should be that it is hoped to trap a very active German agent in this neighbourhood, and it is hoped that sufficient evidence can be obtained by this means to get the Spaniards to eject him. The importance of dealing with this man should be impressed on the crew, together with the fact that any leakage that may *ever* take place about this will compromise our power to get the Spaniards to act in such cases; also that they will never learn whether we were successful in this objective, as the whole matter will have to be conducted in secrecy with the Spaniards or we won't be able to get them to act.

It is in fact most important that the Germans and Spaniards should accept these papers in accordance with Para. I. If they should suspect that the papers are a 'plant,' it might have far-reaching consequences of great magnitude.

(*Signed*) E. E. S. MONTAGU,

Lt.-Cdr., R.N.V.R.

31.3.43.

We then discussed the operation and filled in points of detail.

While all these things were being arranged, we had been busy over the more interesting matters. What document could we provide which could be so impressive that it would make the Germans alter their planning and disposition of forces? How could we provide the document with a sufficiently convincing background to make them accept it as genuine; for Pooh-Bah was right when he spoke of '… corroborative detail, intended to give artistic verisimilitude to an otherwise bald and unconvincing narrative.'

CHAPTER IV

The Vital Document

One thing seemed to me to be crystal clear: if the purpose of this document was to deceive the Germans *so that they would act upon it*, then it had to be on a really high level; no indiscretion or 'leak' from an officer of normal rank would do. Even a security lapse from one brigadier, air commodore or rear-admiral to another would not be weighty enough.

If the German General Staff was to be persuaded, in the face of all probabilities, to bank on our next target being somewhere other than Sicily, it would have to have before it a document which was passing between officers who *must* know what our real plans were, who could not possibly be mistaken and who could not themselves be the victims of a cover plan. If the operation was to be worthwhile, I had to have a document written by someone, and to someone, whom the Germans knew – and whom they knew to be 'right in the know.'

So I put up the proposal that General Sir Archibald Nye, the Vice-Chief of the Imperial General Staff, should write the letter, and that he should write it to General Alexander (who commanded an army in Tunisia under General Eisenhower) at 18th Army Group Headquarters. The letter should be of what we junior officers called 'the old boy type': it should be on the lines of 'Look here, old chap, I want you to understand that we realise your problems, but we have our difficulties too. The C.I.G.S.[1] has had to turn down some of your requests, although you're pressing for them. There really are reasons why you can't have what you want just now, and here they are....' and so on, the sort of friendly letter which can give information and explanations that can't be put into an official communication. That sort of letter, and that sort of letter only, could convey convincingly to the Germans the indication that our next target was not Sicily, and yet could be found in the possession of an officer and not in a bag full of the usual official documents going from home to our army abroad.

I was aiming high, and I had to. I expected something of an explosion, and I got it! For many of even the most able and efficient people failed to

---

[1] Chief of the Imperial General Staff.

appreciate what was wanted for this sort of job, for to realise that needed a particular sort of approach and a peculiar sort of mind that could look at the same puzzle from several different angles at the same time.

You are a British Intelligence officer; you have an opposite number in the enemy Intelligence (as in the last war) in Berlin, and above him is the German operational command. What you, a Briton with a British background, think can be deduced from a document does not matter. It is what *your opposite number*, with his German knowledge and background, will think that matters, what construction *he* will put on the document. Therefore, if you want *him* to think such-and-such a thing, you must give him something which will make *him* (and not *you*) think it. But he may be suspicious and want confirmation. You must think out what enquiries will *he* make (not what enquiries would *you* make) and give him the answers to those enquiries so as to satisfy him. In other words, you must remember that a German does not think and react as an Englishman does, and you must put yourself into his mind.

But you must not forget the operational staff to whom he reports and whom he has to convince if you are to succeed in your plot. The German operational staff does not know all the Allied difficulties. For example, how short you are of, say, landing-craft. They may be prepared to believe that an operation is possible which your own operational staff know is not on the cards at all. You have to remember that your plan has to deceive *them*, and not your own staff. But it is not everyone who can remember, *and apply*, those considerations.

And so we ran into difficulties. But before I record them I should say a word or two about 'cover targets' and 'cover plans.' If you are to prevent there being a concentration at your target ready to meet your landing, you must try to draw the enemy's defensive effort and forces elsewhere. If possible, he should be convinced that you won't attack your real target, but will attack somewhere else – that you will attack what we called the 'cover target.' As I have already mentioned, it is usually certain that there will be some leakage that an operation is intended, and the security measures designed to prevent such leakage giving away the real target may sometimes be adapted to fulfil a second purpose also – to help to put over the cover target. For instance, if any leakage did occur about the operation which I have instanced against the Lofoten Islands, and if sun helmets had been issued, the leakage might well be such that the enemy would deduce that the target was somewhere tropical. If the ships which were to transport the troops received charts or other information which indicated the chosen cover target (let us say Dakar), the various leakages which reached the Germans from those and other factors might well be added together by the German Intelligence Service to make the picture that you wanted them to have.

The best possible cover target would be one so far away from the real one that any sea, air or land defences that the enemy might prepare would be well clear of the real target. To give an exaggerated example: if you were going to invade North Africa and could persuade the enemy that you were going into Norway (oh, what a happy dream!), any extra defences that he put into Norway could not possibly interfere with your real operation.

But in actual war the cover target may have to be in the same general area as the real target, and then it is impossible to divert the whole of the enemy's defences. For instance, if at the time of our North Africa landings in 1942 we had put over a cover target of a landing in Rommel's rear at, say, Tobruk, and if we had succeeded in convincing the Germans, we might have succeeded in diverting some military forces and perhaps the Luftwaffe to that area, but the U-boats would have been drawn to the Straits of Gibraltar through which the real convoys would have to pass for the genuine operation. Often, therefore, it is the case of a compromise between what would be a perfect cover target and what it is possible to get the enemy to believe.

When we came to relate this theory to the particular problem which faced our Intelligence team, our task was to try to convince the Germans that we were not going to attack Sicily – the target which must have been obvious to them – and to persuade them to move their forces elsewhere and to use up time and effort in strengthening the defences of other places.

Looking at the situation from the Allied angle, we had an army under General Eisenhower based on French North Africa at the western end of the Mediterranean and another army under Field-Marshal Sir Henry Wilson based on Egypt, together holding the whole North African coast. We knew that it was intended that both these great forces should be used for a single operation. There were many reasons for this decision which it would take too long to detail here, but I can summarise them by saying that an assault on the defended coast of Sicily, followed by an advance up the peninsula of Italy, would need all the forces that we had available. Apart from the actual troops and aircraft engaged, there was a considerable shortage of landing craft, and the task of providing the shipping and escorts necessary to supply and maintain the campaign would preclude the conduct of two campaigns at once.

When we looked at the same problem from the German viewpoint, the picture was somewhat different. So far as they knew, the Allies could use General Eisenhower's army in the Western Mediterranean to attack the South of France, although this would probably necessitate the reduction of Sicily, Sardinia and Corsica, and would be a risky operation with Italy as an unconquered base for counterattacks on the flank of our supply lines. Equally, the same army or the army based on Egypt could be used for an attack on Italy, although, if the western army was to be used for this purpose, it would almost certainly necessitate the conquest of Sicily as a first step. Finally, the eastern army could be used for an invasion of Greece and an advance through the Balkans.

There was no reason to believe that the Germans knew of our shortage of landing-craft, and it was quite possible that they could be led to believe that we were going to mount two operations, one in the western Mediterranean with General Eisenhower's army and one in the eastern Mediterranean with Sir Henry Wilson's army.

When our team considered the deception that we wanted to convey by 'Operation Mincemeat,' we reasoned as follows. As the Allies had most of their forces in Tunisia, it was hopeless to try to persuade the Germans that we would take our convoys from there through the narrows past their airfields in Sicily. Therefore, any cover target would have to be somewhere west of Italy if the Germans were to believe that it represented the operation in which these troops were involved. Sardinia had already been chosen as the official cover target so as to pretend that we were going to by-pass Sicily and take Sardinia and Corsica, thus opening the whole of the coast of Italy and southern France to attack.

But it seemed to me that, as we would not have to rely on a series of leaks which might or might not reach the Germans, but could use a single document, there could be a second string to our bow. I felt that we could probably convince the Germans that Sir Henry Wilson's army under General Montgomery was not going to take part in the same operation as General Eisenhower's, and that it was going to conduct an invasion of Greece and an advance up the Balkans. There did not seem to be any reason why they should not be led to believe in a double operation with an assault at each end of the Mediterranean, and if we could succeed in convincing them of this we could get a much wider dispersal of their forces than if we based our deception only on the 'official' cover target of Sardinia.

I therefore proposed that the letter to General Alexander should reveal that there were to be two operations: his, under General Eisenhower's command, against Sardinia and perhaps Corsica, with another under Field-Marshal Sir Henry Wilson against Greece. I suggested also that the letter should reveal that we were going to *try to convince the Germans that we were going to invade Sicily!* It seemed to me that the beauty of this was that if there were any actual leakage of our real plans, the Germans would think that what was in fact a leakage was only part of the cover that they had read about in the letter. If they swallowed our deception – that one letter – they would disbelieve any genuine information that might leak through.

So the proposal was put up to the Chiefs of Staff – and then the trouble started! Not many people saw the proposal, for the 'usual channels' were by-passed, but even then, as the plan and the rough draft of the document went up and down to the Chiefs of Staff and back again, so everyone who felt himself to be an expert, and to know the German mind, had bright ideas. It was too dangerous, they said, to try for high stakes, and the letter should be a low-level one, merely putting over a false date; we would never get the Germans to swallow the story and we would be bound to pinpoint Sicily; we must not mention Sardinia as the supposed real target, as, if the Germans saw through the deception, *that* would pinpoint Sicily.

Perhaps the greatest achievement of the whole operation was to persuade our masters that this was an opportunity that would never recur, and that if we were to achieve a real success we must aim high. I have little doubt, as I look back, that to deceive the German High Command was nothing like as difficult as it was to persuade their British opposite numbers we could do that.

Fortunately, after a while, Sir Archibald Nye himself got really intrigued. He tried a letter, based on my draft, which he suggested might do. It had to be pointed out that, although it indicated the cover targets in just the right sort of way, it would be wholly unconvincing. It was the sort of straightforward letter which could and would go in an official bag and would never be given to an officer to carry in his pocket. This was a challenge to which Sir Archibald rose wonderfully, and he produced a truly magnificent letter. To help the deception, in case the Germans heard of 'Husky' (the real code name for the invasion of Sicily), he used that as the code name for the eastern operation against Greece, and used 'Brimstone,' a fake code name, for the western operation against Sardinia. His draft ran as follows:

Telephone: Whitehall 9400.	War Office
Chief of the Imperial	Whitehall,
General Staff.	London, S.W.1.
	23rd April 1943.

Personal and Most Secret

My Dear Alex,

I am taking advantage of sending you a personal letter by hand of one of Mountbatten's officers, to give you the inside history of our recent exchange of cables about Mediterranean operations and their attendant cover plans. You may have felt our decisions were somewhat arbitrary, but I can assure you in fact that the C.O.S. Committee[1] gave the most careful consideration both to your recommendation and also to Jumbo's.[2]

We have had recent information that the Boche have been reinforcing and strengthening their defences in Greece and Crete

---

[1] Chiefs of Staff Committee.
[2] Nickname of Field-Marshal Sir Henry Wilson, Commander-in-Chief, Middle East.

and C.I.G.S. felt that our forces for the assault were insufficient. It was agreed by the Chiefs of Staff that the 5th Division should be reinforced by one Brigade Group for the assault on the beach south of CAPE ARAXOS and that a similar reinforcement should be made for the 56th Division at KALAMATA. We are earmarking the necessary forces and shipping.

Jumbo Wilson had proposed to select SICILY as cover target for 'HUSKY'; but we had already chosen it as cover for operation 'BRIMSTONE.' The C.O.S. Committee went into the whole question exhaustively again and came to the conclusion that in view of the preparations in Algeria, the amphibious training which will be taking place on the Tunisian coast and the heavy air bombardment which will be put down to neutralise the Sicilian airfields, we should stick to our plan of making it cover for 'BRIMSTONE' – indeed, we stand a very good chance of making him think we will go for Sicily – it is an obvious objective and one about which he must be nervous. On the other hand, they felt there wasn't much hope of persuading the Boche that the extensive preparations in the Eastern Mediterranean were also directed at SICILY. For this reason they have told Wilson his cover plan should be something nearer the spot, e.g. the Dodecanese. Since our relations with Turkey are now so obviously closer, the Italians must be pretty apprehensive about these islands.

I imagine you will agree with these arguments. I know you will have your hands more than full at the moment and you haven't much chance of discussing future operations with Eisenhower. But if, by any chance, you do want to support Wilson's proposal, I hope you will let us know soon, because we can't delay much longer.

I am very sorry we weren't able to meet your wishes about the new commander of the Guards Brigade. Your own nominee was down with a bad attack of 'flu and not likely to be really fit for another few weeks. No doubt, however, you know Forster personally; he has done extremely well in command of a brigade at home, and is, I think, the best fellow available.

You must be about as fed up as we are with the whole question of war medals and 'Purple Hearts'. We all agree with you that we don't want to offend our American friends, but there is a good deal more to it than that. If our troops who happen to be serving in one particular theatre are to get extra decorations merely because the Americans happen to be serving there too, we will be faced with a good deal of discontent among those troops fighting elsewhere perhaps just as bitterly – or more so. My own feeling is that we should thank the Americans for their kind offer, but say firmly it would cause too many anomalies and we are sorry we can't accept.

But it is on the agenda for the next Military Members Meeting and I
hope you will have a decision very soon.

Best of luck.

Yours ever,

ARCHIE NYE.

General the Hon. Sir Harold R. L. G. Alexander,
G.C.B., C.S.I., D.S.O., M.C.,
Headquarters, 18th Army Group.

Nothing could have been better: it carried out the scheme put up to him in a
way that only someone who was himself fully in the picture of the personal
relationships among high officers could have devised. Quite by inference,
and so accidentally as to prevent the Germans thinking it a plant, it makes
it clear that there will be an eastern Mediterranean operation with a landing
in Greece, and it also makes it clear that we *want* the Germans to think that
the western Mediterranean operation will be in Sicily (so *that* obviously
can't be the real target). It does all that in an 'off the record' atmosphere
which, together with the very personal matters in the rest of the letter,
makes it natural that it should not go through an official channel.

I had only two regrets. The first was that, knowing my Germans, I
wanted to make certain that they had an absolutely definite target on
which to fix as our Western objective, but the Chiefs of Staff refused to
sanction any mention of Sardinia in the letter. They thought that it would
pinpoint Sicily too clearly if the Germans saw through our operation.
However, after the Prime Minister's completely realistic appreciation
of the situation, which I have already mentioned, I managed to get a
joking reference to Sardinia inserted into another letter that we eventually
drafted for Lord Louis Mountbatten to sign – and that, as will be seen, was
of considerable value.

My second regret was less serious. I had wanted to include in the letter something which would appeal to the mind of the German reader as
being consistent with thoughts that he already had. I felt that the average
mind is readier to believe in the accuracy of a document if some part of it
contains what he already knows. I had thought that the best way of getting
an innocuous reference of this kind into the letter was to suggest a leg-
pull of General Montgomery which might well coincide with the rather
heavy-footed German humour. I therefore suggested that Sir Archibald
should ask General Alexander, 'What's gone wrong with Monty? He
hasn't issued an Order of the Day for at least a week.' Not long before
this time General Montgomery had been issuing a number of Orders of
the Day to encourage the troops, and a certain amount of ribaldry had
resulted in various quarters. However, for some reason that I have never
wholly fathomed, the Chiefs of Staff firmly banned my joke. I admit that

it was a poor one, and its loss was not important, although I felt sure that the Germans would study and appreciate any joke of that kind.

Sir Archibald's letter was typed on his notepaper, addressed 'My Dear Alex' and signed by him, and then enclosed and sealed in the usual double envelopes. The vital document was ready, and it was a pleasing touch that it happened to bear the date of St. George's Day.

CHAPTER V

Major Martin, Royal Marines

While we were preparing the document which we called the 'vital letter', we had to consider the 'man' who was going to carry it, for it was obvious that the first question that our opponent in Berlin would ask was: 'How did the letter come to be at Huelva?' True, it was the sort of letter which would be carried by an officer, and not in an official bag. Nevertheless, the German intelligence officer would ask, 'Was it carried by an officer? Did he seem to be a genuine officer?'

So we had to establish, as a first step, that the body was that of an officer. He had no uniform that we could use, as, for reasons both of security and of keeping my promise to conceal his identity, it was essential that we should provide him with a fresh uniform.

We had taken it for granted that, in his new personality, the body should be that of an Army officer. This had, I think, followed in our minds from the fact that he was carrying a letter from the V.C.I.G.S. to the Commander-in-Chief of an army, and probably also from the fact that the wartime Army was so large.

After a while, however, we decided against putting him in the Army. There were a number of reasons for the decision, but the main and compelling one was concerned with the 'distribution' of the signals and reports which would pass between the appropriate Attaché in Madrid and London after the body came ashore in Spain. Normally telegrams and signals were received in the appropriate office of the Service department concerned, and were then automatically distributed to such officers and departments as might be interested in the subject to which they referred, the distribution being based on a series of distribution lists. As a result, any telegram which reported the finding of a dead body on the Spanish beach would be sent to the Service department concerned and would be automatically distributed to quite a number of people, and any follow-up telegrams would receive the same distribution. Under the Admiralty system, it would be possible for me to arrange, with the authority of D.N.I., that this automatic distribution should be by-passed so that the messages resulting from our operation would be distributed to me only. Such an arrangement would not arouse comment. Under the War Office system, it was not easy to make any such arrangement for distribution to be limited either to me or to any colleague in the War Office.

So we decided that the body should not 'join' the Army, but would have to come under the Admiralty, and at once we found ourselves faced with a number of problems that we had not visualised. He could not easily become a naval officer because, while an Army officer could make such a flight as we were envisaging from London to North African Headquarters wearing a battledress, a naval officer would have had to wear proper uniform, and although a battledress need not fit too accurately, naval uniform would have to be made to measure. We formed a horrid mental picture of Gieves' cutter being brought down to measure and fit our corpse for its uniform, and discarded that suggestion!

The only other possibility which would keep this 'officer' under naval control was that he should join the Royal Marines: that would ease the problem of uniform, but it would bring a number of other problems. Firstly, we had banked on the fact that the wartime Army was so big that there were many units whose officers would not be astonished if they heard of an officer of their unit whom they did not know existed, whereas the Royals are a small corps, and even in wartime most of the officers know one another, or at least know of one another. Secondly, there was the difficulty of obtaining a photograph. For various reasons, we had not got, and could not get, any photograph of the young man whose body we were using which was suitable for an identity card in his new personality, and we had banked on the fact that Army officers did not carry identity cards with photographs when going abroad, but Royal Marine officers did.

We discussed these problems at some length. We easily appreciated the danger that might be caused by the small number that there was of Royal Marine officers, and that if the body *was* sent by the Spaniards to Gibraltar for burial the danger that we had anticipated if the body of an Army officer was sent there would be enormously increased. Nevertheless, we decided that, in view of the distance between Huelva and Gibraltar, we could accept even the increased risk due to his being a Royal Marine. We decided also that we could accept the difficulty of providing a suitable photograph, but in this case we had not appreciated how great the difficulty was.

First, we tried the expedient of taking photographs, of the appropriate type, of the corpse. That was a complete failure. It is a common criticism of photographs taken of living people for the subject to say, 'Oh, it makes me look as if I were dead!' Such criticism may or may not be justified, but I defy anyone to take a photograph of someone who is dead and to make it look as if he could conceivably be alive. It is impossible to describe how utterly and hopelessly dead any photograph of the body looked.

So a feverish search took place for a 'double' of the corpse, or even for someone who resembled him sufficiently for a poor photo to give a reasonable appearance of what the owner of the body must have looked like in life. It was an odd thing, but although we had not thought that our young man had had an appearance which would have singled him out in a crowd, we could not find the man we wanted. All of us walked about for days staring rudely at anyone with whom we came in contact and who might, on some excuse, be persuaded to sit for his photo. Eventually I decided to ask a young naval officer working in N.I.D.[1] to put on a battle-dress blouse and let us photograph him. I forget what excuse I used. The result, as I had anticipated, was not too good, but we decided that the likeness would suffice, bearing in mind the poor quality of such photographs.

And then we had another stroke of luck. Sitting opposite to me at a meeting to deal with quite a different matter, I saw someone who might have been the twin brother of the corpse. He was readily persuaded to let us photograph him, and that obstacle was surmounted.

The final step, before we could 'commission' the body as an officer, was to give him a name and a rank. I felt that a very junior officer would be unlikely to be given such a letter as the vital document to carry, but we could not make him too senior for several reasons. The most important was that our body was too young to have achieved very high rank unless he had been so outstandingly able that his brother officers would be bound to have heard of him. I therefore decided that I would make him a captain (acting major). Then I sat down with a *Navy List*. I steadily went through the list of Royal Marine officers until I found a little group of about that rank who all had the same name. That name was 'Martin'.

There seemed to me to be an advantage in a group of that kind. If the death of a 'Major Martin' *did* arouse discussion in a wardroom, there was always a hope that those present would not know all the Martins in the Royal Marines, or that, if they did, they would think that there was an error in the initial given and would not know whether to write and 'condole.' It might not have worked out that way (indeed for all I knew all the Martins were brothers), but this was only an added precaution against a not too serious risk. Of course, there was bound to be some risk in any name that I gave him. So I added the good normal Christian name of 'William', and our body became 'Captain (Acting Major) William Martin, Royal Marines,' with the approval of the Commandant-General, Royal Marines, who agreed to accept him into that Corps. Finally, I laid on the necessary precautions in case any enquiries were addressed to the C.G.R.M.'s department.

I had got a blank identity card and spent my time, whenever seated, rubbing it up and down my trouser leg to try to produce the 'patina' which

---

[1]   Naval Intelligence Division.

such a document normally gets with time, even when carried in a wallet. I did not do so badly, but I was a little worried by the slow progress of the ageing process when I got another idea. I decided that Major Martin should have lost his original identity card and have had a new one issued. So I got a new blank, stuck in the photograph of Major Martin's double; filled in the particulars and signed it for him, and then got a suitable official to sign it as issued on the 2nd February 1943, 'in lieu of No. 09650 lost' – the latter number being that of my own card, which would help to reduce complications if there were any subsequent enquiry – and got the appropriate stamps and seals put on it.

I had decided that Major Martin's 'ship' should be Combined Operations H.Q., for reasons that I will deal with shortly, and chose Cardiff as his birth-place for no particular reason. The card being complete, I then proceeded to give it a reasonable degree of ageing by the trouser-rubbing process.

So the basis of Major Martin's personality was established; anyone find-ing his body could find *who* he was from his identity card. But I was sure that my German friends in Huelva, Madrid, or Berlin would want to know *why* Major Martin was going to North Africa. If we could let them find evidence answering that question it would increase faith in the 'vital letter.'

Why *should* a Royal Marine officer be flown out to North Africa? And why should he be flown out in such circumstances that the Vice-Chief of the Imperial General Staff would know of his going so that he could be entrusted with an important letter? Why?

After some thought, I found a reason which seemed plausible to our team. A seaborne operation was being mounted against a defended coast; this would involve the use of landing-craft, and it might well be that some hitch in training would call for assistance from an expert in that line. Major Martin could be that expert, and we decided to give him a document that made that clear.

I therefore drafted a letter for signature by Lord Louis Mountbatten, the Chief of Combined Operations, addressed to Admiral Sir Andrew Cunningham, Commander-in-Chief, Mediterranean. It was as follows:

> In reply quote: S.R. 1924/43
> Combined Operations Headquarters,
> 1A Richmond Terrace,
> Whitehall, S.W.1.
> 21st April, 1943.

Dear Admiral of the Fleet,

I promised V.C.I.G.S. that Major Martin would arrange with you for the onward transmission of a letter he has with him for General Alexander. It is very urgent and very 'hot' and as there are some remarks in it that could not be seen by others in the War Office, it could not go by signal. I feel sure that you will see that it goes on safely and without delay.

I think you will find Martin the man you want. He is quiet and shy at first, but he really knows his stuff. He was more accurate than some of us about the probable run of events at Dieppe and he has been well in on the experiments with the latest barges and equipment which took place up in Scotland.

Let me have him back, please, as soon as the assault is over. He might bring some sardines with him – they are 'on points' here!

Yours sincerely,

Louis Moutbatten.

Admiral of the Fleet Sir A. B. Cunningham,
G.C.B., D.S.O.,
Commander in Chief Mediterranean,
Allied Forces H.Q.,
Algiers.

I was rather pleased with that letter. It explained why Major Martin had the 'vital letter' and why that had not been sent through official channels. It explained why Major Martin was being flown out. And, in view of the Prime Minister's clear realisation that it would not matter if Sicily was pin-pointed by a failure of our operation, I was enabled to make a reference to Sardinia. I did this by a joke which was frightfully laboured, but I thought that that sort of joke would appeal to the Germans, who would be able to see the point and understand the reference. This joke, with its indication of Sardinia, was destined to play a part in our eventual success.

But there was yet one more ruse concealed in it. I was sure that the Germans in Berlin would get the 'vital letter' or at least a copy of it, but I could not be sure that they would get more than a précis of what might be called the supporting documents, and I wanted to make certain that they would get this letter in full. I wanted Berlin to have the joke about Sardinia and I wanted them to have the explanation of why this officer was flying out and was carrying the unusual 'vital document'. I therefore put in the bit about Dieppe. I was sure that no German could resist passing on to his superiors what he would feel to be an admission by the Chief of Combined Operations that our raid on Dieppe was not the success that we had hoped it would be. Whether or not I had accurately penetrated the German mind, this was the only one of Major Martin's documents, in addition to the vital document, of which we found a complete copy in the German files and which we know was studied in full by the German Intelligence in Berlin.

The letter was duly typed at Combined Operations H.Q. signed by Lord Louis; and given a fictitious, but plausible, reference number.

In the end we gave Major Martin one more letter to carry in addition to his personal papers. We were a little worried by the fact that an officer would probably put two normal-sized envelopes into his pocket, or perhaps into his personal kit in spite of the secrecy of one of them. If Major Martin were to do this we had no absolute guarantee that the Spaniards would find them before handing over the body. We did not want to risk the German agent at Huelva having to curse his Spanish minions for not having searched the body. If only Major Martin could have an excuse for carrying the letters in a briefcase! We had to find him one.

It so happened that the official 'pamphlet' on the Commandos by Hilary Saunders was about to be published in this country, and was to be accompanied by an American edition. We decided that it would be plausible for Lord Louis Mountbatten to have written a letter to General Eisenhower asking him for a Foreword for inclusion in the pamphlet. So a letter was drafted, making the request, and enclosing the proofs of that pamphlet and the photographs which it would contain, and we took the opportunity to include another little indication that Major Martin was a very responsible officer. This letter ran as follows:

> In reply quote: S.R. 1989/43.
> Combined Operations Headquarters,
> 1A Richmond Terrace,
> Whitehall, S.W.1.
> 22nd April, 1943.

Dear General,

I am sending you herewith two copies of the pamphlet which has been prepared describing the activities of my Command; I have also enclosed copies of the photographs which are to be included in the pamphlet.

The book has been written by Hilary St. George Saunders, the English author of *Battle of Britain, Bomber Command* and other pamphlets which have had a great success both in this country and yours.

The edition which is to be published in the States has already enjoyed pre-publication sales of nearly a million and a half, and I understand the American authorities will distribute the book widely throughout the U.S. Army.

I understand from the British Information Service in Washington that they would like a 'message' from you for use in the advertising for the pamphlet, and that they have asked you direct, through Washington, for such a message.

I am sending the proofs by hand of my Staff Officer, Major W. Martin of the Royal Marines. I need not say how honoured we shall

all be if you will give such a message. I fully realise what a lot is being asked of you at a time when you are so fully occupied with infinitely more important matters. But I hope you may find a few minutes time to provide the pamphlet with an expression of your invaluable approval so that it will be read widely and given every chance to bring its message of co-operation to our two peoples.

We are watching your splendid progress with admiration and pleasure and all wish we could be with you.

You may speak freely to Major Martin in this as well as any other matters since he has my entire confidence.

Yours sincerely,

Louis Mountbatten.

General Dwight Eisenhower,
Allied Forces H.Q.,
Algiers.

This letter also was signed by Lord Louis and, when put into an envelope with its enclosures. It fully justified Major Martin in using a briefcase in which to carry all his official documents.

But our problem over this point did not end here. We had found an excuse for presenting the official documents to the Spaniards in a way that allowed for any inefficiency on their part and made sure that the documents would be discovered, but had we been too clever? Just as we were congratulating ourselves on our ingenuity, a sudden qualm arose: how on earth were we to ensure that the body and the briefcase arrived in Huelva together? Although it might be possible to place the handle of the briefcase into Major Martin's hand, we could not take the risk, on this all-important point, that the fingers might open and let the briefcase be dragged away by the sea. I made enquiries about *rigor mortis*, but, when I had added the complication that the body would have been frozen and then allowed to thaw, it was clear that the imponderables were far too many.

The only solution which we could devise was one which did not appeal to us, because it was the only point in the whole 'set-up' which did not ring true. We decided to assume that an officer who carried really secret and important papers might attach his briefcase to one of the leather-covered chains which some bank-messengers use, wearing them down their sleeves so they are not visible to the normal glance, but prevent their bag of valuables being snatched out of their hands. Such an arrangement seemed horribly phoney to us, but then *we* knew that this method was not one used by British officers. We decided that we would have to take a chance and rely on our opposite numbers in Berlin swallowing this feature. After all, *they* could not be sure that in no circumstances would a British officer adopt this method of safeguarding such documents.

So we decided to take the risk and use a chain. As may have been noted from the instructions to Lieutenant Jewell, we decided that Major Martin would not sit throughout a long flight with the brief-case dangling from his arm, and that it would be reasonable for him, instead of leaving this important bag to get lost or forgotten, to keep the bag on the chain, but to gain comfort by looping the latter through the belt of his trench-coat.

It is hard to be dogmatic: maybe we worried too much. Maybe, on the other hand, the Germans in Berlin would have become suspicious over this point, had it been reported to them. I will not anticipate at this stage what we learned later, and will therefore only say that our luck was good and that question was never put to the test. Still, I would dearly like to know whether the risk that we took was a justifiable one, for we took it on the basis that the Spaniards would report accurately on this obviously important point, but that our opponents would not be sufficiently sure that the chain was a flaw in an otherwise convincing picture for them to take the risk of rejecting the genuineness of the documents. We will never know whether we were right or not. Perhaps it is just as well that we won't!

Finally, as Major Martin was serving at Combined Operations H.Q., he needed a special pass, and we got him one. We felt that we were in danger of making Major Martin into too great a paragon of all the virtues, and that it was about time that he should show some human failing in addition to the loss of his identity card. As will be seen, we were also engaged on building up a personal character for him which would reveal him as a little careless in his personal affairs, in spite of his ability as an officer, and we could not divorce his personal characteristics completely from his military ones. Besides (as is recounted in the next chapter), an event had taken place in his life which would be likely to drive such trivialities as the renewal of a pass from his mind. We therefore decided that he should make the same slip as most of us had done at one time or another, and forget to renew his pass. The one that we gave him expired on the 31st March 1943. We were sure that it would not surprise the Germans (any more than it would us) if Major Martin had been able to get away with the use of this pass until his departure in the third or fourth week of April.

It only remained to provide Major Martin with his uniform. One of us who happened to have approximately the same build as Major Martin got a suitable battledress, to which we added Royal Marine and Commando flashes and a major's crown. An old trench-coat was obtained, and we put similar badges of rank on the shoulder straps after having pierced them for the three 'pips' of his substantive rank. Boots and webbing gaiters were got in addition to a shirt and all his underwear. These last were not new, but all old laundry-marks were removed from them and his handkerchiefs, and they were then all laundered together so as finally to have the same marks.

We had bought a shirt at Gieves, and we thought that Bill Martin might well have stuffed the scrumpled bill into the pocket of his trench-coat. This produced the only real brick which we dropped: the officer who actually bought the shirt was not in the Navy, and he took the unbelievable step of paying cash. As Bill Martin hadn't an account there it would have been difficult for the officer to do otherwise without getting the wrong name on to the bill, but, after the body was out of our reach, I suddenly realised that few naval officers had ever been known to pay cash to Gieves, least of all one who was being dunned for his overdraft! I could, however, comfort myself with the thought that it was the *Germans* that we had to deceive; *they* could not know for certain whether temporary officers were still granted the same privileges by that long-suffering firm as were given to the regulars. Still – it was a mistake and inartistic.

So the body of the 'man who never was' had become that of an officer, Major Martin of the Royal Marines, and anyone who found the body would have ample evidence of who he was and why he was where he was. But it was still the body of an officer and not that of a person. We had still to provide him with his personal effects and with a human personality to make him 'real.'

CHAPTER VI

The Creation of a Person

From quite an early stage Major Martin had become a real person to us and it was obviously desirable that as much of that feeling as possible should be shared by whoever investigated the body. The more real he appeared the more convincing the whole affair would be. Besides, I was quite sure that in a matter of this importance every little detail would be studied by the Germans in an effort to find a flaw in Major Martin's make-up, so as to be sure that the whole thing was genuine and not a plant. That I was not mistaken is evidenced by the fact that, as we learnt later, the Germans even noticed the dates on the two theatre-ticket stubs that we placed in Major Martin's pocket.

The method that we adopted in deciding on Major Martin's personality was to keep on discussing him, rather as if we were pulling a friend to pieces behind his back. In fact, we talked about him until we did feel that he was an old friend whom we had known for years. I must, however, admit that, although he became completely real to us, we did tend to mould his character and history to suit our convenience.

As I have just related, we had decided that Major Martin was a rather brilliant officer and was trusted by his superiors. His only visible lapses were the all too common ones of having lost his identity card and having recently let his pass to Combined Operations H.Q. run out of date.

On that foundation we built a character which could be evidenced by documents in his pockets. That was the only means that we had whereby to convey his personality to the Germans.

We decided that he should be fond of a good time, so he could have an invitation to a night club. It was a probable result of a certain amount of extravagance that he would have a letter from his bank about his over-draft. He could have been staying at a Service club while in London, so he might have a receipted bill for the last part of his stay there. In this way he was developing from an abstraction into something rather more definite.

But how could we make him really 'come to life?' The only way to do it was by letting him carry in his pockets letters which would convey to the reader something really personal about him. On the other hand, if one were able to stop a passer-by in the street and search his pockets, it would be very seldom that one would hit on any occasion when he had letters about him which covered more than trivial details. When we approached our problem in that way, we came to the conclusion that the only times when a man is certain to be carrying 'live' letters conveying a vivid picture of him and his life would be when he had recently become engaged and was carrying love letters on him and making arrangements for married life. We therefore decided that 'a marriage should be arranged' between Bill Martin and some girl just before he was sent abroad.

So Major Martin 'met' a charming girl called Pam early in April, became engaged to her almost at once (those wartime courtships!). She gave him a snap of herself and he gave her an engagement ring. He had a couple of ecstatic letters from her, one written when staying away the week-end and one written in the office (while her boss was out) in an agony of emotion, as he had hinted that he was being sent abroad somewhere. He would have with him the bill for the engagement ring – unpaid, of course, as he had an overdraft to deal with. Lastly, he could have an old-fashioned father who disapproved of war weddings and who would insist on his son making a will if he persisted in so foolish and improvident a step.

We felt that we could not hope to build up a personality more definitely than that with only a pocketful of letters, but they had to sound genuine and they had to be written by someone. We could, of course, have written them ourselves – most of us knew only too well what a letter about an overdraft looked like, and some of us had made wills or received love letters, but I thought it best to rely on the expert hand so that there could be no possibility of any mistake.

Some of the items were easy. For instance, one of our number had an invitation to the Cabaret Club with no name on it, so the night club was easily provided for. The letter about the overdraft was only slightly more difficult. Through another of our number we got a letter from Lloyds Bank dated the 14th April calling on Major Martin to pay off an overdraft of some £79. I was asked, later on, whether it was usual for a letter dealing with such a comparatively small sum to have been signed by the Joint General Manager at Head Office. I had already considered this, as I know from bitter experience that such letters are usually signed by the branch manager. When I raised this question at the time, I was assured that, although it was true that such letters were more usually signed by the manager of the appropriate branch, it did quite often happen that the letter would come from Head Office in certain circumstances. As the officer concerned in getting this letter had a 'lead in' to the Head Office, it was decided to use that. I did not think that the Germans would have had the experience that we had had of overdrafts and, after all, even if the amount was small, Major Martin's father was clearly a man of some importance. This letter was drafted for us personally by Mr. Whitley Jones, the Joint General Manager of Lloyds Bank, typed in his office and signed by him.

It read as follows:

Lloyds Bank Limited
Head Office
London, E.C.3.

Private   14th April, 1943.

Major W. Martin, R.M.,
Army and Navy Club,
Pall Mall,
London, S.W.1.

Dear Sir,

I am given to understand that in spite of repeated application your overdraft amounting to £79. 19s. 2d. still outstands.

In the circumstances, I am now writing to inform you that unless this amount, plus interest at 4% to date of payment, is received forthwith we shall have no alternative but to take the necessary steps to protect our interests.

Yours faithfully,
(*Signed*) E. WHITLEY JONES,
Joint General Manager.

It had been arranged that this letter from the bank should be sent through the post to Major Martin at the Naval and Military Club, but it was erroneously posted addressed to him at the Army and Navy Club, Pall Mall. There the Hall Porter marked the envelope 'Not known at this address' and added 'Try Naval and Military Club, 94 Piccadilly.' This seemed to us to be a most convincing indication that the letter was real and not specially prepared, so we decided that Major Martin should keep this letter in its envelope.

One of us had got the co-operation of the Naval and Military Club. We had been given a bill dated the 24th April which showed that Major Martin had been a temporary member of that club and had stayed there for the nights of the 18th to 23rd April inclusive. Apart from its other purpose of general build-up of the Major's personality, it afforded a strong indication that he was still in London on the 24th.

Similarly, there was but little difficulty in getting the bill for the engagement ring. I chose S. J. Phillips, the Bond Street jewellers, as I knew that they had an international trade, so that it was probable that there would be bill-heads of theirs available in Germany to prove, if comparison were to be made, how genuine Major Martin's bill was. That bill was dated the 19th April, but showed that the ring had actually been bought on the 15th.

We were in some difficulty in getting these and the other documents. Obviously, the true story of why we wanted them could not be told, but I was convinced that just to ask for them and to give no reason, except that it was for something secret, was liable to cause talk. On other hand, once a plausible reason was given, we felt sure that we could rely on those whom we approached.

So my 'cover story' was that there was someone who seemed suspiciously interested in officers who were temporarily hard up. We wanted to have some documents, building up towards a shortage of money, which a particular person could leave about his rooms where they would be seen by this individual. We could then observe what his conduct was. This seemed to be a satisfying story, and we received ready help, and no one ever let us down with the slightest leak.

What might be called the supporting cast among the documents having been provided for, we now had to obtain the 'stars.'

First of all we needed a suitable snapshot of Pam, Major Martin's fiancée. The scheme which we devised was to ask the more attractive girls in our various offices to lend us a snapshot of themselves for use in a photographic identity parade, the sort of thing where the photographs of one or two suspects are shuffled in among those of a number of perfectly innocent persons and the 'witness' is asked to pick out the one of the person whom he had seen. We asked for a variegated lot, and got quite a collection. We eventually chose a charming photograph and returned the remainder. The subject of the photograph was working in the War Office and, as she had access to 'Top Secret' papers, we were able to tell her that we wanted to use the photograph as that of someone's fictitious fiancée in a deception, and she gave her permission.

None of us had felt up to writing the love letters. After all, ours was not the feminine point of view, and it was a bit difficult to ask a girl whether she could write a first-rate pæan of love! So we asked a girl working in one of the offices whether she could get some girl to do it. She took on the job, but never would tell us the name of the girl who produced the two magnificent letters that Major Martin was to carry with him.

I had decided that the first of these should be written on my brother-in-law's notepaper, for I was sure that no German could resist the 'Englishness' of such an address as 'The Manor House, Ogbourne St. George, Marlborough, Wiltshire'. This letter, dated 'Sunday 18th,' ran as follows:

> The Manor House,
> Ogbourne St. George,
> Marlborough, Wiltshire.
> *Telephone*: Ogbourne St. George 242.
> *Sunday, 18th.*

I do think dearest that seeing people like you off at railway stations is one of the poorer forms of sport. A train going out can leave a howling great gap in ones life & one has to try madly – & quite in vain – to fill it with all the things one used to enjoy a whole five weeks ago. That lovely golden day we spent together – oh! I know it has been said before, but if *only* time could sometimes stand still just for a *minute* – But that line of thought is too pointless. Pull your socks up Pam & dont be a silly little fool.

Your letter made me feel slightly better – but I shall get horribly conceited if you go on saying things like that about me – they're utterly unlike ME, as I'm afraid you'll soon find out. Here I am for the weekend in this divine place with Mummy & Jane being too sweet & understanding the whole time, bored beyond words & panting for Monday so that I can get back to the old grindstone again. What an idiotic waste!

Bill darling, do let me know as soon as you get fixed & can make some more plans, & dont *please* let them send you off into the blue the horrible way they do nowadays – now that we've found each other out of the whole world, I dont think I could bear it –

All my love,
Pam.

It was followed by two sheets of plain paper, such as was used in Government offices for carbon copies. The letter was headed 'Office. Wednesday, 21st.' and the writing, which started reasonably good, suddenly degenerated into a scrawl as the letter was hastily brought to an end when the writer's boss was heard returning. It ran:

Office.
Wednesday, 21st.

The Bloodhound has left his kennel for half an hour so here I am scribbling nonsense to you again. Your letter came this morning just as I was dashing out – madly late as usual! You do write such heavenly ones. But what are these horrible dark hints you're throwing out about being sent off somewhere – *of course* I won't say a word to anyone – I never do when you tell me things, but it's not abroad is it? Because I wont have it, I won't, tell them so from me. Darling, why did we go and meet in the middle of a war, such a silly thing for anybody to do – if it weren't for the war we might have been nearly married by now, going round together choosing curtains etc. And I wouldn't be sitting in a dreary Government office typing idiotic minutes all day long – I *know* the futile sort of work I do doesn't make the war one minute shorter –

Dearest Bill, I'm so thrilled with my ring – scandalously extravagant – you know how I adore diamonds – I simply can't stop looking at it.

I'm going to a rather dreary dance tonight with Jock & Hazel, I think they've got some other man coming. You know what their friends always turn out to be like, he'll have the sweetest little Adam's apple & the shiniest bald head! How beastly & ungrateful of me, but it isn't really that – you know – don't you?

Look darling, I've got next Sunday & Monday off for Easter. I shall go home for it of course, *do* come too if you possibly can, or even if you can't get away from London I'll dash up and we'll have an evening of gaiety – (By the way Aunt Marian said to bring you to dinner next time I was up, but I think that might wait?)

Here comes the Bloodhound, masses of love & a kiss

from

Pam.

We felt that we had been well served, and that the letters were ideal for our purpose.

To take the part of Major Martin's father we chose a young wartime officer who produced a brilliant *tour de force*; the letter of the 13th April and the enclosure seemed to me to be so redolent of Edwardian pomposity that no one *could* have invented them – no one but a father of the old school could have written them. The letter and its enclosure read:

Tel. No. 98.

Black Lion Hotel,
Mold,
N. Wales.
13th April, 1943.

My Dear William,

I cannot say that this Hotel is any longer as comfortable as I remember it to have been in pre war days. I am, however, staying here as the only alternative to imposing myself once more upon your aunt whose depleted staff & strict regard for fuel economy (which I agree to be necessary in war time) has made the house almost uninhabitable to a guest, at least one of my age. I propose to be in Town for the nights of the 20th & 21st of April when no doubt we shall have an opportunity to meet. I enclose the copy of a letter which I have written to Gwatkin of McKenna's about your affairs. You will see that I have asked him to lunch with me at the Carlton Grill (which

I understand still to be open) at a quarter to one on Wednesday the 21st. I should be glad if you would make it possible to join us. We shall not however wait luncheon for you, so I trust that, if you are able to come, you will make a point of being punctual.

Your cousin Priscilla has asked to be remembered to you. She has grown into a sensible girl though I cannot say that her work for the Land Army has done much to improve her looks. In that respect I am afraid that she will take after her father's side of the family.

Your affectionate
Father.

Copy.
Tel. No. 98.

Black Lion Hotel,
Mold,
N. Wales.
10th April.

My Dear Gwatkin,

I have considered your recent letter concerning the Settlement which I intend to make on the occasion of William's marriage. The provisions which you outline appear to me reasonable except in one particular. Since in this case the wife's family will not be contributing to the settlement I do not think it proper that they should necessarily preserve, after William's death, a life interest in the funds which I am providing. I should agree to this course only were there children of the marriage. Will you therefore so redraft the Settlement as to provide that if there are children the income is paid to the wife only until such time as she remarries or the children come of age. After that date the children alone should benefit.

I intend to be in London for the two nights of the 20th & 21st of April. I should be glad if you could make it convenient to take luncheon with me at the Carlton Grill at a quarter to one on Wednesday 21st. If you will bring the new draft with you we shall have leisure to examine it afterwards. I have written to William & hope that he will be able to join us.

Yrs. sincerely,
(*Signed*) J. G. Martin.

F. A. S. Gwatkin, Esq.,
McKenna & Co.,
14, Waterloo Place,
London, S.W.1.

We selected the Black Lion Hotel, Mold, not only because it also seemed so British an address that it in itself conveyed an impression of truth, but it was also consistent with Major Martin's birthplace of Cardiff. I hope that they will forgive us for taking and using their notepaper, and especially for questioning the comfort for which that hotel is noted.

Finally, I got a friend who was a partner in the firm to round off the picture by drafting the following letter, and writing it on McKenna & Co.'s notepaper:

McKenna & Co.   14, Waterloo Place,
Solicitors.   London, S.W.1.

Our ref: McL/EG

19th April, 1943.

Dear Sir,

Re your affairs

We thank you for your letter of yesterday's date returning the draft of your will approved. We will insert the legacy of £50 to your batman and our Mr. Gwatkin will bring the fair copy with him when he meets you at lunch on the 21st inst. so that you can sign it there.

The inspector of taxes has asked us for particulars of your service pay and allowances during 1941/2 before he will finally agree to the amount of reliefs due to you for that year. We cannot find that we have ever had these particulars and shall, therefore, be grateful if you will let us have them.

Yours faithfully,
McKenna & Co.

Major W. Martin, R.M.,
Naval & Military Club,
94, Piccadilly,
London, W.1.

When we read all those documents together they conveyed to us the impression of a real person, of a real person who lived, of a man who really was. We did not feel that more could be done with the few papers that a man could reasonably have in his pockets.

However, we took some precautions before we gave the letters to Major Martin. The letters, other than the love letters, I carried in my pockets for the appropriate number of days to get them into the right condition. But the love letters were more of a problem, especially as one of them was on flimsy paper. It was obvious that they would have been read and re-read and would not be in mint condition, but the proper appearance could not be produced quickly by scrumpling them up and then smoothing them out again (as someone foolishly suggested would be the suitable method). Once a piece of paper has been scrumpled no amount of flattening will erase the fact that it has been treated that way – and the one thing that Bill Martin would never have done to those letters was to crush them up. So I did what he would have done: I folded and unfolded the letters again and again, and in addition I rubbed them carefully on my clothing to get a little patina on to them.

CHAPTER VII

Major Martin Gets Ready for War

We had gone steadily on with our preparations although final approval for the launching of the operation had not yet been obtained.

After considering Sir Archibald Nye's letter, the Chiefs of Staff had given approval in principle. We now pressed for authority to start. There was bound to be a conflict of interest at this stage. The Chiefs of Staff were naturally reluctant to become committed to the Germans receiving the information contained in the letter as our strategy *might* be changed. If that had happened it would not have been for the first time! On the other hand, we simply *had* to get the letter to Spain by the beginning of May if the operation was to be of any value. We had to give the German Intelligence Service time to get the information, convince themselves of its genuineness by any check-up that they might want, and then to 'appreciate' it and pass the result on to the operational staff. The latter would then need time to make their arrangements and to send their forces to the wrong places, and, if we wanted them not to fortify Sicily, it was no good waiting until those fortifications were complete.

The Chiefs of Staff accepted this necessity and gave their final approval, subject to reference to the Prime Minister, to whom the matter was submitted through General Ismay.

When the Prime Minister was told that there was some risk of pinpointing Sicily, if the operation went wrong, he replied (as I have already recorded), 'I don't see that that matters. Anybody but a damn' fool would *know* it was Sicily.' We felt that he ought also to be informed that our efforts might be wasted, as there was always the chance that the body *might* be recovered by a Spaniard who was not co-operating with the Germans and the papers might be returned to us intact. The Prime Minister realised that that risk was not great either, and disposed of this point with a grin and a chuckle, saying, 'I don't see that that matters either. We can always try again!'

So we had received the all-clear, subject to General Eisenhower being informed of the plan. If he had had any objection, or any change of strategy had occurred before the body was actually launched, the operation could have been cancelled in the way I had provided in paragraph 8 of the 'operation orders' to Lieutenant Jewell. Meanwhile we had to undertake the least pleasant part of our work – we had to get the body ready for its mission.

We heartily disliked this task. In spite of the great service which we were confident that the body would render to its country, it went against the grain to disturb its rest. In addition, there was an odd psychological reaction on each occasion that we saw the body lying stiff and cold. By this time Major Martin had become a completely living person for us. We felt that we knew him just as one knows one's best friend. After all, one has to be very close to a friend to read his love letters and the very personal letters that he gets from his father. We had come to feel that we had known Bill Martin from his early childhood and were taking a genuine and personal interest in the progress of his courtship and financial troubles. I had thought that I might say that we, who had created him, knew him as a father knows his son, but that would have been inaccurate. We knew him far better than most fathers know their sons. So as to create him we had had to make ourselves know his every thought and his probable reaction to any event that might occur in his life.

We never relished the prospect of a visit to the place where the corpse was in cold storage, and George and I had to pay no less than three visits to him. First we had to disturb him to try to get a suitable photograph, and we took that opportunity to check his measurements, and especially the size that he took in boots. Then we thought it wise to pay a second visit and dress him so that he was fully ready for his journey in case there was any hitch which could not be rectified in haste. It was a good thing that we did, for we had forgotten one point.

I have used the expression 'lying stiff and cold.' We had realised that it would be difficult to dress a body fully, from the underwear up, when it was in such a condition. We had checked on the situation when we took the photographs and found that, although difficult, it was possible. But we had forgotten the boots!

To appreciate what we were up against, it would be necessary for you to try to put a pair of boots on your feet, keeping your ankle and foot absolutely rigid, and with the latter at right angles to the leg – the operation is utterly impossible.

This was a bad check: we knew that to freeze and then to thaw a body, and then to freeze it again is a sure way to hasten the process of decomposition when eventually the body is allowed finally to thaw out. If we had to do this we might well vitiate the whole basis of Sir Bernard Spilsbury's calculations. What were we to do?

Suddenly we thought of the solution. We got an electric fire and thawed the feet and ankles only. Then hurriedly, yet carefully, we dressed the body completely, and finally, with sincere mental apologies for what we were doing to it, replaced it in the cold storage.

Our third visit was on Saturday the 17th April, 1943 at 6 p.m., when we went to fetch Major Martin for the start of his journey. First we put the personal letters and the wallet with his passes and so on into his pockets. Then we added the usual 'junk' that a man carries about on him, or unwittingly collects in his pockets. The final list was somewhat impressive:

Identity discs (2) 'Major W. Martin, R.M., R/C,' attached to braces.
Silver cross on silver chain round neck.
Watch, wrist.
Wallet, containing:
    Photograph of fiancée.
    Book of stamps (2 used).
    2 letters from fiancée.
    St. Christopher plaque.
    Invitation to Cabaret Club.
    C.C.O. Pass $\Big\}$ in cellophane
    Admiralty Identity Card   container.
    Torn-off top of letter.
    1 £5 note – 5th March, 1942 $\frac{227}{C}$ 45827.

    3 £1 notes   X34D527008
                      W21D029293
                      X66D443119
1 half-crown.
2 shillings.
2 sixpences.
4 pennies.
Letter from 'Father.'
Letter from 'Father' to McKenna & Co., solicitors.
Letter from Lloyds Bank.
Bill (receipted) from Naval and Military Club.
Bill (cash) from Gieves Ltd.
Bill for engagement ring.
2 bus tickets.
2 counterfoil stubs of tickets for Prince of Wales'
    Theatre, 22nd April, 1943.
Box of matches.
Packet of cigarettes.
Bunch of keys.
Pencil stub.
Letter from McKerina & Co., solicitors.

I must digress here to explain the item '2 counterfoil stubs of tickets for Prince of Wales' Theatre, 22nd April, 1943.' As I have said, it was on the

17th April that we went to fetch Major Martin, and he was to sail on the 19th. He was due to be launched into the sea off Huelva on about the 29th or 30th April. On the other hand, if he had been travelling by air, as we wanted the Germans to believe, the journey would only have taken a single day. When we considered this difference in time, we decided to work the timetable back the other way: if we deducted from the arrival in Huelva on about the 30th April some five or six days in which the body might have been drifting ashore from an aircraft which had come to grief out at sea (we had reckoned that the eventual degree of decomposition would probably support an immersion of about that period), that would mean that Major Martin would have left London on about the 24th of April, and for that reason the bill for his room at the Naval and Military Club was dated that day. But here George had another of his brilliant ideas, it suddenly came into his ingenious mind that anyone who sees the stub of a theatre ticket at once assumes that the ticket has been used, but there was no reason why we should not buy theatre tickets valid for any date after the body had in fact left London, and then tear off the stubs and waste the tickets. So we decided that Bill Martin and Pam should have a farewell party before he left. We felt that they would enjoy the Sid Fields show at the Prince of Wales' Theatre, and we bought four tickets for that show (the reason why we bought four will be related later), tore off the stubs of two and put them into Major Martin's pocket. Once again a small detail was to play its part in the deception, and this afterthought 'went home' whereas the bill for the room at the Club was overlooked by the Spaniards and Germans.

Finally, we added the briefcase containing the important documents, and here we made a slight alteration from our intended arrangements of which I had notified Lieutenant Jewell. We had intended to take the briefcase up to the Clyde separately from the canister and give it into Lieutenant Jewell's care, but when it came to the point we found that the bag could be inserted into the canister with the body, and we therefore took this course, as it was an obvious safeguard against any forgetfulness during the launching of the body off Huelva. Lieutenant Jewell would have a difficult task, especially if it was rough, and his mind would be fully occupied with that and the safety of his ship. It would have been a pity if Major Martin had floated ashore while his briefcase remained in Lieutenant Jewell's safe.

When we had completed the clothing, filled all the pockets and attached the briefcase, we wrapped the body in a blanket so as to prevent it getting rubbed during its journey. When we had arrived we had stood the canister up on end and filled it with dry ice. When this had melted, we refilled the canister and again waited for the ice to melt. Then we lifted Major Martin and reverently and carefully lowered him into the canister and packed him round with still more dry ice. Finally, we put on the lid and screwed down the nuts. Major Martin was ready to go to war.

CHAPTER VIII

The Journey North

Our party consisted of George and myself, together with Jock Horsfall, the racing motorist, who was on special duty with the War Office, one of whose 30-cwt. Ford vans we had borrowed, and, of course, Major Martin in his canister.

The journey nearly ended almost before it had started for, as we drove out from the 'cold storage' to start back to George's flat in London, we caught sight of a queue waiting to see a spy film at the local cinema. The same thought flashed into each of our minds: what would those people think if we were to stop and say to them, 'Don't bother about the film. We can tell you a much better story, and ours is true. Just look inside this canister'? And we all burst out laughing to such an extent that Jock almost rammed a tram-standard.

But we got safely back to George's flat. There we cooked ourselves some dinner and ate it, taking turns to keep an eye on the van outside. If a thief had got away with the canister, he would have had a disappointment and a shock when he opened it, but his disappointment would have been nothing to ours. So we made ourselves some sandwiches and filled thermos flasks as we realised that we could not leave the van during the journey north.

Our preparations completed, we set off for Greenock, Jock and I taking it in turns to drive. It was a long and tiring journey, as we could, of course, only use masked headlights. At one point we drove straight across a roundabout which, fortunately, only had smooth grass in its centre once we had mounted the kerb. The sound of aircraft overhead added to our worries, for although the *Seraph* was not due to sail until the 19th and we had got a fair amount of time in hand in which to cope, without any really serious consequences, with any traffic diversions through bomb damage, Lieutenant Jewell had asked that we should arrive before midday on the 18th, in case there were any last-minute difficulties in stowing the canister. However, we did not crash the van and, as far as I know, all the aircraft were friendly, so we drove on through the night, taking it in turns to sleep on the floor of the van.

Early on the morning of the 18th we arrived at Greenock and drove to the dock, where we had arranged to meet the launch that was to ferry us out to H.M.S. *Forth*, the submarine depot ship lying in the Holy Loch.

Here we ran up against a snag. I had visualised that there might be some difficulty in lowering the canister into the launch, so I had carefully said in the signal from D.N.I. arranging for our arrival that I would have 'one, repeat one' package weighing over 400 lb. and requesting assistance in embarking it. In spite of that particularity, the signal had been read as if our total baggage weighed 400 lb. in several packages. As a result, we found ourselves faced with a launch surging up and down some feet below the quay and the 'party' for which we had asked consisting of one rating. He was very obliging, but no rope was available, and to lower the canister without disaster was clearly impossible.

Anticipating all sorts of trouble and delay before I, a complete stranger, could arrange for a party to be got together, I hurried off to the Flag Officer in Charge's headquarters. My luck still held. The Duty Officer turned out to be a Wren who had been serving as a rating in the signal office at Hull when I was on the Staff there. We greeted one another as old friends and, all difficulties having been quickly smoothed out, I returned to the dock with half a dozen ratings and some rope with which to lower the canister.

We were soon ferried down to H.M.S. *Forth*, where I handed Major Martin over to Lieutenant Jewell. I also gave him the rubber dinghy which he was to launch with the body. So as to give the impression of an accident and haste, the dinghy was to be launched upside down, and it seemed better to leave only one of the collapsible aluminium oars in it. I therefore kept the other one, and I still have it as a souvenir. As it turned out, however, the launching of the dinghy made no difference: a body might be of no value to a Spanish fisherman, but a rubber dinghy certainly was. Ours was never heard of again. I hope the finder made good use of it.

We had been advised that, if a Catalina flying boat sank out at sea, it was unlikely that any wreckage would float ashore, so we did not provide Lieutenant Jewell with anything more with which to simulate signs of a disaster.

The canister was duly stowed on board H.M.S. *Seraph* and I had final discussions with Lieutenant Jewell. In these I suggested that he might be able to launch the body with only officers present on deck. If he could, it would reduce the number of persons who were 'in the know' and thus make leakage of the story less likely. It was more than usually important to guard against leakage, and the story of the launching of a dead body off the coast of Spain was one that would tempt the best of us to gossip.

If he could launch the body in this way, he would obviously need a 'cover story' for the rest of the crew, who would see a package that they had thought to be destined for Malta taken up on deck off the coast of Spain, after which it would never reappear. I suggested that he might tell them that the so-called optical instruments were, in fact, a secret weather-reporting buoy and that, if the Spaniards learned of its existence, they would remove it. If he had to have the crew on deck during the launching, either because of rough weather or for any other reason, he would use the cover story that I had given him in the 'operation orders'.

All went well with our arrangements, and on our return to London we were able to end our report with the statement: 'On April 19th, 1943 at 1800 British Double Summer Time H.M. s/m *Seraph* sailed from Holy Loch.' Remembering the nature of the cargo, I felt that these names were most suitable and augured well for the success of the operation.

CHAPTER IX

The Launching of the Body

There then came a period of anxiety. I had never had any qualms about the success of the operation, but now that its execution was out of my hands I kept thinking of things that might go wrong. Oddly enough, I still did not worry whether the Germans would see through the deception. I was confident that they would not. My anxiety was confined to the launching of the body. Could we really be sure that the body would float ashore or would I have to confess, after all the effort, that the whole thing was a complete flop? And, in my worst moments, I visualised the *Seraph* getting into trouble off Huelva, where she had gone only because of my plan. Still, I had more than enough to do with my other duties not to have much time for worry, and we did have at least one very cheerful evening during this period.

It had seemed absurd to waste the tickets, the stubs of which Major Martin had in his pocket. So we had, as I have recorded, bought four tickets, and we took care to give Major Martin the stubs of the middle two seats of the four.

George and I then invited 'Pam' and Jill, the girl who had arranged for the writing of the love letters, to 'Bill Martin's farewell party.' We started at the Prince of Wales' Theatre, where the manager let us in after he had inspected the block of tickets and we had explained that someone had torn the stubs off the centre pair 'as a joke'. We did not tell him that the joke was on the Germans.

After the theatre we went on to the Gargoyle Club for dinner. There we were shown to one of the side tables which had a bar faced by two chairs. I suggested that the two girls should take the more comfortable banquette, but Jill turned to George and said, 'Considering Bill and Pam are engaged, they are the least affectionate couple I know. They don't even want to sit together at his farewell party before he goes abroad.' At this the couple at the next table looked round and pricked up their ears.

I 'explained' to Jill that even if Pam and I were engaged we had only known one another for a few days (obvious disapproval of war weddings registered at the next table), and then added, as an afterthought, that it would be different when Pam and I knew one another better, for my boss had said (in the letter that she had seen[1]) that, although I was quiet and shy at first, I really did know my stuff. At this the couple at the next table registered even stronger disapproval and got up and danced.

I might interpolate another result of this joking identification of Bill Martin with me. Pam followed it up by giving me a larger copy of the photograph that was on its way to Spain in Bill Martin's wallet, and signed it 'Till death do us part. Your loving Pam' – a safe inscription, as 'I' was already 'dead.' At that time I was staying with my mother, and to see her reaction I put the photograph on my dressing table. I was disappointed – she said nothing. About a year later, when my wife returned from America, where she had been doing a job in our Security Co-ordination Service, I showed her the photograph, and she astonished me by saying, 'So *that* was why your mother started writing in her letters that she felt that I should come home as soon as my job allowed it!'

While we were waiting in London, the *Seraph* was having an uneventful passage to the coast of Spain. The first news that we got was from the pre-arranged signal which informed us, on the 30th April, that 'Operation Mincemeat' had been completed. This was followed by a letter sent by Lieutenant Jewell from Gibraltar:

Most Secret and Personal

From: The Commanding Officer, H.M. Submarine *Seraph*.
Date: 30th April, 1943.
To Director of Naval Intelligence,
Copy to F.O.S.
(for Lt.-Cdr. The Hon. E. E. S. Montagu, R.N.V.R.) personal.

Operation Mincemeat

1. *Weather*: The wind was variable altering between S.W. and S.E., force 2. It was expected that the sea breeze would spring up in the morning, close inshore, as it had on the previous morning in similar conditions.

Sea and swell – 2.0 – Sky overcast with very low clouds – visibility was patchy, 1 to 2 miles – Barometer 1016.

2. *Fishing Boats*: A large number of small fishing boats were working in the bay. The closest was left, about a mile off, and it is not thought that the submarine was observed by them.

3. *Operation*: The time of 0430 was chosen as being the nearest to Low Water Lisbon (0731), which would allow the submarine to be well clear by dawn. The canister was opened at 0415 and the body extracted. The blanket was opened up and the body examined. The

---

[1] Lord Louis Mountbatten's letter to Admiral Cunningham.

brief case was found to be securely attached.... The 'Mae West' was blown up very hard and no further air was needed. The body was placed in the water at 0430 in a position 148° Portil Pillar 1.3 miles approximately eight cables from the beach and started to drift inshore. This was aided by the wash of the screws going full speed astern. The rubber dinghy was placed in the water blown up and upside down about half a mile further south of this position. The submarine then withdrew to seaward and the canister, filled with water and containing the blanket, tapes and also the rubber dinghy's container, was pushed over the side in position 36°37'30 North 07°18'00 West in 310 fathoms of water by sounding machine. The container would not at first submerge, but after being riddled by fire from Vickers gun and also .455 revolver at very short range was seen to sink. Signal reporting operation complete was passed at 0715.

A sample of the water close inshore is attached.

N. A. Jewell,
Lieutenant-in-Command.

This letter included a description of the condition of the body. There was rather more decomposition than we had expected (perhaps due to oxygen trapped in the clothing and blanket), but not more than was to be expected had the body been floating half immersed in the sea for some days.

Later on I got a more detailed account from a member of the ship's company. I got it at second-hand and, as my go-between was a journalist by profession, the picture that is conjured up by his account is much more vivid than anything that I could record. I therefore give it just as I received it:

As the *Seraph* slid from the shadow of her depot ship and down the Clyde, the commander – he was only twenty-nine – saluted from the conning tower, then went below.

Of the five officers and fifty ratings on board, only he knew the secret of his odd piece of cargo.

Wisecracks

The cylindrical metal canister now rested in a forward chamber of the submarine.

Because of its weight and shape, the six ratings who manoeuvred it into place joked about 'John Brown's body.' And there was many a wisecrack about 'our new shipmate, Charlie.'

To-day, ten years later, those fifty ex-members of the *Seraph's* crew will be shaken to learn how close to the truth they were.

They had been told in the briefing for the trip that the metal canister contained a secret weather-reporting device to be floated experimentally off the coast of Spain. It was actually marked 'Handle with Care – Optical Instruments – for special F.O.S. shipment.'

For ten days the *Seraph* sailed and her crew saw nothing of the sun. Surfacing only at night, she was off Huelva, on the south-west coast of Spain, undetected and according to schedule, on April 30.

The spot selected for floating 'Major Martin' ashore was 1,600 yards off the mouth of the Huelva river.

In the afternoon the *Seraph* ventured an inshore reconnaissance. The periscope revealed a fishing fleet of about fifty vessels. But the prevailing mist and a mile detour helped the submarine to escape detection. Then she went back to the sea bed for the rest of the day.

Mysterious

Zero hour was 4.30 in the morning. When the *Seraph* surfaced again it was dark as pitch. The new moon had set and the ebb tide was just on the turn.

Through the conning tower went the five officers, and the submarine was trimmed down until an inch of the calm sea lapped over the casing. The mysterious canister was hauled aloft.

Only then, with all ratings below, did Lieutenant Jewell let his officers into the secret. Lieutenant Jewell told them that the canister at their feet contained a corpse. The operation, he said, was part of an Allied plan to deceive the enemy into drawing his defensive forces away from the spot selected for the main thrust of the Mediterranean invasion.

Phoney invasion plans were to be 'planted' on the enemy through the medium of the body of this man purporting to be 'Major Martin,' victim of an air crash at sea.

Huelva had been chosen for the 'plant' because it was known that the German agent there was being well fed with military intelligence by local collaborators.

What a story to be sprung on you suddenly in the middle of the night with the Atlantic lapping round your boots! But if the junior officers were shaken by their commander's dramatic and gruesome revelation, they did not betray it.

The only reaction was the comment from one of them: 'Isn't it pretty unlucky carrying dead bodies around?'

Tension

Then quickly and quietly the five set about their task. While three kept watch, the other helped Lieutenant Jewell to unlock the bolts of the canister with the spanner attached to the case. Ten minutes they worked before the lid came away. Then the blanketed body was slid gently from its vacuum coffin. For a moment the tension was relieved as the officers stiffened with silent respect in the presence of death.

On his knees again, Lieutenant Jewell plucked at knotted tapes and the blanket fell away. There followed the final check. Were the Major's uniform and badges intact? Was his hand gripping the handle of the all-important despatch case? Was the case securely strapped to his belt? Everything in order, Jewell bent low to inflate the Major's 'Mae West.'

Only one thing remained, though it was not in the routine instructions. Four young officers bent bare heads in simple tribute as their commander murmured what prayers he could remember from the Burial Service. For them, sworn to secrecy, these words from Psalm 39 held a special significance: 'I will keep my mouth as it were with a bridle: while the ungodly is in my sight. I held my tongue and spake nothing: I kept silence, yea, even from good words, but it was pain and grief to me.'

A gentle push and the unknown warrior was drifting inshore with the tide on his last, momentous journey. 'Major Martin' had gone to the war.

The risk that Lieutenant Jewell had taken in going so close to the shore had given us every possible chance of success. We could now only wait to see how Major Martin Would carry out *his* part of the job.

CHAPTER X

Major Martin Lands in Spain

On the 3rd May we received a signal from the Naval Attaché in Madrid. He had been informed by the Vice-Consul at Huelva that the body of a Major Martin, Royal Marines had been picked up just off-shore by a fisherman on the 30th April. The body had been duly handed over to the Vice-consul and had been given a full military funeral, at which the Spanish Services and civilian authorities were represented, at twelve noon on the following day in the cemetery at Huelva. There was no mention in the Attaché's message of the black official briefcase or of any official papers.

There then followed an exchange of signals between the Admiralty and the Naval Attaché. If the papers had been what they purported to be, it was obvious that, when the death of Major Martin and the arrival of his body in Spain became known at Combined Operations H.Q., there would have been a realisation of the fact that a most secret document had gone astray, and reference to Sir Archibald Nye would have revealed the full measure of the disastrous 'leak' of strategic information that might have taken place. In those circumstances, increasingly pressing messages would have been sent to the Naval Attaché, urging him to try to get the documents back at all costs, but warning him that he must take the utmost care not to show undue anxiety lest that should alert the Spaniards to the importance of the documents and encourage them to open or 'lose' them. We naturally had to act as if the whole affair was genuine, and the signals were therefore on those lines.

We started by a signal on the 4th May stating that Major Martin had some papers with him which were of great secrecy and importance, and instructing the Attaché to make a formal demand for them. If they were not forthcoming, he should make very discreet but searching enquiries at Huelva to see if they had been washed ashore and, if so, what had happened to them. If he did recover them, he was to signal to 'D.N.I. – Personal' the names of the addressees. He was not to open the envelopes, but to return them as quickly as possible to D.N.I.

We followed that by another signal informing him that it had been ascertained that there were three letters of the utmost importance, and that they were believed to be in a black official briefcase with the royal cypher on it. He was again warned on no account to arouse the interest of the Spaniards in the documents.

We learned from the Attaché, in reply to the first signal, that the Minister of Marine had informed him, in answer to a studiously routine enquiry, that the documents had been passed through 'Naval channels' and would only reach Madrid via the Spanish Naval H.Q. at Cadiz. This would take some days. The Attaché had learned that the Vice-Consul at Huelva had had no opportunity to get the briefcase or other documents.

Then, on the 13th May, the Attaché informed us that the Spanish Chief of Naval Staff, in the absence of the Minister of Marine, had just given him all Major Martin's effects, including a black briefcase. The latter was open with a key in the lock. The Chief of Naval Staff had said that 'everything was there,' and the Naval Attaché had thanked him.

Although the Attaché had gained a strong impression that the Chief of Naval Staff knew at least something of the contents of the letters, he considered that there was no reason to think that that officer would divulge his knowledge to anyone. Of course, we did not suspect that officer of any breach of faith, but if *he* knew of the contents it would be certain that others would also know. Things were going well – the 'leak' was starting.

Our optimism was strengthened by the next message that we received from the Attaché. The Minister of Marine himself had referred to the papers when he saw the Attaché on Saturday, the 15th May. Apparently, he had heard, while in Valencia, that the papers had arrived in Madrid, and had immediately given orders to the Chief of Naval Staff to hand them over at once. He had done this lest someone might have had an unauthorised look at them, which might, he said, be a serious matter.

Nothing that had been said to the Minister of Marine before he left Madrid could have given rise to such anxiety about the documents, so we had no doubt at all that the envelopes must have been opened. That being the case, we were confident that there must be at any rate *one* Spaniard 'in the know' who would pass the information on to the Germans. How close the co-operation was in fact we were not to learn until after the end of the war.

Meanwhile, discreet enquiries in Huelva filled in some of the details of what had happened. We learned with absolute certainty that a fisherman had noticed a floating object and had hailed a nearby launch which took it on board. The object, which turned out to be the body of Major Martin, was landed on the nearest beach by the launch and handed over to an officer who happened to be exercising a detachment of infantry there.

A naval judicial officer was summoned, and he took charge of all the documents and personal effects. The body, after identification, was removed to the mortuary at Huelva for medical examination by a doctor who certified that the man had fallen into the sea while still alive and had no bruises, and that death was due to asphyxiation, through immersion in the sea since five to eight days before. An American Air Force pilot who had crashed into the sea on the 27th April was then asked to inspect the body in case he could identify it, but he (naturally) could not do so.

The man whom we knew to be the chief German agent in the vicinity had soon learnt of the landing of the body. He quickly ascertained the details, including the names of the addressees of the letters in the briefcase, and had tried to get copies of all the documents, but he was not successful owing to the chance fact that, as the military patrol had been present to take charge of the body, the naval judicial officer had been called in, and neither he nor his associates had the right kind of contact with that particular official.

Although we were confident that all had gone well, we wanted a final check, and we waited impatiently for the return of the documents that Major Martin had carried. Eventually they reached London and were promptly submitted to scientific tests. Before sending them out, we had taken precautions, which I obviously cannot specify and which would help us to check whether the envelopes had been tampered with. Though the immersion in sea water made certainty impossible, we were now able to say with some degree of confidence from the physical evidence that the letters, or at least two of them, had been removed from the envelopes, although the seals appeared to be intact.

When we added this information to that which we had received from Huelva and from the Naval Attaché, we were quite satisfied. There was little doubt that the Spaniards had extracted the letters and knew what was in them, and that the German Intelligence Service knew of the important addressees. We could rely on the efficiency of the Germans to get all that they wanted out of that situation. We were sure that our confidence in the Spanish end of the German Intelligence Service would not be mis-placed. It was now up to Berlin to play *its* part.

Meanwhile, we must say farewell to Major Martin. He had served his country well, and we felt that it was up to us to see that his last resting-place should be a fitting one and that proper tribute should be paid to him, even if all this had to be done under pseudonyms. We were glad to be able to show respect to him without any danger to the success of the operation in which he had played so vital a part. Indeed, by doing what our instinct required of us, we would make it more difficult for the Germans to check the Spanish doctor's verdict, a verdict with which we were entirely satisfied. Frequent visits to the grave by British officials and their representatives would at least deter any exhumation by the Germans or Spaniards before the tombstone could be laid.

First of all we got the Naval Attaché to arrange for a wreath to be placed on the grave from Pam and the family. Next we arranged that a tombstone should be laid as soon as possible and, finally, I wrote to the Naval Attaché, asking him to thank the Vice-Consul at Huelva on behalf of Major Martin's family for all the trouble he had taken and the consideration that had been shown, and asking also that photographs of the grave might be taken, as they would be treasured by the family and by Major Martin's fiancée, to whom he had so recently become engaged.

The wreath was composed of flowers from the garden of an English mining company at Huelva. The gravestone was of plain white marble and bore the inscription, 'William Martin. Born 29th March, 1907. Died 24th April, 1943. Beloved son of John Glyndwyr Martin and the late Antonia Martin of Cardiff, Wales. *Dulce et decorum est pro patria mori*. R.I.P.'

We could do no more for him, although we were deeply in his debt and felt that very soon many thousands of his fellow countrymen and their American allies might owe their lives to him as they landed on the shores of Sicily. Indeed, my confidence in that probability was shared by now by those in authority. I had sent a message to Lieutenant Jewell to let him know that his part of the operation had been completely successful. As it was undesirable to send my message by signal, in case it aroused talk, I decided that Lieutenant Jewell would know what I meant when I wrote, 'You will be pleased to learn that the Major is now very comfortable' on an ordinary picture postcard. But the Chiefs of Staff went one better; they sent a message to the Prime Minister, who was by then in Washington. It also had of necessity to be cryptic and read: 'Mincemeat swallowed whole.'

CHAPTER XI

We Tidy Up in England

We (and by this I mean all of us on the Allied side) had by now done our part of the job. If I may use a simile, we now had only to stone-wall, keeping our end up until close of play came with the landings in Sicily, leaving the Germans at the other end to do the scoring for us.

So, on the whole, we sat back and waited developments. However, as the days went by, we remembered that *The Times* used to reach Lisbon by air and the Germans might be keeping an eye on the casualty lists which were published from time to time. I therefore checked the average period that elapsed between a death and the subsequent announcement in the newspapers. It appeared as a general rule to be not more than about five weeks, and that, from the 24th April, would bring us to the first week of June.

Should we include Major Martin's name in such a list? Was it worth the complication involved? The landings in Sicily were planned for the second week in July, and the Germans could hardly be certain that the name of a genuine casualty *would* have to appear before then. If the deception had caused them to take any action, they would have done so before the first week of June and could hardly remedy any mistake, or even begin to do so, before we landed. On the other hand, it was always possible that the assault on Sicily might be delayed for some reason. After some hesitation, we decided that an omission to insert the name might do harm and that it was better to be sure than sorry.

Eventually, however, we were indeed sorry that we had added this embellishment to our creation, but fortunately only for the trouble that it gave us and not because it did any harm. As regards our objective of deception, all went smoothly and our phenomenal luck held. It was quite easy to get the Casualty Section of the Commissions and Warrants Branch of the Admiralty to accede to D.N.I.'s request that they should include the name of 'Temporary Captain (Acting Major) William Martin, R.M.' among the 'Killed' in the next casualty list. I forget what explanation I gave when I conveyed the odd request. The announcement duly appeared in the issue of *The Times* dated Friday, the 4th June, 1943. We will probably never know whether the Germans did in fact spot this name, but, if they did, they would have found, in the same list, the names of Rear-Admiral P. J. Mack, D.S.O., and of Acting Captain Sir T. L. Beevor, Bt., R.N. It had already been announced in the newspapers that these two officers, with others whose names had not been given, had died when an aeroplane had been lost at sea. What could be more plausible than that Major Martin had died with them. The fact that it was that list which happened to be the next one was due to pure chance. It makes me hope that the Germans *did* spot that list, as it would be a pity if anything so artistic as that had been wasted.

But it was then that trouble started over here. Casualty lists were studied by departments of whose existence I was blissfully unaware and by others whom I had forgotten. I was given a little experience of the sort of trouble which I would have had on a much larger scale had I allowed the messages passing between us and the Attaché in Madrid to have the normal distribution.

The Naval Wills Department wanted to know whether Major Martin had made a will, and if so, where was it? The Medical Director-General's Department wanted to know whether Major Martin had been killed in action, died of wounds, died on active service, or what, so that their statistics could be kept in order.

Fortunately, the precautions that I had taken to ensure that any enquiries about Major Martin (or any of his documents) were adequately dealt with worked satisfactorily. I heard of these enquiries at a sufficiently early stage for me to be able to prevent their spreading too widely, but I had to deal with the departments concerned. I racked my brains what answer to give. I could not refer the Wills Department to McKenna & Co., the solicitors who had written to Major Martin about his will before he departed.

I had by now fully appreciated the truth of the aphorism, 'O, what a tangled web we weave, when first we practise to deceive' and was getting into the swing of it. I told the heads of each of those departments that they need not worry about Major Martin, or record him or his death. I explained that he was a special agent who had been sent on an important mission after having been given (with the First Sea Lord's authority) the cover of naval rank as an officer in the Royal Marines. After all, that account was perfectly true as far as it went. I only 'forgot' to mention that he was already dead before any of that happened.

With D.N.I.'s authority, I impressed on them the vital need for secrecy, and they undertook to deal with the matter in their respective departments. The nearest we ever came to the operation 'leaking' was over.

I might, perhaps, add that some years later, after I had been demobilised, people were still compiling other lists, and I suddenly got an urgent request to visit the Naval Intelligence Division. They had received other similar enquiries about Major Martin and wanted to know how I had dealt with such enquiries in the past, so that the same answer could be given again.

But apart from this matter of the casualty list, 'Operation Mincemeat' was no longer in our hands. We had played our part and Lieutenant Jewell and Major Martin had played theirs. What were the Germans doing?

CHAPTER XII

The German Intelligence Service Plays its Part

Through the end of May, through June and into July 1943 we had nothing on which to rely for our belief that we had succeeded in our plot, except for our faith in the thoroughness of the German penetration of Spain and the gullibility of the Germans. We were sure that we had succeeded in getting the documents to the Germans and that, now that we had achieved that first step, the picture presented to them was so complete and so authoritative that no intelligence staff could fail to be certain that it had scored an epoch-making triumph.

We could picture the intelligence chiefs rubbing their hands. They would be bound to preen themselves at the thought that the painstaking care and efficiency with which they had built up their organisation in Spain, and the liaison with important Spanish officialdom, which was Admiral Canaris's[1] special pride, had at last proved its worth. In the past that organisation must have provided Berlin with much information about ship movements through the Straits of Gibraltar as well as intelligence gained in the British Isles and America and transmitted through Madrid, but that was to be expected of any such service. Besides, it had clearly been badly at fault before the assault on North Africa, when, so far as we could judge, the Germans had been taken by surprise. Now, at last, it had scored a real triumph.

To be able to provide the Operational Staff with an exact copy of a letter from a Vice-Chief of a General Staff to the Commander of an Army in the field (and such a letter as this one) was beyond the wildest hopes of any experienced intelligence officer – a fulfilment of the daydreams of his hopeful youth. Such information as the letter contained, if acted upon efficiently by the General Staff, might avert a disaster, or might result in the infliction of a crushing defeat on the Allies at a crucial moment in the war, and thus alter the whole history of the world.

---

[1]   The Head of German Military Intelligence and Espionage.

It was for this reason that I had fought so hard against the suggestions that we should play safe, that we should use this plan to plant some minor misinformation contained in documents passing between officers of junior rank. If the letters that Major Martin had carried had been of that sort, not only might the Germans not have made the effort to get copies, but even if they had, they might not have relied on them when making strategic decisions. But what Sir Archibald Nye wrote to General Alexander *must* be true. The Vice-Chief of the Imperial General Staff must *know* what the Allied plans were – *he* could not be himself the victim of a 'cover plan' or misinformed. If the German Intelligence Service swallowed these letters as genuine, they would have to 'go to town' on them, and no General Staff which got such information with its Intelligence Service's *imprimatur* of genuineness could fail to base its strategy upon it.

So we sat back and waited. D-day of 'Operation Husky' came, and the assault went well. Sicily is roughly a triangle standing on its point, and the Allies landed in the early hours of the morning of the 10th July on both sides of this point and advanced rapidly up the sides of the triangle as well as across the middle. There were many elements that added to the surprise which was achieved, such as the rough weather and the 'moon period' which was chosen, but that surprise certainly did nothing to shake the confidence of our group that we had succeeded with 'Operation Mincemeat' and contributed our bit.

As intelligence reports and documents gradually filtered in from Sicily, that view was confirmed. There seemed to be little doubt that the Germans had switched the effort that they had put into preparing the defences of Sicily away from the south (where we in fact landed) to the western angle of the triangle and the northern side, which would have been the danger-points if we had been making a diversionary assault during an invasion of Sardinia, or an assault after Sardinia had been captured. Not only were most of the later minefields, demolitions and defences built in the north of Sicily, but the total of defences and reinforcements in the island was less than had been expected and surprisingly deficient in the south and east. On the information that was available, it was decided officially that our part in the deception had been successful. The view formed by those in authority on the whole operation was summed up when Admiral Cunningham reported, 'The very efficient cover plan and the deceptive routeing of convoys played their part' in the surprise achieved. How preponderantly it was due to the former we were only to know later.

Real knowledge of the extent and degree of our success did not come until very much later – not, in fact, until some months after 'V.E.-Day.'

I was quietly slogging away one morning in my stuffy and ill-ventilated room in the bowels of the Admiralty, winding up my work, writing records of what had been done for the guidance of those in future wars who would never have time to read them (or think them worth reading), and impatiently waiting for the date for the demobilisation of my 'Group' to come round, when the telephone bell rang. It was D.D.N.I.,[1] and his voice was so distorted with laughter that I found it hard to understand what he was saying, though I gathered that he wanted me in his room. So I went up there and, still shaking with laughter, he pushed some documents across the table to me. I picked them up and recognised them, in spite of the fact that the first words that caught my eye on the upper one were *'Lieber Grossadmiral'*! They were the 'Mincemeat' letters, or at least the German translations of them, finishing their long journey!

D.D.N.I. then explained the cause of his laughter. An officer was in charge of the sorting and translation of the German Naval archives which had been captured at Tambach in Germany. He had come up to D.D.N.I.'s room that morning with a very worried face, and had asked for instructions. His report was as follows:

In the file of documents that he was examining he had discovered 'these two documents': one was a copy of a most secret letter from the V.C.I.G.S. to General Alexander and (he said) it looked as if there had been a fearful breach of security, as well as probable breaches of all sorts of regulations. Normally, he ought to hand copies of letters of military importance over to his opposite number in the War Office, but this affair seemed to be so 'hot' and fraught with high level complications that he felt that D.N.I. might like to handle it himself on his level!

D.D.N.I. had recognised the letters and put the officer's mind at rest. There then began a search for other documents bearing on the matter, and we soon found evidence of the completeness of our triumph over the German Intelligence Service. As we had anticipated, they had immediately recognised the vital importance to their Operational Staff of these documents, if genuine, and had wasted no time.

Their agents in Madrid must have telegraphed the contents of the documents and an account of their discovery to Berlin early in the first week of May, because we have found reference in a later document to the fact that an Intelligence appreciation of Allied intentions had been circulated by signal on the 9th May before the 'original documents' had been received in Berlin.

When the German Intelligence Service in Berlin received this information, they had obviously reacted as we expected them to do, and had demanded evidence to support the authenticity of the documents, for the first written report from Madrid had been followed by a second and more detailed one. This latter indicated that still further enquiries would be made. But time was short; Berlin had clearly appreciated the importance

---

[1] Deputy Director of Naval Intelligence.

of the information and had decided that the details given by Madrid were convincing. They had indeed, 'gone to town' on it! The first document of importance was an Intelligence appreciation which had been attached to a translation into German of the letter from Sir Archibald Nye to General Alexander. It was dated the 14th May, 1943, and had been stamped with the 'most secret' instructions: 'To be circulated personally! Not through Registry!' The circulation marked on it was to the Commander-in-Chief of Naval Staff, Admiral Doenitz, and on the 15th May his Chief of Staff had initialled it and marked it with a cross in blue pencil to signify that Doenitz should read it himself. This the latter did, obliterating the cross in green pencil with his personal 'squiggle' and the figures 18 to indicate the date when he read it on his return to his H.Q. from his visits to Mussolini and Hitler. There were also two other officers included in the circulation.

This document read as follows:

Subject: Captured Enemy Document on Mediterranean Operations. Attached herewith are:

(*a*) Translation of the captured letter from the Imperial Staff to General Alexander.

(*b*) Appreciation thereof by the (German) General Staff.

The contents of further captured documents are unimportant. Exhaustive examination by 3 Skl. revealed the following:

1. The genuineness of the captured documents is above suspicion. The suggestion that they have intentionally fallen into our hands – of which the probability is slight – and the question whether the enemy is aware of the capture of the documents by us or only of their loss at sea is being followed up. It is possible that the enemy has no knowledge of the capture of the documents.

Against that it is certain that he knows that they did not reach their destination.

2. Whether the enemy will now alter his intended operations or will set an earlier date for their commencement must be taken into consideration, but seems unlikely.

3. *Probable Date of the Operation*

The matter is being treated as urgent; yet there is still time on the 23rd April to inform General Alexander by air courier of General Wilson's proposal to use Sicily as cover-target for the assault in the Eastern Mediterranean, wherein he is requested to reply immediately in the event of his supporting Wilson's opinion, 'as we cannot postpone the matter much longer.' In this case the Imperial General Staff considers altering the planning both in the Eastern and Western Mediterranean, for which there is still time.

4. *Sequence of the Operations.*

It is presumed that both operations will take place simultaneously, since Sicily is unsuitable as a cover-target simultaneously for both.

5. The Tobruk area comes into consideration as a starting-point for the operations in the Eastern Mediterranean. Alexandria is not considered, as in this case Sicily would have been absurd as a cover-target.

6. It is not clear whether the deception worked by the cover-target concerns only the period up to the beginning of the operations or whether in fact a cover-operation would be used as well as the actual assault.

7. It is *not* clear from the attached whether *only* the 5th and 56th Divisions will be landed in the Eastern Mediterranean (at Araxos and Kalamata). However *only* these two Divisions are to be reinforced for their assault. It is always possible that all assault troops and targets are included with them.

8. It should be emphasised that it is obvious from this document that big preparations are in course in the Eastern Mediterranean *as well.* This is important, because considerably less intelligence about preparations has reached us from this area than from Algeria, owing to their geographical situation.

The first point that strikes one is that the German Intelligence Service is already committing itself to the categorical assertion that 'The genuineness of the captured documents is above suspicion,' and, although they do prudently cover themselves with a reservation that they are enquiring into the possibility of a 'plant' and the extent of our knowledge of the fate of the documents, they are already saying that the possibility of the first 'is slight.' They have also already decided that we would be 'unlikely' to change our plans or hasten the date of the assault. Anyone with experience of the complexity and detail involved in the planning and launching of large-scale operations would agree with that view at least!

Another point which illustrates how, when one is working a deception of this kind, one has to put oneself into the mind of the enemy and to try to assume *his* degree of general knowledge is the statement in Paragraph 5. The Germans say that Sicily is impossible as a cover-target for an operation by troops based on Alexandria, presumably because they consider the distance to be too great. Had it been *our* Staff who read the document, the reaction would have been different: they knew that the distance was not too great and that troops from Alexandria could be used in an assault on Sicily, as, in fact, took place.

I need not consider the rest of the document in detail, as I will deal in the next chapter with the Operational Staffs' appreciations of the documents. But this appreciation does reveal the care with which every word and implication of the V.C.I.G.S.'s letter was studied.

This document was followed by another report circulated by the German Intelligence Service which was dated the 15th May, 1943. It read as follows:

Subject: *British Official Mail Washed Ashore Near Huelva*

The following points were cleared up in a conversation on 10.5.43 with the official concerned, a Spanish staff officer with whom we have been in contact for many years:

1. Clutched in the hand of the corpse was an ordinary briefcase which contained the following documents:

(a) A piece of ordinary white paper containing letters addressed to General Alexander and Admiral Cunningham. This white paper bore no writing on it.

Each of the three letters was in a separate envelope with the usual form of address and directed personally to the addressee, sealed apparently with the sender's private seal (signet ring).

The seals were in perfect condition. The letters themselves, which I have had in my hands in their re-sealed envelopes, are in good condition. For reproduction purposes the Spaniards had dried them with artificial heat and then placed them in salt water for twenty-four hours, without greatly altering their condition.

(b) Also in the briefcase were the proofs of the pamphlet on the operations of the Combined Operations Command mentioned by Mountbatten in his letter of the 22nd April, as well as the photographs mentioned therein.

The proofs were in perfect condition, but the photographs were quite ruined.

2. The messenger also carried a note-case in the breast pocket of his coat with personal papers, including his military papers with photographs (according to these, he was the Major Martin referred to in Mountbatten's letter of the 22nd April), a letter to Major Martin from his fiancée and one from his father, and a London night-club bill dated the 27th April.

Major Martin therefore left London on the morning of the 28th April, the same day that the aircraft came to grief near Huelva.

3. The British Consul was present at the discovery and is fully informed about it. The expected suggestions by the British Consul that the documents should be handed over to him were set aside under the pretext that all articles found on the body, including all papers, must be laid before the local Spanish magistrate.

After being reproduced, all documents were returned to their original condition by the Spanish General Staff and definitely give the impression – as I was able to see for myself – that they had not been opened. They will be returned to the English to-day through the Spanish Foreign Office.

Further enquiries are being made by the Spanish General Staff concerning the whereabouts of the pilot of the aircraft, who was presumably injured in the crash, and an interrogation of the latter about any other passengers.

From the point of view of our little group, this was a most fascinating document. It fully justified the care with which we had built up the personality of Major Martin, so that the very 'reality' of that officer carried conviction as to the genuineness of the documents that he was carrying, although it does reveal how chance would render some details important and others unimportant. It also reveals how accurate we were in our belief, on which the whole operation was based, that the Germans would have complete access to anything that interested them once it was placed in the hands of the Spanish Staff.

The first point that emerges is that, as I have already said, we need not have worried whether the attachment of the briefcase to Major Martin by a chain was plausible or not as the Germans were told that he had the briefcase clutched in his hand. So the inefficiency of the Spaniards, as well as their cooperation with the Germans, helped us.

I do not follow the reference in Paragraph 1 (a) to a 'piece of plain white paper' round the envelopes. Either this was something that some Spaniard put round them to preserve them from stains or some paper from the bundle of proofs of the Combined Operations pamphlet had become misplaced. Anyhow, we had not wrapped up the envelopes. Also the seals were official seals with the Royal Coat of Arms.

Then we noted that the personal papers in the wallet had been extracted and inspected, and we were glad that the letters from Pam and Major Martin's father had not been missed – that artistic effort was not wasted! Lord Louis Mountbatten's letter to Admiral Cunningham is also shown to have played its intended part in establishing who Major Martin was.

But this report illustrates one of the greatest difficulties that has to be faced in carrying out a deception. The deceiver can only supply his opponent with the material and has to leave that opponent to draw the deductions from it. For that reason he has to gauge both the efficiency and the intelligence with which his material will be treated. I feel that our deduction as to the intelligence of the Germans was about right, but we may have put their efficiency too high, for they made two extremely careless mistakes – both about dates.

As can be seen by a comparison of the photographs in the plate section of Lord Louis Mountbatten's letter to Admiral Cunningham and the photostat of the German translation of the same document, the Germans were too careless to copy the date correctly. The letter was dated 21st April, but the Germans, either in copying the letter or in translating it into German, altered the date to the 22nd April.

As it happened, that did not matter, but the other mistake was much more dangerous. There is a reference in the report to 'a London night-club bill dated the 27th April'. We came to the conclusion that that must be based on a careless reading of the stubs of the theatre tickets. The invitation to the Cabaret Club was not only not a bill, but it was not dated at all. It could not have been the bill dated the 24th April for his room for several nights at the Naval and Military Club, since that did not look like a night-club bill, and surely even the Spaniards would not have mistaken the 'In and Out' for a night-club! So we came to the conclusion that this error was due to a careless confusion between the stubs from the Prince of Wales' Theatre and the invitation to the Cabaret Club. That did not matter, but the mistake in the date might have been more serious.

The report decided, as we intended the Germans to believe, that Major Martin flew from England the day after he had had his farewell party, but the error in the date fixed that departure as having taken place 'on the morning of the 28th April, the same day that the aircraft came to grief near Huelva.' Had the Germans considered the opinion of the Spanish doctor, of which at least their agent in Huelva must have been aware, as to the date of death, and linked it with this date of departure, they might have become suspicious. The Spanish doctor had, not unreasonably, put the date as several days before the body was recovered on the 30th May. The shortest time that was suggested was some five days. So, on that basis, the aircraft disaster which caused Major Martin's death must have taken place on about the 25th April.

I am not sufficient of a philosopher to work out what can be deduced from this. It could be argued that we had been lucky that no one noticed this discrepancy and that our deception ought to have been 'blown.' I hope it is not too egotistical to say that I do not accept that. We had provided the Spaniards and Germans with all the clues from which they could draw the deductions that we wanted. While I suppose it would be absurd to say that we were entitled to reasonably competent and intelligent cooperation from the other side, I think we can say that we *had* provided the right clues and that they *did* draw the right deductions, even if those deductions were only reached by a cancelling out of compensating errors!

Anyhow, the report shows that the Germans did deduce that Major Martin *must* have travelled by air and that the disaster to the aircraft took place on a date consistent both with his departure and his state when he arrived.

The next paragraph of the report also interested us. It revealed that our view of the efficiency of German-Spanish co-operation at Huelva was fully justified. It recorded how, when the fortuitous intervention by a military unit and a naval judicial officer precluded immediate access to the documents, the efforts of the British Vice-Consul to take charge of them were 'set aside' under a 'pretext.' We knew that we could 'trust' the Spaniards!

Finally, there is the record of the fact that the envelopes, with the letters restored to them, and other papers were not returned until after the German agent had himself inspected and handled them. That he thought that the letters 'gave the impression that they had not been opened' does not surprise me. They would have given me the same impression if we had not taken precautions.

So, as far as the German Intelligence Service was concerned, we had won. As far as they were concerned, one could repeat the view of the Chiefs of Staff, as regards the Spaniards, 'Mincemeat Swallowed Whole.' The Intelligence Service, at any rate, had accepted the whole thing as genuine. But, as I have indicated before, that would have been only a hollow victory if the German Operational Staff had failed to take the same view and had continued to go all out in preparing to meet an invasion of Sicily. But they swallowed it also, and they also 'went to town.'

CHAPTER XIII

The German High Command Gets Busy

The information that we gleaned from the German naval archives cap-tured at Tambach was equally revealing with regard to the reactions that 'Operation Mincemeat' produced from the German High Command. The results that we gained were far beyond our wildest hopes.

Our guess as to what the Germans originally thought the Allies were going to do after Tunisia had fallen had been right, and we had even underestimated the difficulties that we were up against. We found a copy of a message sent by the German High Command to their army in Tunisia in February of 1943. They had decided that our next operation would be in the Mediterranean, and that it would be against one of the large islands. They put the order of probability as Sicily first, with Crete second and Sardinia and Corsica following behind. So, when we were doing our planning in London we were right in thinking that, from a very early stage, the Germans would put Sicily at the head of the betting, and as our preparations grew in the western Mediterranean they would have realised that *those* could not be for an assault on Crete, with an un-reduced Sicily barring the way. We had guessed right about that, but the message included the statement 'from reports coming in about Anglo-American landing intentions it is apparent that the enemy is practising deception on a large scale.' They were going to turn out to be accurate about that also, but had the Chiefs of Staff known how alert the Germans were for deception, I wonder whether we ever *would* have got permission to launch 'Mincemeat'!

The documents reveal that this strategic appreciation was maintained right up to the beginning of May, 1943. And then, on the 9th May, the whole picture changed: the news of the capture of Major Martin's docu-ments had reached the High Command.

On the 9th May an Intelligence appreciation must have reached the High Command, for we found the following document in the file just after the appreciation dated the 14th May mentioned in the last chapter:

Further to my 2144/43 dated 9.5.43, following appreciation has been made on receipt of original material:

1. A landing in the eastern and western Mediterranean on a fairly large scale is anticipated.

(a) Target of the operation in Eastern Mediterranean under General Wilson is the coast near Kalamata and the stretch of coast south of Cape Araxos (both on the West coast of the Peloponnese). The reinforced 56th Infantry Division is detailed for the landing at Kalamata and the reinforced 5th Infantry Division at Cape Araxos. It is not known whether both divisions will land in force or in part only. In the first instance, a lapse of at least 2–3 weeks would be required as the 56th Division on 9.5.43 was engaged at Enfidaville with two brigades and must first be rested and embarked. This solution, which embraces a certain delay before the landing can take place, appears to be the more probable from the way in which the letter is written. However, if the landing is to be effected by only certain units of both divisions, it could be made at any time, as one brigade of the 56th Division and 1–2 brigades of the 5th Division are probably already available in the actual starting-area (Egypt-Libya). Code-name for the landing on the Peloponnese is 'HUSKY' The Anglo-American General Staff has proposed a simultaneous cover operation against the Dodecanese to General Wilson. Wilson's decision thereon was not yet taken on 23.4.43.

(b) Target for the operation under General Alexander in the western Mediterranean is not mentioned. A joking reference in the letter points to Sardinia. Code-name for this operation is 'BRIMSTONE.' The proposed cover target for operation 'BRIMSTONE' is Sicily.

2. Maintenance of completest secrecy over this discovery and utmost limitation of circulation of this information is essential.

On a point of detail, this document gave me great pleasure. I had already congratulated myself that the German agent in Madrid had bothered to send on a copy of the seemingly unimportant letter from Lord Louis Mountbatten to Admiral Cunningham, unlike his treatment of the equally unimportant letter to General Eisenhower. *Was* it because of the hint that we thought we had failed at Dieppe? But Paragraph 1 (b) of this appreciation showed that my heavy-footed joke about sardines had gone home – 'a joking reference in the letter points to Sardinia'. It was not the same letter, but that can be excused in an appreciation of this kind. The German sense of humour is a great asset.

The German Intelligence Service had swallowed the deception: now the High Command accepted this view. It may well be that we have Hitler to thank for this, for we know, from the diary of Admiral Doenitz's conferences with the Fuehrer, that by the 14th May Hitler was convinced of the genuineness of the documents, and what they foretold. Doenitz had been sent to Italy to try to stiffen Mussolini after the North African disasters, and he reported to Hitler on his way back to his own headquarters before he himself had seen the documents. In reply to a question by Hitler as to Mussolini's views on 'Anglo-American intentions,' he reported that the Duce was convinced that we would attack Sicily, and here is his record of Hitler's reply:

> The Fuehrer does not agree with the Duce that the most likely invasion point is Sicily. Furthermore, he believes that the discovered Anglo-Saxon order confirms the assumption that the planned attack will be directed mainly against Sardinia and the Peloponnesus.

It is clear that Hitler was completely sold on the idea that we were intending to land in Greece and, now that he had come to this conclusion, he stuck firmly to it. So much so that, on the 23rd July, nearly a fortnight after the Allied landing in Sicily, Hitler *still* believed that the main operation was going to be an invasion of Greece, and appointed his favourite general, General Rommel, to command the forces that were being assembled there. On the 25th July Rommel flew to Greece, whence he had to be hurriedly recalled to take over the command in Italy and rally the defence of that country after the fall of Mussolini.

But it would be unfair to put too much blame on Hitler. On the very same day that Hitler had corrected the Duce's opinion, the 14th May, the Official War Diary of the German Naval High Command recorded the fact that the General Staff of the Army had come to the definite conclusion that the documents were genuine. They concluded that the assault would be on Sardinia, but that there might be a diversionary attack on Sicily.

So, by the 14th May, 1943, the Operational Staffs, the Supreme Command and the Fuehrer himself were all convinced. 'Operation Mincemeat' was completely successful. It remained for us to discover just what this eventually meant to the 'Anglo-American' forces.

I do not know in any detail what the German Army and the Luftwaffe were doing, but that they were doing something considerable is evidenced by an order sending the 1st German Panzer Division all the way across Europe from France to establish its headquarters at Tripolis, a town in the Peloponnesus ideally situated to command resistance against landings which included Kalamata and Araxos. When one considers the enormous effort involved in a journey of this kind for a complete Panzer Division, and how it put that force 'out of the war' for the time being, one might say that that alone would have far more than repaid the effort that we put into 'Operation Mincemeat,' even if we had not assisted the invasion of Sicily at all.

We also found in the German records a memorandum of the fact that the German Foreign Office had been asked to warn the Turkish Government that troops and shipping were being moved to Greece, but to stress that there were no hostile intentions against Turkey.

This precaution was not surprising when we consider the extent of the German preparations, for, although, as I have said, I have no details of the Army and Luftwaffe movements and activities, they may well have been large if we judge by the German naval activity, of which we naturally found a much more detailed picture among these documents.

By the 20th May the Naval High Command had ordered[1] the laying or the completion of three new German minefields off Greece, including one off Kalamata itself. The German Admiral commanding in the Ægean was ordered to take over control of minefields that the Italians were laying off the western coast of Greece, and German coastal-defence batteries were to be set up in territory under Italian control. These were only some of the steps that were 'envisaged or have already been taken' by that date as the Germans had appreciated that almost the whole coast of Greece, as well as the Greek islands, was threatened, though it was hoped that the Allied assaults might be beaten off in spite of German weakness in that area.

These instructions were completed by orders to establish R-boat[2] bases, command stations, naval sea patrol services and other safeguards. The effort to be put in was intense.

The dividend from 'Mincemeat' was growing, and that it was a dividend from 'Mincemeat' alone is established by documents which show that these orders were based on Major Martin's letters (a point that would have to be concealed in the operational orders themselves for reasons of security). Another indication is given by the statement in the orders that the likelihood of a large scale Allied landing in the eastern as well as the western Mediterranean had been established in spite of the fact that 'so far indications of the preparation of large numbers of landing craft have reached us only from the western Mediterranean'. In addition, it is possible for those who compare both documents – the 'Mincemeat' letter and these orders – to trace the connection.

Shortly after this, in early June, a whole group of German R-boats was sent *from* Sicily to the Ægean! Our dividend was indeed growing fast.

Meanwhile, things were moving in the western Mediterranean area also. I can summarise the main reaction best by reference to an order sent out on the 14th June in Hitler's name by General Keitel, Commander-in- Chief of the Supreme Command of the German Armed Forces. These orders[3] are clearly based on the German appreciation that the use of Sicily as a 'cover-target' for the assault on Sardinia might involve a diversionary attack on that island (they took a similar view of our use of the Dodecanese as a cover target for the eastern Mediterranean operation: see Appendix I

---

[1] See Appendix I.

[2] German Motor Torpedo Boats.

[3] Appendix II.

and the appreciation of the 14th May). The operation of that factor on the mind of the German Staff is evidenced also by the location of the German defensive measures which we found in Sicily, as I have already recorded.

We also found a record of the fact that a strong Panzer force with its ancillaries and supplies for two months was sent to Corsica in June by an order issued in Hitler's name, and from now on there was a growing emphasis on the reinforcement of Sardinia and Corsica, with the north coast of Sicily coming next in priority.

On the 9th July, *the day before we landed in Sicily*, Keitel sent out a long appreciation which he says is that of Doenitz. This appreciation covered not only both the eastern and western Mediterranean, but also future Allied strategy based on operations in both those areas. In it he concludes that an attack on all three islands, Corsica, Sardinia and Sicily (either all together or one at a time), as well as the Greek operation, is possible. Doenitz estimates that there are enough Allied troops in the whole of North Africa to provide for both operations and then to exploit the bridgehead that the Allies may be able to form in Greece. His appreciation is that a major landing on the coast of Italy (after the capture of the Italian islands) is unlikely, as the Germans could react fast in Italy, whereas in Greece their reinforcements and supplies would necessarily be slow. From Greece the Allies could attack the Roumanian oilfields, and the political effect of such an operation on Hungary, as well as Roumania, might be great. Finally, Doenitz's conclusion, promulgated by Keitel, is that 'the western assault forces appear to be ready for an immediate attack,' which could begin at any time (how right he was!), whereas 'the eastern force appears still to be forming up' (how wrong he was: they in fact took part in the invasion of Sicily).

On the early morning of the 10th July our forces had landed in Sicily, but the Germans still could not believe that that was the real assault (and that the documents must have been a plant). The German High Command asked that a special look-out should be kept by the German agents on the shores of the Straits of Gibraltar for convoys which would be going to attack Corsica and Sardinia. They presumably still thought that the landings in Sicily (although on the side of the island that they did not anticipate) were a diversion to draw attention from the main operation.

But by the 12th July even the German belief in the accuracy of the 'Mincemeat' documents had begun to weaken. After all, the invasion of Sicily was obviously genuine and had been going on for two days.

We found two messages passing between the German Naval Commander-in-Chief in Italy and the Naval High Command. In the first the Commander-in-Chief complains bitterly that the departure of the 1st R-boat Group (which had been sent to the Ægean for the defence of Greece) had prejudiced the defence of Sicily, as a gap had been left in the patrols which were consequently ineffective. He stated that the shortage of small craft was 'chronic' and that the departure of any more boats, as ordered, would have a serious effect both on defensive work and on escort work. The reply stated that reconnaissance reports had shown the Allies to have engaged so much in Sicily that there was little probability of landings in Greece until the Sicilian operation was over. The defence of Greece could take second place 'for the time being' (was 'Mincemeat' *still* having some influence on the High Command as well as on Hitler?), and the order for seven boats of the 11th R-boat Flotilla to go to the Ægean was cancelled: these boats could remain under the orders of the Commander-in-Chief, Italy.

So the immediate repercussions of 'Operation Mincemeat' had finally ended, except for the German forces still sitting idle in Greece. The survey that has been made of its results can be summarised as follows:

As regards the working out of the 'Operation', we fooled those of the Spaniards who assisted the Germans, we fooled the German Intelligence Service both in Spain and in Berlin, we fooled the German Operational Staff and Supreme Command, we fooled Keitel, and, finally, we fooled Hitler himself, and kept him fooled right up to the end of July.

As regards the Eastern Mediterranean, we caused immense effort to be put into the defence of Greece, with the creation of minefields, shore batteries, etc. We caused a concentration of troops in Greece which justified the appointment by Hitler of Rommel to command them. These troops included a panzer division which had to be sent right across Europe. All this was completely wasted effort from the German point of view and diminished the potential defence of Sicily and of Italy.

As regards the western Mediterranean, we caused an increase in the fortification and reinforcement of Corsica and Sardinia at the expense of that of Sicily, we caused the defensive preparations in Sicily to be largely diverted from those coasts of the island where the Allies in fact landed to the coasts where they did not land, and we caused the Germans to send R-boats away from Sicily to the Ægean, thus opening a gap in their defences which 'prejudiced the defence of Sicily' as well as creating a shortage of escort vessels.

All this can be traced from the contemporary documents, and I think that I can fairly claim that our dividends from the 'Operation' were indeed enormous, far greater than we had anticipated in even our most sanguine moments. It is for others to assess how many British and American lives were saved by 'The Man Who Never Was' during the conquest of Sicily, and what effect his exploit had on the course of the war.

Envoi

Rather than conclude on a somewhat bombastic note, a note that I feel to be owed to the memory of the man who really was, and who became 'Major Martin, Royal Marines', I would like to add something that puts my own part in the 'Operation' into its proper perspective.

As the result of what we already knew of the success of 'Operation Mincemeat,' I was awarded the Military O.B.E. in 1944. When he was pinning the medal on to my uniform jacket, His Majesty asked me where it was that I had earned it, and on my replying, 'At the Admiralty, Sir,' I could see his eyebrows go up in some astonishment. He followed with another question: 'What did you get it for?' Taken by surprise, I could only ejaculate: 'Part of the planning of 'Operation Husky,' Sir.'

That reply of mine made me realise how the entire thing fitted together and, as I have said, put the whole picture into its proper perspective. 'Operation Mincemeat,' with all its thrill and glamour, was just an integral part of the planning of a modern operation.

Appendix I

*Copy of 1st Naval War Staff 1 Ops. 1942/43,
Most Secret, S.O. only, of May 20.43*

From a teleprinted signal (outgoing) to:

Supreme Command of the Armed Forces/Operations Staff of the
Armed Forces.

Copy to: Naval Group Command South, C.-in-C. G.A.F., Operations
Staff of the G.A.F. la (Naval), Captain Mossel, Supreme Command
of the Army/Army General Staff Naval Liaison Officer, Captain
Weygoldt.

Cleared as Single Address Message.

Most Secret for S.O. only.

The Naval War Staff has examined exhaustively the possibilities of enemy
landing operations in the South-Eastern Area and has come to the following conclusions:

(1) (i) The possibility of enemy landings in the Western as well as the
Eastern Mediterranean must be reckoned with although reliable evidence
about the preparation of a large number of landing craft is so far available
from the W. Med. only.

(ii) Possible starting-points for landing operations:

(a) ARTA-PYRGOS area: Gulf of Arta, Gulf of Patras, the coast
South of Cape Araxos and on both sides of Pyrgos and also
islands off these areas, especially Corfu and Cephalonia.

(b) The South coast of the Peloponnese: Navarino, Gulf of Corone
(Kalamata) and Gulf of Marathon.

(c) CRETE: Preferably the North coast, on the South coast Mesara
Bay and Hierapetra, but only with limited forces.

(d) RHODES.

(e) Islands in the ÆGEAN: Leros, Milos, Chios, Mytilene and
Lemnos.

(f) The East coast of the PELOPONNESE and Central GREECE: Gulf
of Nauplia, Gulf of Petali (East coast of Attica).

(g) SALONICA: Gulf of Salonica, Gulf of Orphani.

(h) THRACE: Gulf of Cavalla and the coast to the East of Thasos.

(iii) It can be assumed that the enemy will probably make an initial landing where he believes there will be the least resistance and where he expects the greatest results in the shortest time. Therefore an initial landing on CRETE can be ruled out for the moment. In view of the advanced state of the development and equipment of the Fortress of CRETE a very considerable expenditure of strength would be required and a prerequisite would be subsidiary operations to obtain airfields in the Dodecanese and Peloponnese close to the scene of operations. Further, the capture of CRETE would only represent a partial accomplishment of his aims. A thrust past CRETE into the ÆGEAN, the occupation of the most important islands and a landing attempt on the East coast of the PELOPONNESE and Central GREECE is likewise improbable. An attempt at an immediate thrust into the area of SALONICA and THRACE need not be reckoned with. For such operations the enemy would require very large forces to protect his supply-routes. Considerable losses would be unavoidable as long as German air and light Naval forces (S-boats) can be operated from CRETE.

(iv) In the opinion of the Naval War Staff landing attempts are most likely to be made in the Greek West coast area where the CORFU-ARTA-PYRGOS region offers the greatest prospects of success.

Possibilities: a thrust from the North towards LARISSA-VOLOS, cutting off Central GREECE with the PELOPONNESE, in the centre an advance towards Central GREECE and ATICA, in the South a drive for the CORINTH Isthmus. The islands off this coast (especially CORFU and CEPHALONIA) would become very valuable bases in enemy hands. Special attention is drawn to the exceptional importance of these islands.

Simultaneous subsidiary landings are probable at NAVARINO (a good harbour for Naval forces operating for the protection of landings and supplies), KALAMATA (airfield) and perhaps also the Gulf of MARATHON. A subsidiary thrust might be made through TRIPOLIS to CORINTH. Simultaneously or shortly beforehand a diversionary operation against the DODECANESE (RHODES) is to be expected.

(2) The defensive power of the areas in the greatest danger is still weak. Nevertheless, in the opinion of the Naval War Staff it should be possible to throw back attempted enemy landings if he attacks with only limited forces. According to evidence from the Army General Staff available to Naval War Staff the enemy has at present only a few divisions available in the E. Med. Also the available transport space is sufficient for these forces only.

All measures must therefore be taken to reinforce rapidly the defensive strength of the areas which are specially threatened. The construction of a secondary line of defence in the rear (roughly in the N. GREECE–SALONICA area) is only to be considered when the other has been accomplished.

(3) The following immediate steps are envisaged or have already been taken by the Naval War Staff:

(i) Laying of German minefields: off KALAMATA in the process of completion, CERIGO Strait complete, CERIGOTTO Strait in preparation. Group Command South (Admiral Ægean) to exert his influence for the laying of mines by the Italians on the West coast of GREECE.

(ii) The installation of coastal batteries, also in the Italian-occupied area (the decision of the Supreme Commander of the Armed Forces has been requested).

(iii) PIRÆUS and SALONICA are intended as the principal bases for Naval forces and are or will be appropriately supplied. MELOS, LEROS and LEMNOS as auxiliary bases will receive only limited supplies for Naval forces.

(iv) The possibility of installing operational bases for S-boats on the PELOPONNESE and CRETE is being explored.

(v) Preliminary discussion with C.-in-C. G.A.F. South East concerning reconnaissance and offensive action by the G.A.F. after the approach of enemy operations has been established (air attacks on the landing fleet where possible while it is still in its port of departure and mining these harbours from the air).

(vi) Preparation of a patrol-service with coastal defence vessels to the West, South and East of CRETE.

(vii) Preparation of a Command Station for Admiral Ægean at SALONICA to ensure uninterrupted control in the event of it proving necessary to move the headquarters.

Naval War Staff Reg. No. 1st Naval War
Staff 1 Op. 1492/43. Most Secret. S.O. only.

Appendix II

Reg. No. Naval War Staff I 17 189/43. Most Secret.
Distribution: Copy No. 1. Chief Naval War Staff
                        2. Naval War Staff
                        3. 1a
                        4. 1 ops
                        5. 1 m
                        6. Naval War Staff qu A
                        7.   ,,   ,,   ,,   ,,   ,,
                        8. 1f
                        9. 1b
                        File 13.
Teleprint MBBZ 02175 of 14.6.43 23.34.
Most Immediate GWASL 02633 14.6 2130.
To Supreme Command of the Navy, Naval War Staff.
Also for: General Staff of the Army, Inspector-General of Armoured Troops, Supreme Command of the Navy (Naval War Staff, C.-in-C. South, Home Staff, Overseas Branch).

MOST SECRET

(A) The FUEHRER has issued the following orders for the reinforcement of SARDINIA and SICILY.

(1) Measures to be taken by the Army General Staff:

(i) Every island to be provided with a Fortress Infantry Regiment to the strength of one regimental staff with an H.Q. Coy. and 4 battalions. 3 March Battalions of the June draft to ITALY may be used if necessary. In this connection the FUEHRER stressed especially the need to be strongly equipped with local weapons suitable for defence against armour and land attack. For this purpose recourse can even be had to French 2.5 and 3.7 centimetre anti-tank guns with stick grenades.

The regiments must be ready to move by 28.6.43. If it is not possible to procure the anti-tank guns needed for SICILY by this time, the remaining anti-tank guns must be sent on by 20.7 at the latest.

(ii) SARDINIA to be provided with a Fortress Artillery Abteilung for coastal defence.

Equipment – 2 batteries of 17-cm. guns.

               1 battery of 10-cm. guns.

(The latter are available from C.-in-C. South.)

To be prepared to depart as soon as possible.

(iii) The SARDINIA detachment to be provided with 1 anti-tank coy. with 12 anti-tank guns for each regiment.

Every lorried infantry coy. of the SICILY detachment to be equipped with 2 anti-tank guns. If heavy and medium anti-tank guns are not at first available, recourse must be had to light anti-tank guns firing stick grenades. The anti-tank coys. should, however, be equipped with heavy and medium anti-tank guns.

(iv) The SARDINIA Armoured Coy. to be expanded to an armoured Abteilung with at least 50 tanks (of which at least 25 will be Mark IV) by supplying the necessary units and weapons. To be prepared to move off as soon as possible.

(v) The setting up of an armoured coy. of 20 tanks Mark IV for the 215th Armoured Abteilung in SICILY. (This coy. to be transferred to compensate for the Tiger coy. which was handed over to the Hermann Goering Division.) To be prepared to move off by 15.7.43.

(vi) Several W/T detachments to reinforce the Signals Coy. of the SARDINIA Command.

(2) The Supreme Command of the Navy is to form a coastal artillery Abteilung from 3 newly-commissioned batteries and is to transfer them to C.-in-C. South for despatch to SICILY on call.

(3) C.-in-C. South's other requirements must be given lower priority unless a special order to the contrary is given.

(B) (1) The Army General Staff will report to the Supreme Command of the Allied Forces/Operations Staff of the Armed Forces:

(i) The proposed equipment of the Fortress Regiments with anti-tank guns (statement of calibre) and other heavy weapons (including rifle-grenade apparatus).

(ii) Details of the distribution of the anti-tank guns according to calibre amongst the other newly-created units and reinforcements required.

(iii) The times at which the individual reinforcements will be ready to move off (to be reported also to Home Staff (Overseas Branch)).

(2) The Supreme Command of the Armed Forces will report to Operations Staff of the Armed Forces and Home Staff (Overseas Branch)

when the coastal artillery Abteilungen are ready to move off.

(3) Home Staff (Overseas Branch) will be responsible for the rapid passage of these reinforcements.

(Signed) Keitel,
Supreme Command of the Armed Forces/
Operations Staff of the Armed Forces.
Op. No. 002820. Most Secret.

BLACK LION HOTEL,
MOLD,
N. WALES.

13th April 1943.

TEL. NO. 98

My dear William,

    I cannot say that this Hotel is any longer as comfortable as I remember it to have been in pre war days. I am, however, staying here as the only alternative to imposing myself once more upon your aunt whose depleted staff & strict regard for fuel economy (which I agree to be necessary in war time) has made the house almost uninhabitable to a guest, at least one of my age. I propose to be in Town for the nights of the 20th & 21st of April when no doubt we shall have an opportunity to meet. I enclose the copy of a letter which I have written to Gwatkin of McKenna's about your affairs. You will see that I have asked him to lunch with me at the Carlton Grill (which I understand still to be open)

Above and opposite: Father's letter to 'Major Martin'.

at a quarter to one on Wednesday the 21st. I should be glad if you would make it possible to join us, we shall not however wait luncheon for you, so I trust that, if you are able to come, you will make a point of being punctual.

Your cousin Priscilla has asked to be remembered to you. She has grown into a sensible girl though I cannot say that her work for the Land Army has done much to improve her looks.

In that respect I am afraid that she will take after her father's side of the family.

Your affectionate

Father.